WELLBEING, FREEDOM AND SOCIAL JUSTICE

Wellbeing, Freedom and Social Justice

The Capability Approach Re-Examined

Ingrid Robeyns

https://www.openbookpublishers.com

All external links were active at the time of publication unless otherwise stated and have been archived via the Internet Archive Wayback Machine at https://archive.org/web

Digital material and resources associated with this volume are available at https://www.openbookpublishers.com/product/682#resources

Every effort has been made to identify and contact copyright holders and any omission or error will be corrected if notification is made to the publisher.

ISBN Paperback: 978-1-78374-421-3
ISBN Hardback: 978-1-78374-422-0
ISBN Digital (PDF): 978-1-78374-423-7
ISBN Digital ebook (epub): 978-1-78374-424-4
ISBN Digital ebook (mobi): 978-1-78374-425-1
DOI: 10.11647/OBP.0130

Cover image: Weaving by Aaron Robeyns (2015). Photo by Roland Pierik (2017), CC-BY 4.0. Cover design by Heidi Coburn.

All paper used by Open Book Publishers is SFI (Sustainable Forestry Initiative) and PEFC (Programme for the Endorsement of Forest Certification Schemes) Certified.

Printed in the United Kingdom, United States, and Australia
by Lightning Source for Open Book Publishers (Cambridge, UK)

Contents

To Roland, Aaron and Ischa

Acknowledgements

In 1998, when I started to work on my PhD dissertation at Cambridge University on the capability approach and gender inequality, there were very few scholars working on the capability approach. I recall searching on the internet for publications on the topic, not receiving more than a few hundred hits (rather than the, roughly, 440,000 hits one gets today). I had studied economics and additional courses in social and political sciences and gender studies, and I had a strong intuition that, for the study of gender inequalities, the capability approach was a much more suitable framework than the prevailing ways in which economists as well as political theorists analysed unjustified gender inequalities. I was extremely lucky that Amartya Sen had agreed to supervise my doctoral studies. He not only opened a world that was new for me (being the first in my family to study for a PhD and the first to study abroad), but also taught me not to be afraid of developing myself as an interdisciplinary scholar. And, importantly, he very patiently helped me to grasp the capability approach in all its details. The privilege of having Amartya Sen as my PhD supervisor meant that I had the best possible access to the scholar who had developed the capability approach as it emerged at the end of the twentieth century. When I graduated from Cambridge University, I asked Amartya whether he was planning to write another book on the capability approach, such as his classic *Commodities and Capabilities*. He smiled, shook his head and responded: "No, it has grown over my head". His judgement was probably very accurate — in essence the problem of a literature becoming unwieldy — and that challenge only became much worse over the next two decades. One way to read this book is to see it as an attempt to tame the proliferation of scholarship about the capability approach since the turn of the last century.

Over the last fifteen years, I have published quite a number of articles, book chapters and online pieces on the capability approach, including many that had as their main aim to clarify or explain certain aspects of it. But I kept receiving many emails from students who had questions about the capability approach. Their emails, as well as conversations with scholars sceptical of the importance of this approach, made it clear that a general introduction was necessary to answer as many of these questions as possible. I decided to write an introductory overview of the capability approach, in which the aim was not to develop my own, novel version of a capability theory, but rather to try to present a general helicopter view of the approach. In addition, I felt that too many claims about or critiques of the capability approach that were circulating were based either on some scholar's own interest in seeing the approach develop exclusively in a certain direction, or else were based on misunderstandings, often due to miscommunication between different disciplines.

The result lies in front of you. Unfortunately, it took me much longer to write this than I had originally planned; almost twelve years lie between the initial idea and its completion. Yet in hindsight, despite that at many points the ambition of writing this book felt like a heavy psychological burden, I have no regrets that I'm only now completing it. Only in the last year, after the publication of an article in the *Journal of Human Development and Capabilities* in which I offered a general definition of the capability approach (Robeyns 2016b), did it became clear to me exactly what the general anatomy of the approach looked like. Thanks to discussions with students and other scholars, the generalisation of the capability approach that emerged from that journal article was further crystallised and polished. That generalisation is the heart of this book, and it is presented in chapter 2. In addition, I also provide what one could see as an F.A.Q. guide to the capability literature — the most frequently voiced questions and criticisms will be clarified and discussed in chapters 3 and 4.

Over the many years of developing my own understanding of the capability approach, I have learnt a lot from other scholars as well as from those whom I taught. Intellectually, my biggest debt is no doubt to Amartya Sen, who had the single most important influence on my intellectual development. I also learnt a lot from conversations on the capability approach with people working in different disciplines and in different corners of the world. I cannot possibly list everyone who contributed to my understanding and thinking, yet I would like to express my gratitude to Bina Agarwal, Sabina Alkire, Constanze Binder, Harry Brighouse, Morten Fibieger Byskov, Enrica Chiappero-Martinetti, Rutger Claassen, Ina Conradie, Andrew Crabtree, David Crocker, Séverine Deneulin, Avner De-Shalit, Jay Drydryk, Des Gasper, Pablo Gilabert, Reiko Gotoh, Govert den Hartogh, Martin van Hees, Jane Humphries, Sakiko Fukuda-Parr, Matthias Kramm, Sem de Maagt, Martha Nussbaum, Ilse Oosterlaken, Antonella Picchio, Roland Pierik, Mozaffar Qizilbash, Erik Schokkaert, Elaine Unterhalter, Robert van der Veen, Sridhar Venkatapuram, Polly Vizzard, Melanie Walker, Krushil Watene, Tom Wells, Jonathan Wolff, as well as my late friend and co-author Wiebke Kuklys. I also benefited a lot from teaching the capability approach to hundreds of students, but in particular during a week-long course at the University of the Western Cape, Cape Town, in 2011; during a workshop at Hitotsubashi University in Tokyo in March 2016; during a Masterclass at the London School of Economics in which I worked on a draft of this book manuscript in February 2017; and during a Research Master's tutorial in practical philosophy at Utrecht University during the academic year 2016–2017.

I benefited from the comments I received at two book manuscript workshops that were held over the last year, one at the Erasmus University Rotterdam organised by Constanze Binder and Sem de Maagt, and the other as a session at the 2017 Human Devolpment & Capability Association (HDCA) conference in Cape Town, organised by Morten Fibieger Byskov and Rebecca Gutwald. I benefited from the comments I received at those occasions from Morten Fibieger Byskov, Willem van der Deijl, Monique Deveaux, Akshath Jitendranath, Caroline Suransky and Miriam Teschl in Rotterdam, and from Solava Ibrahim, Serene Khader and Henry Richardson in Cape Town. In addition, I also received comments on parts of the draft manuscript from Conrad Heilmann, Chris Lyon, Bart Mijland, Raphael Ng, Petra van der Kooij, Roland Pierik and Polly Vizard. I owe special thanks to Constanze Binder, Séverine Deneulin, Morten Fibieger Byskov, Matthias Kramm, Sem de Maagt and Henry Richardson, whose comments led to multiple substantive changes. Thanks also to the two anonymous reviewers who reviewed the book proposal in 2011 and especially to Tania Burchardt, who reviewed the final manuscript and provided very valuable suggestions for final revisions.

My thanks are also due to Robert van der Veen, for his permission to draw on our joint work in section 3.8. I would furthermore like to acknowledge generous research funding from the Netherlands Organisation for Scientific Research (NWO), who awarded me three grants over the last 15 years that allowed me to further develop my research on the capability approach: a four-year postdoctoral scholarship (2002–2006) to work on the capability approach and theories of justice; a VIDI grant (2006–2011) to work on demographic changes and social justice using the capability approach as one of the normative tools; and finally the Horizon grant (2011–2016) awarded to a consortium of scholars from three universities and led by Marcus Düwell, for an interdisciplinary analysis of practical self-understanding. Thanks also to the team at Open Book Publishers — in particular Lucy Barnes, Bianca Gualandi, Alice Meyer, and Alessandra Tosi — who have been a real pleasure to work with.

This book is dedicated to my family — to my husband Roland Pierik and our children Aaron and Ischa. This book contains not only almost half a million characters typed and retyped by me, but also visible and less visible contributions from my three (little) men. Obviously, as a fellow political philosopher with interdisciplinary leanings, there are insights from Roland in various places in this book, including some direct citations. Moreover, Roland helped me not to let the best be the enemy of the good, and kept encouraging me to finish this book. If I waited until I was happy with each sentence and paragraph, this book probably would never see the light of day. Ischa's contribution may be the least visible, yet it is there. It is his unconventional view of human affairs that keeps prompting me not to accept norms or practices that are unjust or make no sense. Aaron provided the artwork for the cover. The woven piece very well represents the multi-dimensional nature of the capability approach, as well as the fact that life is made up by one's own choice of functionings, which follows a dynamic and always unfinished pattern. If one has enough bright and colourful functionings, they can be woven together to become something bigger than the mere functionings taken separately — a flourishing life worth living.

1. Introduction

1.1 Why the capability approach?

Many people who encounter the capability approach for the first time find the ideas embedded within it intuitively attractive. The basic claim of the capability approach is that, when asking normative questions, we should ask what people are able to do and what lives they are able to lead. That claim resonates with widespread ideas among citizens, academics, and politicians about how to make policies, views about what social justice requires, or bottom-up views about development and social progress. Perhaps the most important contribution the capability approach makes is to prompt us to ask alternative questions, and to focus on different dimensions when we make observations or when we gather the relevant data for making evaluations or judgements.

What is the capability approach? This book will answer that question in detail. But let us start with a first, preliminary description, taken from a quote by Amartya Sen, who introduced the theoretical idea of the capability approach in his 1979 Tanner Lecture (Sen 1980a) and soon after in empirical work (Sen and Sengupta 1983; Sen 1985a). According to Sen, the capability approach "is an intellectual discipline that gives a central role to the evaluation of a person's achievements and freedoms in terms of his or her actual ability to do the different things a person has reason to value doing or being" (Sen 2009a, 16). As we will see later in this book, I will propose a definition and an account of the capability approach that does not exactly equal Sen's but rather can be interpreted

https://doi.org/10.11647/OBP.0130.01

as a *generalisation* of Sen's definition.[1] Yet Sen's definition is a good way to start, since it highlights that the capability approach is concerned with aspects of people's lives such as their health, the education they can enjoy and the support they enjoy from their social networks; it is also concerned with what people can do, such as being able to work, raise a family, travel, or be politically active. The capability approach cares about people's real freedoms to do these things, and the level of wellbeing that they will reach when choosing from the options open to them. It is a rich, multidimensional approach.

Here's an example illustrating the difference the capability approach makes. Everyone agrees that poverty needs to be combatted — but who are the people that suffer from poverty? Which conceptual and normative framework do we use when we identify the poor? Which definition of poverty do we use when we analyse the incidence of poverty in a country? As empirical research has shown, it *does matter* whether one uses the widespread income-based metric, or whether one takes a capability perspective and focuses on a set of thresholds of basic functionings, the lack of which indicates a dimension of poverty. Caterina Ruggeri Laderchi (1997) used data from a Chilean household survey to investigate the extent to which an income-based measure is able to capture some basic functionings that could arguably be seen as central to poverty analysis: basic education, health and nutrition. She found that the income variable *in itself* is insignificant as a determinant of the shortfall in health, schooling and child nutrition and that the role that income plays is highly non-linear and depends on a number of other personal, household and regional characteristics. In other words, looking at the income level in a household to determine whether the members of that household are poor may be an unreliable indicator for the prevalence of poverty. The difference between, on the one hand, the income-based measurements and, on the other hand, measurements based on a selection of basic indicators that reflect how people are doing has also been confirmed by a large number of other studies in the last twenty-five years.[2] It is for that income-based approach that the

---

1   The exact definition and description of the capability approach that I will develop in this book is broader than Sen's own. The reason, as will become clear in due course, is that the "having reason to value" clause in Sen's definition is, in my view, a special case of the general definition of the capability approach.

2   See, among others, Klasen 2000; Laderchi, Saith and Stewart 2003; Qizilbash 2002; Reddy, Visaria and Asali 2009; Alkire et al. 2015.

capability approach offers an alternative — but, as will be explained in this book, it is also an alternative to many other approaches and theories, such as the happiness approach or resources-based theories of justice.

While the capability approach has been used to identify the poor, it has also been used for many other purposes. Over the last twenty-five years, the range of fields in which the capability approach has been applied and developed has expanded dramatically, and now includes global public health, development ethics, environmental protection and ecological sustainability, education, technological design, welfare state policies and many, many more.[3] Nor has the use of the capability approach been restricted to empirical research only. Some of its purposes have been theoretical, such as the construction of theories of justice (Anderson 1999; Nussbaum 2000; Nussbaum 2006b; Claassen 2016), or the development of a riches-line, which allows us to identify the rich (Robeyns 2017b). Other uses of the capability approach have combined theoretical and empirical research, such as Jonathan Wolff and Avner De-Shalit's (2007) study of disadvantage.

For all these endeavours, the capability approach asks: *What are people really able to do and what kind of person are they able to be?* It asks what people can do and be (their capabilities) and what they are actually achieving in terms of beings and doings (their functionings). Do the envisioned institutions, practices and policies focus on people's capabilities, that is, their opportunities to do what they value and be the kind of person they want to be? Do people have the same capabilities in life?[4] Or do global economic structures, domestic policies or brute bad luck make people's capabilities unequal, and if so, is that unfair and should we do something about that? Do development projects focus on

---

3 See section 1.4 for a more detailed discussion of the scope of the capability approach, and some references to the various fields in which it is now applied and developed.

4 Some capability scholars, in particular Martha Nussbaum, have extended the capability approach to include the functionings of non-human animals. In this book, I restrict the discussion to *human* functionings and *human* capabilities. This is not to deny that the functionings of non-human animals are important, nor that for some ethical questions we need to consider both humans and non-human animals. There is a literature that analyses whether the capability approach can plausibly be extended to include non-human animals, which will not be discussed here, given the focus on humans (e.g. Nussbaum 2006b; Schinkel 2008; Cripps 2010; Wissenburg 2011; Holland and Linch 2016). Note that there is also a large literature on 'the capabilities of firms', which is not related to how the term 'capabilities' is used in the capability approach. In this book, the term 'capabilities' refers only to the capabilities of members of the human species.

expanding people's capabilities, or do they have another public policy goal (such as economic growth), or are they merely serving the interests of a dominant group? The capability approach thus offers a different perspective than alternative approaches that focus on the accumulation of material resources, or the mental states of people, such as their overall satisfaction with their lives.

1.2 The worries of the sceptics

Although the capability approach appeals to many readers, others have wondered whether this theory is really any different from other more established theories, or whether the capability approach is promising as a theory with sufficient bite. For example John Rawls (1999, 13), while acknowledging that the idea of basic capabilities is important, calls it "an unworkable idea" for a liberal conception of justice. John Roemer (1996, 191–93) has criticized the capability approach for being insufficiently specified — a complaint that is also echoed in the critique made by Pratab Bhanu Mehta (2009). Others have questioned the practical significance of the capability approach for policy making and empirical assessment. For instance, Robert Sugden (1993, 1953) has questioned the usefulness of the capability approach for welfare economics — a critique to which we will return in section 4.10. In addition, at seminars and other scholarly gatherings, an often-heard criticism is that the capability approach is old wine in new bottles — it aims to do what the non-economic social sciences have been doing all along. If that is the case, then why should we bother?[5]

There are two types of answer to the sceptics. The first is conceptual or theoretical and that answer will be given in the remainder of this book. In a nutshell, the reason the capability approach is worth our time and attention is that it gives us a new way of evaluating the lives of individuals and the societies in which these people live their lives. The attention is shifted to public values currently not always considered most important — such as wellbeing, freedom and justice. It is an alternative discourse or paradigm, perhaps even a 'counter-theory' to a range of more mainstream discourses on society, poverty and prosperity.

---

5   Several more specific critiques on the capability approach will be discussed in chapter 4.

Moreover, it brings insights from several disciplines together, and gives scholars a common interdisciplinary language. Nevertheless, it doesn't follow that the capability approach will always offer a framework that is to be preferred over other frameworks: as this book will show, the capability approach can contribute something, but we should be careful not to overplay our hand and believe that it can do a better job for *all* ethical questions.

The second answer to the sceptic is empirical — to *show* the sceptic what difference the capability approach makes. The earlier mentioned study by Ruggeri Laderchi (1997) and dozens of similar studies do exactly that. In 2006, I provided a survey of the studies in which the capability approach had been put into practice (Robeyns 2006b) — a task that I think is no longer feasible today in a single paper or chapter, given that the empirical literature of applications of the capability approach has grown dramatically. But in order to illustrate in somewhat greater depth this kind of answer to the sceptic, let us focus on one type of empirical application of the capability approach: namely how we perceive and evaluate our lives at a macro level, and how we evaluate the social arrangements in which we live those lives.

1.3 A yardstick for the evaluation of prosperity and progress

For many decades, the dominant way to measure prosperity and social progress has been to focus on Gross Domestic Product (GDP) or Gross National Product (GNP) per capita. The more we produce, the more developed our country has been taken to be. Yet a large literature has emerged showing that GDP per capita is limited and often flawed as a measure of social and economic progress (Fleurbaey 2009; Stiglitz, Sen and Fitoussi 2010; Fleurbaey and Blanchet 2013; Coyle 2015).

In one of the very first empirical applications of the capability approach, Amartya Sen (1985a) used some very simple statistics to illustrate how deceiving GDP per capita can be as a measure of prosperity and progress.[6] Sen showed that, in the early 1980s, the (roughly

---

6   An even earlier empirical study, in which the capability approach is referred to as the right evaluative framework, was done by Amartya Sen and Sunil Sengupta (1983).

equivalent) GNP per capita of Brazil and Mexico was more than seven times the (roughly equivalent) GNP per capita of India, China and Sri Lanka — yet performances in life expectancy, infant mortality and child death rates were best in Sri Lanka, better in China compared to India and better in Mexico compared to Brazil. Important social indicators related to life, premature death and health, can thus not be read from the average national income statistic. Another finding was that India performs badly regarding basic education but has considerably higher tertiary education rates than China and Sri Lanka. Thus, Sen concluded that the public policy of China and especially Sri Lanka towards distributing food, public health measures, medical services and school education have led to their remarkable achievements in the capabilities of survival and education. What can this application teach us about the capability approach? First, the ranking of countries based on GNP per capita can be quite different from a ranking based on the selected functionings. Second, growth in GNP per capita should not be equated with growth in living standards.

Sen has often made use of the power of comparing the differences in the ranking of countries based on GDP per capita with indicators of some essential functionings. Recently Jean Drèze and Amartya Sen (2013, 46–50) used the capability approach to develop an analysis of India's development policies. For example, as table 1.1 shows, they compared India with the fifteen other poorest countries outside sub-Saharan Africa in terms of development indicators.[7]

Of those sixteen countries, India ranks on top in terms of GDP per capita, but ranks very low for a range of functionings, such as life expectancy at birth, infant mortality, undernourishment, schooling and literacy. Other countries, with fewer financial means, were able to achieve better outcomes in terms of those functionings. Once again, the point is made that focussing on income-based metrics such as disposable income at the household level, or GDP per capita at the national level, gives limited information on the lives people can lead.

---

7   Those other countries are Afghanistan, Bangladesh, Burma, Cambodia, Haiti, Kyrgyzstan, Laos, Moldova, Nepal, Pakistan, Papua New Guinea, Tajikistan, Uzbekistan, Vietnam and Yemen.

Table 1.1 Selected Indicators for the World's Sixteen Poorest Countries Outside Sub-Saharan Africa

	India	Average for other poorest countries	India's rank among 16 poorest countries
GDP per capita, 2011 (PPP Constant 2005 international $)	3,203	2,112	1
Life expectancy at birth, 2011 (years)	65	67	9
Infant mortality rate, 2011 (per 1,000 live births)	47	45	10
Under-5 mortality rate, 2011 (per 1,000 live births)	61	56	10
Total fertility rate, 2011 (children per woman)	2.6	2.9	7
Access to improved sanitation, 2010 (%)	34	57	13
Mean years of schooling, age 25+, 2011	4.4	5.0	11
Literacy rate, age 14–15 years, 2010 (%)			
Female	74	79	11
Male	88	85	9
Proportion of children below 5 years who are undernourished, 2006–2010 (%)			
Underweight	43	30	15
Stunted	48	41	13
Child immunization rates, 2011 (%)			
DPT	72	88	13
Measles	74	87	11

Source: Drèze and Sen (2013, 47).

This type of illustration of the power of the capability approach, whereby at the macro level the quality of life in a country is compared with GDP per capita, is not restricted to poor countries only. For example, the capability approach has recently also been taken up by the 'Better Life Initiative' of the OECD, the Organisation for Economic Co-operation and Development. The aim of this initiative is to track wellbeing, both in the present day and historically, by looking at ten dimensions of wellbeing: per capita GDP, real wages, educational attainment, life expectancy, height, personal security, the quality of political institutions, environmental quality, income inequality and gender inequality. Several of these dimensions can be conceptualized through a capability lens and others (such as per capita GDP or real wages) are needed for a comparison between capability dimensions and income dimensions, or can be seen as core capability determinants or capability inputs. In a recent report, which reconstructed the outcomes on those dimensions between 1820 and 2000, it was found that some dimensions, such as education and health outcomes, are strongly correlated with per capita GDP, but others are not — such as the quality of political institutions, homicide rates and exposure to conflicts (Van Zanden et al. 2014).

Another example that illustrates the difference the capability approach can make is the analysis of gender inequality, for which it is clear that we are missing out the most important dimensions if we only focus on how income is distributed. There are two main problems with an income-based approach to gender inequalities. The first is that it is often assumed that income within households will be shared. Yet that assumption makes most of the economic inequalities between women and men invisible (Woolley and Marshall 1994; Phipps and Burton 1995; Robeyns 2006a). Moreover, gender scholars across the disciplines have argued that one of the most important dimensions of gender inequality is the distribution of burdens between men and women (paid work, household work and care work); the fact that women are expected to do the lion's share of unpaid household work and care work makes them financially vulnerable and restricts their options. Any account of gender inequality that wants to focus on what really matters should talk about the gender division of paid and unpaid work, and the capability approach allows us to do that, since both paid and unpaid work can be conceptualized as important capabilities of human beings (e.g. Lewis and Giullari 2005; Robeyns 2003, 2010; Addabbo, Lanzi and Picchio 2010).

Moreover, for millions of girls and women worldwide, the most important capability that is denied to them is extremely basic — the capability to live in the first place. As Sen showed in an early study and as has been repeatedly confirmed since, millions of women are 'missing' from the surface of the Earth (and from the population statistics), since newborn girls have been killed or fatally neglected, or female foetuses have been aborted, because they were females in a society in which daughters are more likely to be seen as a burden, especially when compared to sons (Sen 1990b, 2003b, 1992b; Klasen 1994; Klasen and Wink 2003). In sum, tracking the gap between women's achievements in income and wealth or labour market outcomes will not reveal some crucial dimensions of gender inequality, whereas the capability approach draws attention to these non-income-based dimensions.

Using the capability approach when thinking about prosperity and social progress has another advantage: it will impede policy makers from using mistaken assumptions about human beings in their policies, including how we live together and interact in society and communities, what is valuable in our lives and what kind of governmental and societal support is needed in order for people (and in particular the disadvantaged) to flourish. For example, in their study of disadvantage in affluent societies, in particular the UK and Israel, Jonathan Wolff and Avner De-Shalit discuss the effects of a government policy of clearing a slum by moving the inhabitants to newly built tower blocks. While there may be clear material advantages to this policy — in particular, improving the hygiene conditions in which people live — a capabilitarian analysis will point out that this policy damages the social aspects of people's wellbeing, since social networks and communities are broken up and cannot simply be assumed to be rebuilt in the new tower blocks (Wolff and De-Shalit 2007, 168, 178–79). Since social relationships among people are key to their wellbeing, this may well have additional derivative effects on other dimensions of people's lives, such as their mental health. Understanding people as beings whose nature consists of a *plurality* of dimensions can help governments to think carefully through *all* the relevant effects of their policies.

1.4 Scope and development
of the capability approach

The previous section provides one type of answer to those who are sceptical about the capability approach, namely by showing what difference it makes in practice. The other strand in answering the sceptic who asks "Why bother?" is to explain in detail how one should understand the capability approach as a conceptual and theoretical frame and how it differs from other theoretical frameworks. After all, a proper understanding of what the capability approach precisely is (and is not) should also help in making clear what difference it can make. While this book is not framed as a reply to the sceptic, implicitly such an argument is made in the chapters to come.

Nevertheless, we should not simply assume that the added value of the capability approach is equal across cases, fields and disciplines. In some areas, the difference between the capability approach and the dominant ways of thinking and evaluating are so significant that we can rightly speak of a 'counter-theory'. In other debates and discussions, the difference that the capability approach makes to the prevailing modes of analysis has been more limited. Moreover, the development of the capability approach *itself* is uneven within different disciplines.

In some debates, the capability approach has been so much studied, developed or applied that we should no longer speak of "the potential of the capability approach" or "the promises of the capability approach", since the work that has been done has made quite clear what difference the capability approach *actually makes*. The prime example is the literature and debate on the very idea of what development is. The capability approach has made a crucial foundational contribution to the growth of the human development paradigm which is now well-known, especially through the work of the *Human Development Reports*, which are annually published by the United Nations Development Programme (UNDP). In addition, the most well-known of Sen's books among the wider public is *Development as Freedom*, which uses the capability approach as a key element of his alternative vision on development (Sen 1999a). In economics, Sabina Alkire, James Foster and their collaborators have made major contributions to the development of poverty measures based on the capability approach, with the development of the Multidimensional Poverty Index (Alkire and Foster 2011; Alkire et al. 2015). In the area of development studies, the capability approach is no longer a new and emerging alternative (as it was twenty to thirty years ago), but rather one of the major established frameworks.[8]

Another area is philosophical thinking about the metric of distributive justice (that is: what we ought to compare between individuals when we make statements about whether certain inequalities between people are unjust). In this literature too, the capability approach has by now established itself as an important alternative.[9] And while work on development and on justice perhaps stands out, there are now significant bodies of literature on the capability approach in many fields, such as health economics and public health,[10] technology,[11] sustainability analysis and environmental policy studies,[12] disability studies,[13] and

---

8   For some examples from the huge body of literature in development economics, development studies and development ethics that builds on the capability approach, see Alkire (2002); Clark (2002, 2005); Conradie (2013); Crocker (2008); Deneulin (2006a, 2006b, 2014); Drydyk (2011, 2013); Gasper (2004); Ibrahim (2011); Klasen (2000); Qizilbash (1996) and Qizilbash and Clark (2005).

9   See e.g. Anderson (1999, 2010); Nussbaum (1988); Nussbaum (2000; 2006b); Richardson (2000); Kaufman (2007); Wolff and De-Shalit (2007); Brighouse and Robeyns (2010); Arneson (2010, 2013); Claassen (2014, 2016); Nielsen and Axelsen (2017). See also section 3.13.

10   E.g. Grewal et al. (2006); Ruger (2006, 2010); Coast et al. (2008); Coast, Smith and Lorgelly (2008); Venkatapuram (2009, 2011, 2013); Bleichrodt and Quiggin (2013); Entwistle and Watt (2013); Mitchell et al. (2016, 2017).

11   E.g. Oosterlaken (2009, 2011, 2015); Zheng (2009); Zheng and Stahl (2011); Kleine (2010, 2011, 2013); Fernández-Baldor et al. (2014).

12   E.g. Anand and Sen (1994, 2000); Robeyns and Van der Veen (2007); Scholtes (2010); Schlosberg and Carruthers (2010); Rauschmayer, Omann and Frühmann (2012); Schlosberg (2012); Crabtree (2013); Voget-Kleschin (2013, 2015); Schultz et al. (2013); Holland (2014).

13   E.g. Nussbaum (2002a); Burchardt (2004); Zaidi and Burchardt (2005); Terzi (2005, 2007, 2008); Wasserman (2005); Mitra (2006); Qizilbash (2011); Harnacke (2013); Robeyns (2016c).

the vast amount of literature in educational studies that works with the capability approach.[14]

However, in other academic fields it is more disputed to what extent the capability approach has been shown to make a real difference. For example, in ethical theories within the systematic/analytical strand of philosophy, the capability approach hasn't yet been much developed. Similarly, one can doubt whether the capability approach has contributed to a significant change in mainstream economic thinking. The development of the capability approach within different academic disciplines and discussions thus differs significantly, and the effect the capability approach has had on developing new policies also differs drastically between different policy fields.

In the debates where the capability approach is now well-established, the development of that literature has often raised new questions. For example, in philosophical theories of justice there are now enough convincing arguments that the capability approach makes a difference, but the very possibility of a capability theory of justice has also allowed us to be much more explicit about which questions remain unaddressed in case one wants to make a substantive theory of (distributive) justice (Freeman 2006; Robeyns 2016d). This is a 'normal' way in which a paradigm develops. It therefore shouldn't be surprising that we have just as many questions about the capability approach as we had a few years ago. We may even have more, but they are different to those that were raised a decade or two ago.

Whatever the unevenness in its uptake and development between disciplines, and independently of the new questions that the capability approach has raised, the current state of the literature which I will present in this book confirms that the capability approach is here to stay. It makes a difference in many debates. It is one of those rare theories that strongly connects disciplines and offers a truly interdisciplinary language. And it leads to recommendations on how to organise society and choose policies that are often genuine alternatives for prevailing views.

---

14   E.g. Terzi (2008); Walker and Unterhalter (2007); Lozano et al. (2012); Boni and Walker (2013); Apsan Frediani, Boni and Gasper (2014); Unterhalter (2003a, b, 2009, 2013); Hart (2009, 2012); Peppin Vaughan (2011, 2016); Peppin Vaughan and Walker (2012); Saito (2003); Nussbaum (2002b, 2006a); Walker (2003, 2005, 2008, 2010, 2012a, 2012b), Loots and Walker (2015, 2016); Mutanga and Walker (2015); Wilson-Strydom and Walker (2015).

1.5 A guide for the reader

This book has an extremely simple structure. There are five chapters — an introduction (this chapter), a short concluding chapter (chapter 5) and three very long chapters in the middle. In chapter 2 we start with a rather simple explanation of the capability approach, and then present a more detailed account of capability theories, focusing in particular on their structure and properties. I will present the capability approach by describing it as having *a modular structure* — whereby each specific capability theory combines the core elements of the non-optional module with a range of non-core modules. This way of looking at the capability approach helps those who want to apply the capability approach to a particular question or problem to see clearly which elements are needed for such an application; it also makes it very clear that the capability approach can be specified in diverse ways. One could see chapter 2 as trying to provide the anatomy of the capability approach — to try to see behind its skin, to detect what its various organs are, how they interact and which ones are essential, whereas others may be more tangential.

In chapter 3 we discuss further details and try to clear up some misunderstandings. The capability approach is a field that is notoriously prone to misunderstandings, in part because of its interdisciplinary nature, but also because the terminology differs somewhat between different authors. Chapter 3 tries to present the literature as neutrally as possible and describes how it has been evolving.

Chapter 4 then zooms in on a range of critiques that have been made of the capability approach, such as the argument that it is too individualistic, or that it cannot properly account for power. In this chapter, my own voice will be more prominent, as I will engage with these claims, agreeing with some of them (and, as philosophers do, giving *reasons* why I agree), but also arguing against some other critiques. Here, it will become clear what the value is of the distinction between the general capability approach and more specific capability theories, which I introduced elsewhere (Robeyns 2016b) and explain again in section 2.3. As it turns out, some of the critiques are valid against particular capability *theories*, but make no sense against the capability *approach* in general. I hope that the adoption of this distinction between capability theories or applications on the one hand, and capability approach on the other, will clear the capability literature of many confusing and unnecessary criticisms, so that we can devote our energy to those that are powerful and with which we need to engage. Moreover, let us not forget that the capability approach is a *tool* and not an end in itself; we should master it as well as we can, perhaps also as efficiently as we can, and then move on to use it in the work that really matters.

2. Core Ideas and the Framework

2.1 Introduction

The previous chapter listed a range of fields in which the capability approach has been taken up, and in chapters 3 and 4 we focus in more detail on how the capability approach can (or cannot) make a difference for thinking about wellbeing, social and distributive justice, human rights, welfare economics and other topics. This broad uptake of the capability approach across disciplines and across different types of knowledge production (from theoretical and abstract to applied or policy oriented) is testimony to its success. But how is the capability approach understood in these different fields, and is it possible to give a coherent and clarifying account of how we can understand the capability approach *across* those fields?[1] In other words, how should we understand the capability approach as an overarching framework, that unites its more specific uses in different fields and disciplines?

---

[1] In developing the account of the capability approach as presented in this book, I have started in an inductive way by trying to generalize from how the capability approach has been used in the literature. However, that literature has been critically scrutinized, and in some cases I have come to the conclusion that some ideas in this broad 'capabilities literature' do not survive careful analysis, and should be rejected. Put differently, my methodology has been to be as inclusive as possible, but not at the cost of endorsing (what I believe to be) confusions or errors.

   https://doi.org/10.11647/OBP.0130.02

This chapter gives an account of that general framework. It provides explanations and insights into what the capability approach is, what its core claims are, and what additional claims we should pay attention to. This chapter will also answer the question: what do we mean exactly when we say that the capability approach is a *framework* or an *approach*?

In other words, in this chapter, I will give an account (or a description) of the capability approach at the most general level. I will bracket additional details and questions about which disagreement or confusion exists; chapter 3 will offer more detailed clarifications and chapter 4 will discuss issues of debate and dispute. Taken together, these three chapters provide my understanding of the capability approach.

Chapter 2 is structured as follows. In the next section, we look at a preliminary definition of the capability approach. Section 2.3 proposes to make a distinction between 'the capability approach' and 'a capability theory'. This distinction is crucial — it will help us to clarify various issues that we will look at in this book, and it also provides some answers to the sceptics of the capability approach whom we encountered in the previous chapter. Section 2.4 describes, from a bottom-up perspective, the many ways in which the capability approach has been developed within particular theories, and argues why it is important to acknowledge the great diversity within capabilitarian scholarship. Sections 2.5 to 2.11 present an analytic account of the capability approach, and show what is needed to develop a particular capability theory, application or analysis. In 2.5, I propose the modular view of the capability approach, which allows us to distinguish between three different types of modules that make up a capability theory. The first, the A-module, consists of those properties that each capability theory *must* have (section 2.6). This is the non-optional core of each capability theory. The B-modules are a set of modules in which the module itself is non-optional, but there are different possible choices regarding the content of the module (section 2.7). For example, we cannot have a capability theory or application without having chosen a purpose for that theory or application — yet there are many different purposes among which we can choose. The third group of modules, the C-modules, are either non-optional but dependent on a choice made in the B-modules, or else are completely optional. For example, if the purpose you choose is to measure poverty, then you need to decide on some empirical methods in the C-modules; but if your aim is to make a theory of justice, you don't need to choose empirical methods and hence the C-module for empirical methods (module C3) is not relevant for your capability application (section 2.8).[2] In the next section, 2.9, I discuss the possibility of hybrid theories — theories that give a central role to functionings and capabilities yet violate some other core proposition(s). Section 2.11 rounds up the discussion of the modular view by discussing the relevance and advantages of seeing the capability approach from this perspective.

Section 2.12 summarises the conceptual aspects that have been explained by presenting a visualisation of the conceptual framework of the capability approach. Section 2.13 uses the modular view to illuminate the observation, which has been made by several capability scholars, that the capability approach has been used in a narrow and in a broad sense, and explains what difference lies behind this distinction. In the broader use of the capability approach, supporting or complementary theories or additional normative principles are added to the core of the approach — yet none of them is itself *essential* to the capability approach. These are choices made in B-modules or the C-modules. The modular view of the capability approach that will be central to this chapter can thus help to formulate in a sharper manner some observations that have already been made in the capability literature. The chapter closes by looking ahead to the next chapter.

2.2 A preliminary definition of the capability approach

The capability approach has in recent decades emerged as a new theoretical framework about wellbeing, freedom to achieve wellbeing, and all the public values in which either of these can play a role, such as development and social justice. Although there is some scholarly disagreement on the best description of the capability approach (which will be addressed in this chapter), it is generally understood as a

---

2   To the reader who finds this ultra-brief summary of the modular account of the capability approach here unclear: please bear with me until we have reached the end of this chapter, when the different modules will have been unpacked and explained in detail.

conceptual framework for a range of evaluative exercises, including most prominently the following: (1) the assessment of individual levels of achieved wellbeing and wellbeing freedom; (2) the evaluation and assessment of social arrangements or institutions;[3] and (3) the design of policies and other forms of social change in society.

We can trace some aspects of the capability approach back to, among others, Aristotle, Adam Smith, Karl Marx and John Stuart Mill,[4] yet it is Sen who pioneered the approach and a growing number of other scholars across the humanities and the social sciences who have significantly developed it — most significantly Martha Nussbaum, who has developed the capability approach into a partial theory of social justice.[5] Nussbaum also understands her own capabilities account as a version of a theory of human rights.[6] The capability approach purports that freedom to achieve wellbeing is a matter of what people are able to do and to be, and thus the kind of life they are effectively able to lead. The capability approach is generally conceived as a flexible and multipurpose framework, rather than a precise theory (Sen 1992a, 48; Alkire 2005; Robeyns 2005b, 2016b; Qizilbash 2012; Hick and Burchardt 2016, 78). The open-ended and underspecified nature of the capability approach is crucial, but it has not made it easier for its students to understand what kind of theoretical endeavour the capability approach exactly is. How should we understand it? Isn't there a better account possible than the

---

3   Amartya Sen often uses the term "*social arrangement*", which is widely used in the social choice literature and in some other parts of the literature on the capability approach. Yet this term is not very widely used in other disciplines, and many have wondered what "social arrangement" exactly means (e.g. Béteille 1993). Other scholars tend to use the term "institutions", using a broad definition — understood as the formal and informal rules in society that structure, facilitate and delineate actions and interactions. "Institutions" are thus not merely laws and formal rules such as those related to the system of property rights or the social security system, but also informal rules and social norms, such as social norms that expect women to be responsible for raising the children and caring for the ill and elderly, or forbid members of different castes to work together or interact on an equal footing.

4   See Nussbaum (1988, 1992), Sen (1993a, 1999a, 14, 24); Walsh (2000); Qizilbash (2016); Basu and López-Calva (2011, 156–59).

5   A partial theory of justice is a theory that gives us an account of some aspects of what justice requires, but does not comment on what justice requires in other instances or areas.

6   On the relationship between capabilities and human rights, see section 3.14.

somewhat limited description of the capability approach as 'an open, flexible and multi-purpose framework'? Answering these questions will be the task of this chapter.[7]

The open and underspecified nature of the capability approach also explains why the term 'capability approach' was adopted and is now widely used rather than 'capability theory'. Yet as I will argue in section 2.3, we could use the terms 'capability theory' and 'capability approach' in a more illuminating way to signify a more substantive difference, which will help us to get a better grip on the capability literature.

It may be helpful to introduce the term *'advantage'* here, which is a technical term used in academic debates about interpersonal comparisons and in debates about distributive justice.[8] A person's advantage is those aspects of that person's interests that matter (generally, or in a specific context). Hence 'advantage' could refer to a person's achieved wellbeing, or it could refer to her opportunity to achieve wellbeing, or it could refer to her negative freedoms, or to her positive freedoms, or to some other aspect of her interests. By using the very general term 'advantage', we allow ourselves to remain agnostic between the more particular specifications of that term;[9] our analysis will apply to all the different ways in which 'advantage' could be used. This technical term 'advantage' thus allows us to move the arguments to a higher level of generality or abstraction, since we can focus, for example, on which conditions interpersonal comparisons of advantage need to meet, without having to decide on the exact content of 'advantage'.

---

7   For earlier attempts to describe the capability approach, see amongst others Deneulin (2014); Gasper (2007, 1997); Alkire, Qizilbash and Comim (2008); Qizilbash (2012); Robeyns (2005b, 2016b).

8   A 'technical term' is a term which is used in a specialist debate, and has a meaning that is defined within that debate. In many cases, the term refers to something other than its referent in common-sense language (that is, a layperson's use of language).

9   To 'remain agnostic' means that, for the purpose of that analysis, one does not make a choice between different options, and hence proceeds with an analysis that should be valid for all those options. This does not mean that one cannot make a choice, or really believes that all available options are equally good, but rather that one wants to present an analysis that is applicable to as wide a range of choices as possible.

Within the capability approach, there are two different specifications of 'advantage': achieved wellbeing, and the freedom to achieve wellbeing. The notions of 'functionings' and 'capabilities' — which will be explained in detail in section 2.6.1 — are used to flesh out the account of achieved wellbeing and the freedom to achieve wellbeing.[10] Whether the capability approach is used to analyse distributive injustice, or measure poverty, or develop curriculum design — in all these projects the capability approach prioritises certain people's beings and doings and their opportunities to realize those beings and doings (such as their genuine opportunities to be educated, their ability to move around or to enjoy supportive social relationships). This stands in contrast to other accounts of advantage, which focus *exclusively* on mental categories (such as happiness) or on the material means to wellbeing (such as resources like income or wealth).[11]

Thus, the capability approach is a conceptual framework, which is in most cases used as a normative framework for the evaluation and assessment of individual wellbeing and that of institutions, in addition to its much more infrequent use for non-normative purposes.[12] It can be used to evaluate a range of values that draw on an assessment of people's wellbeing, such as inequality, poverty, changes in the wellbeing of persons or the average wellbeing of the members of a group. It can also be used as an evaluative tool providing an alternative for social cost-benefit analysis, or as a framework within which to design and

---

10 Following Amartya Sen (1985c), some would say there are four different ideas of advantage in the capability approach: achieved wellbeing, freedom to achieve wellbeing, achieved agency, and freedom to achieve agency. Yet whether the capability approach should always and for all purposes consider agency freedom to be an end in itself is disputed, and depends in large measure on what one wants to use the capability approach for.

11 Of course, it doesn't follow that mental categories or the material means play *no role at all*; but the normative *priority* lies with functionings and capabilities, and hence happiness or material resources play a more limited role (and, in the case of resources, a purely instrumental role). The relations between functionings/capabilities and resources will be elaborated in 3.12; the relationship between functionings/capabilities and happiness will be elaborated in more detail in section 3.8.

12 On whether the capability approach can be used for explanatory purposes, see section 3.10.

evaluate policies and institutions, such as welfare state design in affluent societies, or poverty reduction strategies by governments and non-governmental organisations in developing countries.

What does it mean, exactly, if we say that something is a normative analysis? Unfortunately, social scientists and philosophers use these terms slightly differently. My estimate is that, given their numerical dominance, the terminology that social scientists use is dominant within the capability literature. Yet the terminology of philosophers is more refined and hence I will start by explaining the philosophers' use of those terms, and then lay out how social scientists use them.

What might a rough typology of research in this area look like? By drawing on some discussions on methods in ethics and political philosophy (O. O'Neill 2009; List and Valentini 2016), I would like to propose the following typology for use within the capability literature. There are (at least) five types of research that are relevant for the capability approach. The first type of scholarship is *conceptual* research, which conducts conceptual analysis — the investigation of how we should use and understand certain concepts such as 'freedom', 'democracy', 'wellbeing', and so forth. An example of such conceptual analysis is provided in section 3.3, where I offer a (relatively simple) conceptual analysis of the question of what kind of freedoms (if any) capabilities could be. The second strand of research is *descriptive*. Here, research and analyses provide us with an empirical understanding of a phenomenon by describing it. This could be done with different methods, from the thick descriptions provided by ethnographic methods to the quantitative methods that are widely used in mainstream social sciences. The third type of research is *explanatory* analysis. This research provides an explanation of a phenomenon — what the mechanisms are that cause a phenomenon, or what the determinants of a phenomenon are. For example, the social determinants of health: the parameters or factors that determine the distribution of health outcomes over the population. A fourth type of research is *evaluative*, and consists of analyses in which values are used to evaluate a state of affairs. A claim is evaluative if it relies on evaluative terms, such as good or bad, better or worse, or desirable or undesirable. Finally, an analysis is *normative* if it is prescriptive — it entails a moral norm that tells us what we *ought* to do.[13] Evaluative analyses and prescriptive analyses are closely intertwined, and often we first conduct an evaluative analysis, which is followed by a prescriptive analysis, e.g. by policy recommendations, as is done, for example, in the evaluative analysis of India's development conducted by Jean Drèze and Amartya Sen (2013). However, one could also make an evaluative analysis while leaving the prescriptive analysis for someone else to make, perhaps leaving it to the agents who need to make the change themselves. For example, one can use the capability approach to make an evaluation or assessment of inequalities between men and women, without drawing prescriptive conclusions (Robeyns 2003, 2006a). Or one can make a prescriptive analysis that is not based on an evaluation, because it is based on universal moral rules. Examples are the capability theories of justice by Nussbaum (2000; 2006b) and Claassen (2016).

The difference with the dominant terminology used by economists (and other social scientists) is that they only distinguish between two types of analysis: 'positive' versus 'normative' economics, whereby 'positive' economics is seen as relying only on 'facts', whereas 'normative economics' also relies on values (e.g. Reiss 2013, 3). Hence economists do not distinguish between what philosophers call 'evaluative analysis' and 'normative analysis' but rather lump them both together under the heading 'normative analysis'. The main take-home message is that the capability approach is used predominantly in the field of ethical analysis (philosophers' terminology) or normative analysis (economists' terminology), somewhat less often in the fields of descriptive analysis and conceptual analysis, and least in the field of explanatory analysis. We will revisit this in section 3.10, where we address whether the capability approach can be an explanatory theory.

---

13   Alkire (2008) calls these normative applications "prospective analysis", and argues that we need to distinguish the evaluative applications of the capability approach from the "prospective applications" of the capability approach. I agree, but since we should avoid introducing new terms when the terms needed are already available, it would be better to use the term 'prescriptive applications' or, as philosophers do, 'normative analysis', rather than introducing 'prospective applications' as a new term.

2.3 The capability approach versus capability theories

The above preliminary definition highlights that the capability approach is an open-ended and underspecified framework, which can be used for multiple purposes. It is *open-ended* because the general capability approach can be developed in a range of different directions, with different purposes, and it is *underspecified* because additional specifications are needed before the capability approach can become effective for a particular purpose — especially if we want it to be normative (whether evaluative or prescriptive). As a consequence, 'the capability approach' itself is an open, general idea, but there are many different ways to 'close' or 'specify' this notion. What is needed for this specifying or closing of the capability approach will depend on the aim of using the approach, e.g. whether we want to develop it into a (partial) theory of justice, or use it to assess inequality, or conceptualise development, or use it for some other purpose.

This distinction between the general, open, underspecified capability approach, and its particular use for specific purposes is absolutely crucial if we want to understand it properly. In order to highlight that distinction, but also to make it easier for us to be clear when we are talking about the general, open, underspecified capability approach, and when we are talking about a particular use for specific purposes, I propose that we use two different terms (Robeyns 2016b, 398). Let us use the term *'the capability approach'* for the general, open, underspecified approach, and let us employ the term *'a capability theory'* or *'a capability analysis, capability account or capability application'* for a specific use of the capability approach, that is, for a use that has a specific goal, such as measuring poverty and deriving some policy prescriptions, or developing a capabilitarian cost-benefit analysis, or theorising about human rights, or developing a theory of social justice. In order to improve readability, I will speak in what follows of *'a capability theory'* as a short-hand for *'a capability account, or capability application, or capability theory'*.[14]

---

14 I kindly request readers who are primarily interested in the capability approach for policy design and (empirical) applications to read 'capability application' every time the term 'capability theory' is used.

One reason why this distinction between 'capability approach' and 'capability theory' is so important, is that many theories with which the capability approach has been compared over time are *specific* theories, not general open frameworks. For example, John Rawls's famous theory of justice is not a general approach but rather a specific theory of institutional justice (Rawls 2009), and this has made the comparison with the capability approach at best difficult (Robeyns 2008b). The appropriate comparison would be Rawls's theory of justice with a properly developed capability theory of justice, such as Nussbaum's *Frontiers of Justice* (Nussbaum 2006b), but not Rawls's theory of justice with the (general) capability approach.

Another reason why the distinction between 'capability approach' and 'capability theory' is important, is that it can help provide an answer to the "number of authors [who] 'complain' that the capability approach does not address questions they put to it" (Alkire 2005, 123). That complaint is misguided, since the capability *approach* cannot, by its very nature, answer all the questions that should instead be put to particular capability *theories*. For example, it is a mistake to criticise Amartya Sen because he has not drawn up a specific list of relevant functionings in his capability approach; that critique would only have bite if Sen were to develop a particular capability theory or capability application where the selection of functionings is a requirement.[15]

In short, there is one capability approach and there are many capability theories, and keeping that distinction sharply in mind should clear up many misunderstandings in the literature.

However, if we accept the distinction between capability theories and the capability approach, it raises the question of what these different capability theories have in common. Before addressing that issue, I first want to present a bottom-up description of the many modes in which capability analyses have been conducted. This will give us a better sense of what the capability approach has been used for, and what it can do for us.

---

15   Yet even for capability theories, it is unlikely that Sen would agree that he has to *draw up a list* of capabilities, since he is a proponent of a procedural method for selecting capabilities. At the beginning of this century, there was a fierce discussion in the capability literature about whether it was a valid critique of Sen's work that it lacked a specific list (Nussbaum 2003a; Robeyns 2003; Sen 2004a; Qizilbash 2005). Luckily that debate seems to be settled now. For an overview of the different ways in which dimensions can be selected in the capability approach, see section 2.7.2.

2.4 The many modes of capability analysis

If the capability approach is an open framework, then what are the ways in which it has been closed to form more specific and powerful analyses? Scholars use the capability approach for different types of analysis, with different goals, relying on different methodologies, with different corresponding roles for functionings and capabilities. Not all of these are capability *theories*; some are capability *applications*, both empirical as well as theoretical. We can observe that there is a rich diversity of ways in which the capability approach has been used. Table 2.1 gives an overview of these different usages, by listing the different types of capability analyses.

Normative theorising within the capability approach is often done by moral and political philosophers. The capability approach is then used as one element of a normative theory, such as a theory of justice or a theory of disadvantage. For example, Elizabeth Anderson (1999) has proposed the outlines of a theory of social justice (which she calls "democratic equality") in which certain basic levels of capabilities that are needed to function as equal citizens should be guaranteed to all. Martha Nussbaum (2006b) has developed a minimal theory of social justice in which she defends a list of basic capabilities that everyone should be entitled to, as a matter of human dignity.

While most normative theorising within the capability approach has related to justice, other values have also been developed and analysed using the capability approach. Some theorists of freedom have developed accounts of freedom or rights using the capability approach (van Hees 2013). Another important value that has been studied from the perspective of the capability approach is ecological sustainability (e.g. Anand and Sen 1994, 2000; Robeyns and Van der Veen 2007; Lessmann and Rauschmayer 2013; Crabtree 2013; Sen 2013). Efficiency is a value about which very limited conceptual work is done, but which nevertheless is inescapably normative, and it can be theorised in many different ways (Le Grand 1990; Heath 2006). If we ask what efficiency is, we could answer by referring to Pareto optimality or x-efficiency, but we could also develop a notion of efficiency from a capability perspective (Sen 1993b). Such a notion would answer the question 'efficiency of what?' with 'efficiency in the space of capabilities (or functionings, or a mixture)'.

Table 2.1 The main modes of capability analysis

Epistemic goal	Methodology/discipline	Role of functionings and capabilities	Examples
Normative theories (of particular values), e.g. theories of justice, human rights, wellbeing, sustainability, efficiency, etc.	Philosophy, in particular ethics and normative political philosophy.	The metric/currency in the interpersonal comparisons of advantage that are entailed in the value that is being analysed.	Sen 1993b; Anand and Sen 1994; Crabtree 2012, 2013; Lessmann and Rauschmayer 2013; Robeyns 2016c; Nussbaum 1992, 1997; Nussbaum 2000; Nussbaum 2006b; Wolff and De-Shalit 2007.
Normative applied analysis, including policy design.	Applied ethics (e.g. medical ethics, bio-ethics, economic ethics, development ethics etc.) and normative strands in the social sciences.	A metric of individual advantage that is part of the applied normative analysis.	Alkire 2002; Robeyns 2003; Canoy, Lerais and Schokkaert 2010; Holland 2014; Ibrahim 2017.
Welfare/quality of life measurement.	Quantitative empirical strands within various social sciences.	Social indicators.	Kynch and Sen 1983; Sen 1985a; Kuklys 2005; Alkire and Foster 2011; Alkire et al. 2015; Chiappero-Martinetti 2000.
Thick description/descriptive analysis.	Qualitative empirical strands within various humanities and social sciences.	Elements of a narrative.	Unterhalter 2003b; Comradie 2013.
Understanding the nature of certain ideas, practices, notions (other than the values in the normative theories).	Conceptual analysis.	Used as part of the conceptualisation of the idea or notion.	Sen 1993b; Robeyns 2006c; Wigley and Akkoyunlu-Wigley 2006; van Hees 2013.
[Other goals?]	[Other methods?]	[Other roles?]	[Other studies may be available/are needed.]

Source: Robeyns (2005a), expanded and updated.

Quantitative social scientists, especially economists, are mostly interested in measurement. This quantitative work could serve different purposes, e.g. the measurement of multidimensional poverty analysis (Alkire and Foster 2011; Alkire et al. 2015), or the measurement of the disadvantages faced by disabled people (Kuklys 2005; Zaidi and Burchardt 2005). Moreover, some quantitative social scientists, mathematicians, and econometricians have been working on investigating the methods that could be used for quantitative capability analyses (Kuklys 2005; Di Tommaso 2007; Krishnakumar 2007; Krishnakumar and Ballon 2008; Krishnakumar and Nagar 2008).

Thick description or descriptive analysis is another mode of capability analysis. For example, it can be used to describe the realities of schoolgirls in countries that may have formal access to school for both girls and boys, but where other hurdles (such as high risk of rape on the way to school, or the lack of sanitary provisions at school) mean that this formal right is not enough to guarantee these girls the corresponding capability (Unterhalter 2003b).

Finally, the capability approach can be used for conceptual work beyond the conceptualisation of values, as is done within normative philosophy. Sometimes the capability approach lends itself well to providing a better understanding of a certain phenomenon. For example, we could understand education as a legal right or as an investment in human capital, but we could also conceptualise it as the expansion of a capability, or develop an account of education that draws on both the capability approach and human rights theory. This would not only help us to look differently at what education is; a different conceptualisation would also have normative implications, for example related to the curriculum design, or to answer the question of what is needed to ensure that capability, or of how much education should be guaranteed to children with low potential market-related human capital (McCowan 2011; Nussbaum 2012; Robeyns 2006c; Walker 2012a; Walker and Unterhalter 2007; Wigley and Akkoyunlu-Wigley 2006).

Of course, texts and research projects often have multiple goals, and therefore particular studies often mix these different goals and methods. Jean Drèze and Amartya Sen's (1996, 2002, 2013) comprehensive analyses of India's human development achievements are in part an evaluative analysis based on various social indicators, but also in part a prescriptive analysis. Similarly, Nussbaum's (2000) book *Women and Human Development* is primarily normative and philosophical, but also includes thick descriptions of how institutions enable or hamper people's capabilities, by focussing on the lives of particular women.

What is the value of distinguishing between different uses of the capability approach? It is important because functionings and capabilities — the core concepts in the capability approach — play different roles in each type of analysis. In quality of life measurement, the functionings and capabilities are the social indicators that reflect a person's quality of life. In thick descriptions and descriptive analysis, the functionings and capabilities form part of the narrative. This narrative can aim to reflect the quality of life, but it can also aim to understand some other aspect of people's lives, such as by explaining behaviour that might appear irrational according to traditional economic analysis, or revealing layers of complexities that a quantitative analysis can rarely capture. In philosophical reasoning, the functionings and capabilities play yet another role, as they are often part of the foundations of a utopian account of a just society or of the goals that morally sound policies should pursue.

The flexibility of functionings and capabilities, which can be applied in different ways within different types of capability analysis, means that there are no hard and fast rules that govern how to select the relevant capabilities. Each type of analysis, with its particular goals, will require its own answer to this question. The different roles that functionings and capabilities can play in different types of capability analyses have important implications for the question of how to select the relevant capabilities: each type of analysis, with its particular goals, will require its own answer to this question. The selection of capabilities as social indicators of the quality of life is a very different undertaking from the selection of capabilities for a utopian theory of justice: the quality standards for research and scholarship are different, the epistemic constraints of the research are different, the best available practices in the field are different. Moral philosophers, quantitative social scientists, and qualitative social scientists have each signed up to a different set of meta-theoretical assumptions, and find different academic practices acceptable and unacceptable. For example, many ethnographers tend to reject normative theorising and also often object to what they consider the reductionist nature of quantitative empirical analysis, whereas many economists tend to discard the thick descriptions by ethnographers, claiming they are merely anecdotal and hence not scientific.

Two remarks before closing this section. First, providing a typology of the work on the capability approach, as this section attempts to do, remains work in progress. In 2004, I could only discern three main modes of capability analysis: quality of life analysis; thick description/descriptive analysis; and normative theories — though I left open the possibility that the capability approach could be used for other goals too (Robeyns 2005a). In her book *Creating Capabilities*, Nussbaum (2011) writes that the capability approach comes in only two modes: comparative qualify of life assessment, and as a theory of justice. I don't think that is correct: not all modes of capability analysis can be reduced to these two modes, as I have argued elsewhere in detail (Robeyns 2011, 2016b). The different modes of capability analysis described in table 2.1 provide a more comprehensive overview, but we should not assume that this overview is complete. It is quite likely that table 2.1 will, in due course, have to be updated to reflect new types of work that uses the capability approach. Moreover, one may also prefer another way to categorise the different types of work done within the capability literature, and hence other typologies are possible and may be more illuminating.

Second, it is important that we fully acknowledge the diversity of disciplines, the diversity of goals we have for the creation of knowledge, and the diversity of methods used within the capability approach. At the same time, we need not forget that some aspects of its development might need to be discipline-specific, or specific for one's goals. As a result, the capability approach is at the same time multidisciplinary, interdisciplinary, but also forms part of developments *within* disciplines and methods. These different 'faces' of the capability approach *all* need to be fully acknowledged if we want to understand it in a nuanced and complete way.

2.5 The modular view of the capability approach

It is time to take stock. What do we already know about the capability approach, and what questions are raised by the analysis so far? The capability approach is an open approach, and depending on its purpose can be developed into a range of capability theories or capabilitarian applications. It is focused on what people can do and be (their capabilities) and on what they are actually achieving in terms of beings and doings (their functionings). However, this still does not answer the question of what kind of framework the capability approach is. Can we give an account of a capability theory that is more enlightening regarding what exactly makes a theory a capabilitarian theory, and what doesn't?

In this book, I present an account of the capability approach that, on the one hand, makes clear what all capability theories share, yet on the other hand allows us to better understand the many forms that a capability theory or capability account can take — hence to appreciate the diversity within the capability approach more fully. The modular view that I present here is a modified (and, I hope, improved) version of the cartwheel model that I have developed elsewhere (Robeyns 2016b). The modular view shifts the focus a little bit from the question of how to understand the capability approach in general, to the question of how the various capability accounts, applications and theories should be understood and how they should be constructed. After all, students, scholars, policy makers and activists are often not concerned with the capability approach in general, but rather want to know whether it would be a smart idea to use the capability approach to construct a particular capability theory, application or account for the problem or question they are trying to analyse. In order to answer the question of whether, for their purposes, the capability approach is a helpful framework to consider, they need to know what is needed for a capability theory, application or account. The modular view that will follow will give those who want to develop a capability theory, application or analysis a list of properties their theory has to meet, a list of choices that need to be made but in which several options regarding content are possible, and a list of modules that they could take into account, but which will not always be necessary.

Recall that in order to improve readability, I use the term 'a capability theory' as a short-hand for 'a capability account, or capability analysis, or capability application, or capability theory'. A capability theory is constructed based on three different types of module, which (in order to facilitate discussion) will be called the A-module, B-modules and C-modules. The A-module is a single module which is compulsory for all capability theories. The A-module consists of a number of propositions (definitions and claims) which a capability theory should not violate. This is the core of the capability approach, and hence entails those properties that all capability theories share. The B-modules consist of a range of non-optional modules with optional content. That is, if we construct a capability theory, we have to consider the issue that the module addresses, but there are several different options to choose from in considering that particular issue. For example, module B1 concerns the 'purpose' of the theory: do we want to make a theory of justice, or a more comprehensive evaluative framework for societal institutions, or do we want to measure poverty or inequality, or design a curriculum, or do we want to use the capability approach to conceptualise 'social progress' or 'efficiency' or to rethink the role of universities in the twenty-first century? All these purposes are possible within the capability approach. The point of seeing these as B-modules is that one *has to* be clear about one's purpose, but there are many different purposes possible. The C-modules are either contingent on a particular choice made in a B-module, or they can be fully optional. For example, one can offer a comprehensive evaluation of a country's development path, and decide that as part of this evaluation, one wants to include particular accounts of the history and culture of that country, since this may make more comprehensible the reasons why that country has taken this particular development path rather than another. The particular historical account that would be part of one's capability theory would then be optional.[16]

---

16 To say that the insertion of those theories is fully optional is not the same as saying that capability theories that will be developed with different types of additional complementary theories will all be equally good. For example, historians are very likely to think that most theories, even normative theories, have to be historically informed, and hence the relevant historical knowledge will need to be added to a capability theory. But these are matters of dispute that have to be debated, and cannot be settled by narrowing down *the definition* of a capability theory.

Given this three-fold structure of the modular view of capability theories, let us now investigate what the content of the compulsory module A is, as well as what the options are within the B-modules and C-modules.

2.6 The A-module: the non-optional core of all capability theories

What, then, is the content of the A-module, which all capability theories should share? Table 2.2 presents the keywords for the eight elements of the A-module.

Table 2.2 The content of the compulsory module A
A1: Functionings and capabilities as core concepts
A2: Functionings and capabilities are value-neutral categories
A3: Conversion factors
A4: The distinction between means and ends
A5: Functionings and/or capabilities form the evaluative space
A6: Other dimensions of ultimate value
A7: Value pluralism
A8: Valuing each person as an end

2.6.1 A1: Functionings and capabilities

Functionings and capabilities are the core concepts in the capability approach. They are also the dimensions in which interpersonal comparisons of 'advantage' are made (this is what property A5 entails).[17] They are the most important distinctive features of all capabilitarian theories. There are some differences in the usage of these notions between different capability theorists,[18] but these differences do not affect the essence of these notions: capabilities are what people are able to be and to do, and functionings point to the corresponding achievements.

---

17 See section 2.2 for an explanation of the technical term 'advantage'.
18 For some core differences in the way Martha Nussbaum and Amartya Sen use the terms 'functionings' and 'capabilities', see section 3.2.

Capabilities are real freedoms or real opportunities, which do not refer to access to resources or opportunities for certain levels of satisfaction. Examples of 'beings' are being well-nourished, being undernourished, being sheltered and housed in a decent house, being educated, being illiterate, being part of a supportive social network; these also include very different beings such as being part of a criminal network and being depressed. Examples of the 'doings' are travelling, caring for a child, voting in an election, taking part in a debate, taking drugs, killing animals, eating animals, consuming great amounts of fuel in order to heat one's house, and donating money to charity.

Capabilities are a person's real *freedoms* or *opportunities* to achieve functionings.[19] Thus, while travelling is a functioning, the real opportunity to travel is the corresponding capability. A person who does not travel may or may not be free and able to travel; the notion of capability seeks to capture precisely the fact of whether the person *could* travel *if* she wanted to. The distinction between functionings and capabilities is between the realized and the effectively possible, in other words, between achievements, on the one hand, and freedoms or opportunities from which one can choose, on the other.

Functionings are constitutive of human life. At least, this is a widespread view, certainly in the social sciences, policy studies, and in a significant part of philosophy — and I think it is a view that is helpful for the interdisciplinary, practical orientation that the vast majority of capability research has.[20] That means one cannot be a human being without having at least a range of functionings; they make the lives of human beings both *lives* (as opposed to the existence of innate objects) and *human* (in contrast to the lives of trees or animals). Human functionings are those beings and doings that constitute human life and that are central to our understandings of ourselves as human beings. It is hard to think of any phenomenological account of the lives of

---

19 See also section 3.3 which discusses in more depth *the kind* of freedoms or opportunities that capabilities are.

20 The exceptions are those philosophers who want to develop normative theories while steering away from *any* metaphysical claims (that is, claims about how things are when we try to uncover their essential nature). I agree that the description of 'functionings' and 'capabilities' in this section makes metaphysical claims, but I think they are very 'minimal' (in the sense that they are not wildly implausible, and still leave open a wide variety of theories to be developed) and hence we should not be troubled by these metaphysical assumptions.

humans — either an account given by a human being herself, or an account from a third-person perspective — which does not include a description of a range of human functionings. Yet, not all beings and doings are functionings; for example, flying like a bird or living for two hundred years like an oak tree are not *human* functionings.

In addition, some human beings or doings may not be constitutive but rather contingent upon our social institutions; these, arguably, should not qualify as 'universal functionings' — that is, functionings no matter the social circumstances in which one lives — but are rather 'context-dependent functionings', functionings that are to a significant extent dependent on the existing social structures. For example, 'owning a house' is not a universal functioning, yet 'being sheltered in a safe way and protected from the elements' is a universal functioning. One can also include the capability of being sheltered in government-funded housing or by a rental market for family houses, which is regulated in such a way that it does not endanger important aspects of that capability.

Note that many features of a person could be described either as a being or as a doing: we can say that a person *is* housed in a pleasantly warm dwelling, or that this person *does consume* lots of energy to keep her house warm. Yet other functionings are much more straightforwardly described as either a being or a doing, for example 'being healthy' (a being) or 'killing animals' (a doing).

A final remark. Acknowledging that functionings and capabilities are the core concepts of the capability approach generates some further conceptual questions, which have not all been sufficiently addressed in the literature. An important question is whether additional structural requirements that apply to the relations between various capabilities should be imposed on the capability approach in general (not merely as a particular choice for a specific capability theory). Relatively little work has been done on the question of the conceptual properties of capabilities understood as freedoms or opportunities and on the question of the minimum requirements of the opportunity set that make up these various capabilities. But it is clear that more needs to be said about which properties we want functionings, capabilities, and capability sets to meet. One important property has been pointed out by Kaushik Basu (1987), who argued that the moral relevance lies not in the various capabilities each taken by themselves and only considering the choices made by one person. Rather, the moral relevance lies in whether capabilities are truly available to us given the choices made by others, since that is the real freedom to live our lives in various ways, as it is truly open to us. For example, if a teenager lives in a family in which there are only enough resources for one of the children to pursue higher education, then he only truly has the capability to pursue higher education if none of his older siblings has made that choice before him.[21]

2.6.2 A2: Functionings and capabilities are value-neutral categories

Functionings and capabilities are defined in a value-neutral way. Many functionings are valuable, but not all functionings necessarily have a positive value. Instead, some functionings have no value or even have a negative value, e.g. the functioning of being affected by a painful, debilitating and ultimately incurable illness, suffering from excessive levels of stress, or engaging in acts of unjustifiable violence. In those latter cases, we are better off without that functionings outcome, and the functionings outcome has a negative value. Functionings are constitutive elements of human life, which consist of both wellbeing and ill-being. The notion of functionings should, therefore, be value-neutral in the sense that we should conceptually allow for the idea of 'bad functionings' or functionings with a negative value (Deneulin and Stewart 2002, 67; Nussbaum 2003a, 45; Stewart 2005, 190; Carter 2014, 79–81).

There are many beings and doings that have negative value, but they are still 'a being' or 'a doing' and, hence, a functioning. Nussbaum made that point forcefully when she argued that the capability to rape should not be a capability that we have reason to protect (Nussbaum 2003: 44–45). A country could *effectively* enable people to rape, for example, either when rape is not illegal (as it is not between husband and wife in many countries), or when rape is illegal, but *de facto* never leads to any

---

21 Arguably, some of that work is being done by social choice theorists and others working with axiomatic methods, but unfortunately almost none of the insights of that work have spread among the disciplines within the capability literature where axiomatic and other formal methods are not used (and, presumably, not well understood). See, for example, Pattanaik (2006); Xu (2002); Gotoh, Suzumura and Yoshihara (2005); Gaertner and Xu (2006, 2008).

punishment of the aggressor. If there is a set of social norms justifying rape, and would-be rapists help each other to be able to rape, then would-be rapists in that country effectively enjoy the capability to rape. But clearly, rape is a moral bad, and a huge harm to its victims; it is thus not a capability that a country should want to protect. This example illustrates that functionings as well as capabilities can be harmful or have a negative value, as well as be positive or valuable. At an abstract and general level, 'functionings' and 'capabilities' are thus in themselves neutral concepts, and hence we cannot escape the imperative to decide which ones we want to support and enable, and which ones we want to fight or eliminate. Frances Stewart and Séverine Deneulin (2002, 67) put it as follows:

> [...] some capabilities have negative values (e.g. committing murder), while others may be trivial (riding a one-wheeled bicycle). Hence there is a need to differentiate between 'valuable' and non-valuable capabilities, and indeed, within the latter, between those that are positive but of lesser importance and those that actually have negative value.

The above examples show that some functionings can be unequivocally good (e.g. being in good health) or unequivocally bad (e.g. being raped or being murdered). In those cases, there will be unanimity on whether the functionings outcome is bad or good. But now we need to add a layer of complexity. Sometimes, it will be a matter of doubt, or of dispute, whether a functioning will be good or bad — or the goodness or badness may depend on the context and/or the normative theory we endorse. An interesting example is giving care, or 'care work'.[22] Clearly being able to care for someone could be considered a valuable capability. For example, in the case of child care, there is much joy to be gained, and many parents would like to work less so as to spend more time with their children. But care work has a very ambiguous character if we try to answer whether it should be considered to be a valuable functioning from the perspective of the person who does the care. Lots of care is performed primarily because there is familial or social pressure put on someone (generally women) to do so, or because no-one else is doing it

---

22   On the complex nature of 'care', and what the need to care and be cared for requires from a just society, see e.g. Tronto (1987); Kittay (1999); Nussbaum (2006b); Folbre (1994); Folbre and Bittman (2004); Engster (2007); Gheaus (2011); Gheaus and Robeyns (2011).

(Lewis and Giullari 2005). There is also the hypothesis that care work can be a positive functioning if done for a limited amount of time, but becomes a negative functioning if it is done for many hours. Hence, from the functionings outcome in itself, we cannot conclude whether this is a positive element of that person's quality of life, or rather a negative element; in fact, sometimes it will be an ambiguous situation, which cannot easily be judged (Robeyns 2003).

One could wonder, though, whether this ambiguity cannot simply be resolved by reformulating the corresponding capability slightly differently. In theory, this may be true. If there are no empirical constraints related to the observations we can make, then one could in many cases rephrase such functionings that are ambiguously valued into another capability where its valuation is clearly positive. For example, one could say that the *functioning* of providing care in itself can be ambiguous (since some people do too much, thereby harming their own longer-term wellbeing, or do it because no-one else is providing the care and social norms require them to do it). Yet there is a closely related capability that is clearly valuable: the capability to provide hands-on care, which takes into account that one has a robust choice not to care if one does not want to, and that one does not find oneself in a situation in which the care is of insufficient quantity and/or quality if one does not deliver the care oneself. If such a robust *capability* to care is available, it would be genuinely valuable, since one would have a real option not to choose the functioning without paying an unacceptable price (e.g. that the person in need of care is not properly cared for). However, the problem with this solution, of reformulating functionings that are ambiguously valuable into capabilities that are unequivocally valuable, is the constraints it places on empirical information. We may be able to use these layers of filters and conditions in first-person analyses, or in ethnographic analyses, but in most cases not in large-scale empirical analyses.

Many specific capability theories make the mistake of *defining* functionings as those beings and doings that one has reason to value. But the problem with this value-laden definition is that it collapses two aspects of the development of a capability theory into one: the definition of the relevant space (e.g. income, or happiness, or functionings) and, once we have chosen our functionings and capabilities, the normative decision regarding which of those capabilities will be the focus of our theory. We may agree on the first issue and not on the second and still both rightly believe that we endorse a capability theory — yet this is only possible if we analytically separate the normative choice for functionings and capabilities from the additional normative decision of which functionings we will regard as valuable and which we will not regard as valuable. Collapsing these two normative moments into one is not a good idea; instead, we need to acknowledge that there are two normative moves being made when we use functionings and capabilities as our evaluative space, and we need to justify each of those two normative moves separately.

Note that the value-laden definition of functionings and capabilities, which defines them as always good and valuable, may be less problematic when one develops a capability theory of severe poverty or destitution. We all agree that poor health, poor housing, poor sanitation, poor nutrition and social exclusion are dimensions of destitution. So, for example, the dimensions chosen for the Multidimensional Poverty Index developed by Sabina Alkire and her colleagues — health, education and living standard — may not elicit much disagreement.[23] But for many other capability theories, it is disputed whether a particular functionings outcome is valuable or not. The entire field of applied ethics is filled with questions and cases in which these disputes are debated. Is sex work bad for adult sex workers, or should it be seen as a valuable capability? Is the capability of parents not to vaccinate their children against polio or measles a valuable freedom? If employees in highly competitive organisations are not allowed to read their emails after working hours, is that then a valuable capability that is taken away from them, or are we protecting them from becoming workaholics and protecting them from the pressure to work all the time, including at evenings and weekends? As these examples show, we need to allow for the conceptual possibility that there are functionings that are always valuable, never valuable, valuable or non-valuable in some contexts but not in others, or where

---

23   The Multidimensional Poverty Index is developed by the Oxford Poverty and Human Development Initiative (OPHI), under the leadership of Sabina Alkire. See http://www.ophi.org.uk/multidimensional-poverty-index/ for a clear introduction of the Multidimensional Poverty Index. For scholarly papers on the Index, as well as other work done by the scholars in OPHI, see http://www.ophi.org.uk/resources/ophi-working-papers/

we simply are not sure. This requires that functionings and capabilities are conceptualised in a value-neutral way, and hence this should be a core requirement of the capability approach.

2.6.3 A3: Conversion factors

A third core idea of the capability approach is that *persons have different abilities to convert resources into functionings*. These are called *conversion factors*: the factors which determine the degree to which a person can transform a resource into a functioning. This has been an important idea in Amartya Sen's version of the capability approach (Sen 1992a, 19–21, 26–30, 37–38) and for those scholars influenced by his writings. Resources, such as marketable goods and services, but also goods and services emerging from the non-market economy (including household production) have certain characteristics that make them of interest to people. In Sen's work in welfare economics, the notion of 'resources' was limited to material and/or measurable resources (in particular: money or consumer goods) but one could also apply the notion of conversion factors to a broader understanding of resources, including, for example, the educational degrees that one has.

The example of a bike is often used to illustrate the idea of conversion factors. We are interested in a bike not primarily because it is an object made from certain materials with a specific shape and colour, but because it can take us to places where we want to go, and in a faster way than if we were walking. These characteristics of a good or commodity enable or contribute to a functioning. A bike enables the functioning of mobility, to be able to move oneself freely and more rapidly than walking. But a person might be able to turn that resource into a valuable functioning to a different degree than other persons, depending on the relevant conversion factors. For example, an able-bodied person who was taught to ride a bicycle when he was a child has a high conversion factor enabling him to turn the bicycle into the ability to move around efficiently, whereas a person with a physical impairment or someone who never learnt to ride a bike has a very low conversion factor. The conversion factors thus represent how much functioning one can get out of a resource; in our example, how much mobility the person can get out of a bicycle.

There are several different types of conversion factors, and the conversion factors discussed are often categorized into three groups (Robeyns 2005b, 99; Crocker and Robeyns 2009, 68). All conversion factors influence how a person can be or is free to convert the characteristics of the resources into a functioning, yet the sources of these factors may differ. *Personal conversion factors* are internal to the person, such as metabolism, physical condition, sex, reading skills, or intelligence. If a person is disabled, or if she is in a bad physical condition, or has never learned to cycle, then the bike will be of limited help in enabling the functioning of mobility. *Social conversion factors* are factors stemming from the society in which one lives, such as public policies, social norms, practices that unfairly discriminate, societal hierarchies, or power relations related to class, gender, race, or caste. *Environmental conversion factors* emerge from the physical or built environment in which a person lives. Among aspects of one's geographical location are climate, pollution, the likelihood of earthquakes, and the presence or absence of seas and oceans. Among aspects of the built environment are the stability of buildings, roads, and bridges, and the means of transportation and communication. Take again the example of the bicycle. How much a bicycle contributes to a person's mobility depends on that person's physical condition (a personal conversion factor), the social mores including whether women are generally allowed to ride a bicycle (a social conversion factor), and the availability of decent roads or bike paths (an environmental conversion factor). Once we start to be aware of the existence of conversion factors, it becomes clear that they are a very pervasive phenomenon. For example, a pregnant or lactating woman needs more of the same food than another woman in order to be well-nourished. Or people living in delta regions need protection from flooding if they want to enjoy the same capability of being safely sheltered as people living in the mountains. There are an infinite number of other examples illustrating the importance of conversion factors. The three types of conversion factor all push us to acknowledge that it is not sufficient to know the resources a person owns or can use in order to be able to assess the wellbeing that he or she has achieved or could achieve; rather, we need to know much more about the person and the circumstances in which he or she is living. Differences in conversion factors are one important source of human diversity, which is a central concern in the capability approach, and will be discussed in more detail in section 3.5.

Note that many conversion factors are not fixed or given, but can be altered by policies and choices that we make. And the effects of a particular conversion factor can also depend on the social and personal resources that a person has, as well as on the other conversion factors. For example, having a physical impairment that doesn't allow one to walk severely restricts one's capability to be mobile if one finds oneself in a situation in which one doesn't have access to a wheelchair, and in which the state of the roads is bad and vehicles used for public transport are not wheelchair-accessible. But suppose now the built environment is different: all walking-impaired people have a right to a wheelchair, roads are wheelchair-friendly, public transport is wheelchair-accessible and society is characterised by a set of social norms whereby people consider it nothing but self-evident to provide help to fellow travellers who can't walk. In such an alternative social state, with a different set of resources and social and environmental conversion factors, the same personal conversion factor (not being able to walk) plays out very differently. In sum, in order to know what people are able to do and be, we need to analyse the full picture of their resources, and the various conversion factors, or else analyse the functionings and capabilities directly. The advantage of having a clear picture of the resources needed, and the particular conversion factors needed, is that it also gives those aiming to expand capability sets information on where interventions can be made.

2.6.4 A4: The means-ends distinction

The fourth core characteristic of the capability approach is the means-ends distinction. The approach stresses that we should always be clear, when valuing something, whether we value it as an end in itself, or as a means to a valuable end. For the capability approach, when considering interpersonal comparisons of advantage, the ultimate ends are people's valuable capabilities (there could be other ends as well; see 2.6.6). This implies that the capability approach requires us to evaluate policies and other changes according to their impact on people's capabilities as well as their actual functionings; yet at the same time we need to ask whether the preconditions — the means and the enabling circumstances — for those capabilities are in place. We must ask whether people are able to be healthy, and whether the means or resources necessary for this capability, such as clean water, adequate sanitation, access to doctors, protection from infections and diseases and basic knowledge on health issues are present. We must ask whether people are well-nourished, and whether the means or conditions for the realization of this capability, such as having sufficient food supplies and food entitlements, are being met. We must ask whether people have access to a high-quality education system, to real political participation, and to community activities that support them, that enable them to cope with struggles in daily life, and that foster caring friendships. Hence we do need to take the means into account, but we can only do so if we first know what the ends are.

Many of the arguments that capability theorists have advanced against alternative normative frameworks can be traced back to the objection that alternative approaches focus on particular means to wellbeing rather than the ends.[24] There are two important reasons why the capability approach dictates that we have to start our analysis from the ends rather than the means. Firstly, people differ in their ability to convert means into valuable opportunities (capabilities) or outcomes (functionings) (Sen 1992a, 26–28, 36–38). Since ends are what ultimately matter when thinking about wellbeing and the quality of life, means can only work as fully reliable proxies of people's opportunities to achieve those ends if all people have *the same* capacities or powers to convert those means into equal capability sets. This is an assumption that goes against a core characteristic of the capability approach, namely claim A3 — the inter-individual differences in the conversion of resources into functionings and capabilities. Capability scholars believe that these inter-individual differences are far-reaching and significant, and hence this also explains why the idea of conversion factors is a compulsory option in the capability approach (see 2.6.3). Theories that focus on

---

24 This is a critique that the capability approach shares with the happiness approach, which also focusses on what it considers to be an end in itself — happiness. Still, capability scholars have reasons why they do not endorse the singular focus on happiness, as the happiness approach proposes. See section 3.8.

means run the risk of downplaying the normative relevance of not only these conversion factors, but also the differences in structural constraints that people face (see 2.7.5).

The second reason why the capability approach requires us to start from ends rather than means is that there are some vitally important ends that do not depend very much on material means, and hence would not be picked up in our analysis if we were to focus on means only. For example, self-respect, supportive relationships in school or in the workplace, or friendship are all very important ends that people may want; yet there are no crucial means to those ends that one could use as a readily measurable proxy. We need to focus on ends directly if we want to capture what is important.

One could argue, however, that the capability approach does not focus entirely on ends, but rather on the question of whether a person is being put in the conditions in which she can pursue her ultimate ends. For example, being able to read could be seen as a means rather than an end in itself, since people's ultimate ends will be more specific, such as reading street signs, the newspaper, or the Bible or Koran. It is therefore somewhat more precise to say that the capability approach focuses on people's ends in terms of beings and doings expressed in general terms: being literate, being mobile, being able to hold a decent job. Whether a particular person then decides to translate these general capabilities into the more specific capabilities A, B or C (e.g. reading street signs, reading the newspaper or reading the Bible) is up to them. Whether that person decides to stay put, travel to the US or rather to China, is in principle not important for a capability analysis: the question is rather whether a person has these capabilities in more general terms.[25] Another way of framing this is to say that the end of policy making and institutional design is to provide people with general capabilities, whereas the ends of persons are more specific capabilities.[26]

Of course, the normative focus on ends does not imply that the capability approach does not at all value means such as material or

---

25 However, while a focus on available options rather than realised choices is the default normative focus of capability theories, there are some capability applications where, for good reasons, the focus is on achieved functionings rather than capabilities. This will be elaborated in the next section.

26 On the distinction between general capabilities and specific capabilities, see 3.2.4.

financial resources. Instead, a capability analysis will typically focus on resources and other means. For example, in their evaluation of development in India, Jean Drèze and Amartya Sen (2002, 3) have stressed that working within the capability approach in no way excludes the integration of an analysis of resources such as food. In sum, all the means of wellbeing, like the availability of commodities, legal entitlements to them, other social institutions, and so forth, *are* important, but the capability approach presses the point that they are not the ends of wellbeing, only their means. Food may be abundant in the village, but a starving person may have nothing to exchange for it, no legal claim on it, or no way of preventing intestinal parasites from consuming it before he or she does. In all these cases, at least some resources will be available, but that person will remain hungry and, after a while, undernourished.[27]

Nevertheless, one could wonder: wouldn't it be better to focus on means only, rather than making the normative analysis more complicated and more informationally demanding by also focusing on functionings and capabilities? Capability scholars would respond that starting a normative analysis from the ends rather than means has at least two advantages, in addition to the fundamental reason mentioned earlier that a focus on ends is needed to appropriately capture inter-individual differences.

First, if we start from being explicit about our ends, the valuation of means will retain the status of an *instrumental* valuation rather than risk taking on the nature of a valuation of ends. For example, money or economic growth will not be valued for their own sake, but only in so far as they contribute to an expansion of people's capabilities. For those who have been working within the capability framework, this has become a deeply ingrained practice — but one only needs to read the newspapers for a few days to see how often policies are justified or discussed without a clear distinction being made between means and ends.

Second, by starting from ends, we do not a priori assume that there is only one overriding important means to those ends (such as

---

27   The relationship between means and capabilities is analysed in more depth in section 3.12.

income), but rather explicitly ask the question: which types of means are important for the fostering and nurturing of a particular capability, or set of capabilities? For some capabilities, the most important means will indeed be financial resources and economic production, but for others it may be a change in political practices and institutions, such as effective guarantees and protections of freedom of thought, political participation, social or cultural practices, social structures, social institutions, public goods, social norms, and traditions and habits. As a consequence, an effective capability-enhancing policy may not be increasing disposable income, but rather fighting a homophobic, ethnophobic, racist or sexist social climate.

2.6.5 A5: Functionings and capabilities as the evaluative space

If a capability theory is a normative theory (as is often the case), then functionings and capabilities form the entire evaluative space, or are part of the evaluative space.[28] A normative theory is a theory that entails a value judgement: something is better than or worse than something else. This value judgement can be used to compare the position of different persons or states of affairs (as in inequality analysis) or it can be used to judge one course of action as 'better' than another course of action (as in policy design). For all these types of normative theories, we need normative claims, since concepts alone cannot ground normativity.

The first normative claim which each capability theory should respect is thus that functionings and capabilities form the 'evaluative space'. According to the capability approach, the ends of wellbeing freedom, justice, and development should be conceptualized in terms of people's functionings and/or capabilities. This claim is not contested

---

28   I am using the term 'normative' here in the way it is used by social scientists, hence encompassing what philosophers call both 'normative' and 'evaluative'. For these different uses of terminology, see section 2.2. It is also possible to use the notions of 'functionings' and 'capabilities' for non-normative purposes (see section 3.10). In that case, the basic notions from the core are all that one takes from the capability approach; one does not need this normative part of the core. I will suggest in the concluding chapter 5 that explanatory applications of the capability approach are part of how it could be fruitfully developed in the future.

among scholars of the capability approach; for example, Sabina Alkire (2005, 122) described the capability approach as the proposition "that social arrangements should be evaluated according to the extent of freedom people have to promote or achieve functionings they value". However, if we fully take into account that functionings can be positive but also negative (see 2.6.2), we should also acknowledge that our lives are better if they contain fewer of the functionings that are negative, such as physical violence or stress. Alkire's proposition should therefore minimally be extended by adding "and to promote the weakening of those functionings that have a negative value".[29]

However, what is relevant is not only which opportunities are open to us individually, hence in a piecemeal way, but rather which combinations or sets of potential functionings are open to us. For example, suppose you are a low-skilled poor single parent who lives in a society without decent social provisions. Take the following functionings: (1) to hold a job, which will require you to spend many hours on working and commuting, but will generate the income needed to properly feed yourself and your family; (2) to care for your children at home and give them all the attention, care and supervision they need. In a piecemeal analysis, both (1) and (2) are opportunities open to that parent, but they are not *both together* open to her. The point about the capability approach is precisely that it is comprehensive; we must ask which *sets* of capabilities are open to us, that is: can you simultaneously provide for your family and properly care for and supervise your children? Or are you rather forced to make some hard, perhaps even tragic choices between two functionings which are both central and valuable?

Note that while most types of capability analysis require interpersonal comparisons, one could also use the capability approach to evaluate the wellbeing or wellbeing freedom of one person at one point in time (e.g. evaluate her situation against a capability yardstick) or to evaluate the changes in her wellbeing or wellbeing freedom over

---

29 Moreover, further extensions of this proposition may be needed. One issue is that we should not only focus on capabilities that people value, but also on capabilities that they do not, but should, value (see section 2.7.2). Another issue is that the evaluative space should not necessarily be restricted to capabilities only, but could also be functionings, or a combination of functionings and capabilities (see section 2.6.5).

time. The capability approach could thus also be used by a single person in her deliberate decision-making or evaluation processes, but these uses of the capability approach are much less prevalent in the scholarly literature. Yet all these normative exercises share the property that they use functionings and capabilities as the evaluative space — the space in which personal evaluations or interpersonal comparisons are made.

2.6.6 A6: Other dimensions of ultimate value

However, this brings us straight to another core property of module A, namely that *functionings and/or capabilities are not necessarily the only elements of ultimate value.* Capabilitarian theories might endorse functionings and/or capabilities as their account of ultimate value but may add other elements of ultimate value, such as procedural fairness. Other factors may also matter normatively, and in most capability theories these other principles or objects of evaluation *will* play a role. This implies that the capability approach is, in itself, incomplete as an account of the good since it may have to be supplemented with other values or principles.[30] Sen has been a strong defender of this claim, for example, in his argument that capabilities capture the opportunity aspect of freedom but not the process aspect of freedom, which is also important (e.g. Sen 2002a, 583–622).[31]

At this point, it may be useful to reflect on a suggestion made by Henry Richardson (2015) to drop the use of the word 'intrinsic' when describing the value of functionings and capabilities — as is often done in the capability literature. For non-philosophers, saying that something has 'intrinsic value' is a way to say that something is much more important than something else, or it is used to say that we don't need to investigate what the effects of this object are on another object. If we think that something doesn't have intrinsic value, we would hold that it is desirable if it expands functionings and capabilities; economic

---

30   For example, if Henry Richardson (2007) is right in arguing that the idea of capabilities cannot capture basic liberties, then one need not reject the capability approach, but instead could add an insistence on basic liberties to one's capability theory, as Richardson (2007, 394) rightly points out.

31   This distinction, and its relevance, will be discussed in more detail in section 3.3.

growth is a prominent example in both the capability literature and in the human development literature. Yet in philosophy, there is a long-standing debate about what it means to say of something that it has intrinsic value, and it has increasingly been contested that it is helpful to speak of 'intrinsic values' given what philosophers generally would like to say when they use that word (Kagan 1998; Rabinowicz and Rønnow-Rasmussen 2000).

In philosophy, the term 'intrinsic' refers to a metaphysical claim; something we claim to be intrinsically valuable *only* derives its value from some internal properties. Yet in the capability approach, this is not really what we want to say about functionings (or capabilities). Rather, as Richardson rightly argues, we should be thinking about what we take to be worth seeking for its own sake. Richardson prefers to call this 'thinking in terms of final ends'; in addition, one could also use the terminology 'that which has ultimate value' (see also Rabinowicz and Rønnow-Rasmussen 2000, 48).[32] This has the advantage that we do not need to drop the widely used, and in my view very useful, distinction between instrumental value and ultimate value. Those things that have ultimate value are the things we seek because they are an end (of policy making, decision making, evaluations); those things that do not have ultimate value, hence that are not ends, will be valued to the extent that they have instrumental value for those ends.

Of course, non-philosophers may object and argue they are using 'intrinsic value' and 'ultimate value' as synonyms. But if we want to develop the capability approach in a way that draws on the insights from all disciplines, we should try to accommodate this insight from philosophy into the interdisciplinary language of the capability approach, especially if there is a very easy-to-use alternative available to us. We can either, as Richardson proposes, speak of the selected functionings and capabilities as *final ends*, or we can say that the selected functionings and capabilities have *ultimate value* — that is, they have value as ends in themselves and not because they are useful for some

---

32   "[...] the relevant values can be said to be 'end-point values', insofar as they are not simply conducive to or necessary for something else that is of value. They are 'final', then, in this sense of being 'ultimate'" (Rabinowicz and Rønnow-Rasmussen 2000, 48).

further end. It is of course possible for a capability to have ultimate value and for the corresponding functioning to have instrumental value. For example, being knowledgeable and educated can very plausibly be seen as of ultimate value, but is also of instrumental value for various other capabilities, such as the capability of being healthy, being able to pursue projects, being able to hold a job, and so forth.

However, the question is whether it is possible to change the use of a term that is so widespread in some disciplines yet regarded as wrong from the point of view of another discipline. It may be that the best we can hope for is to become aware of the different usages of the term 'intrinsic value', which in the social sciences is used in a much looser way than in philosophy, and doesn't have the metaphysical implications that philosophers attribute to it.

2.6.7 A7: Value pluralism

There are at least two types of value pluralism within the capability approach. One type is the other objects of ultimate value, which was briefly addressed in the previous section. This is what Sen called in his Dewey lectures *principle pluralism* (Sen 1985c, 176). Expanding capabilities and functionings is not all that matters; there are other moral principles and goals with ultimate value that are also important when evaluating social states, or when deciding what we ought to do (whether as individuals or policy makers). Examples are deontic norms and principles that apply to the processes that lead to the expansion of capability sets. This value pluralism plays a very important role in understanding the need to have the C-module C4, which will be discussed in section 2.8.4.

It is interesting to note that at some stage in Sen's development of the capability approach, his readers lost this principle-pluralism and thought that the capability approach could stand on its own. But a reading of Sen's earlier work on the capability approach shows that all along, Sen felt that capabilities can and need to be supplemented with other principles and values. For example, in his 1982 article 'Rights and Agency', Sen argues that "goal rights, including capability rights, and other goals, can be combined with deontological values [...], along with other agent-relative considerations, in an integrated system" (Sen 1982, 4). Luckily, the more recent publications in the secondary literature on the capability approach increasingly acknowledge this principle pluralism; the modules A7 and C4 of the modular view presented in this book suggest that it is no longer possible not to acknowledge this possibility.

The second type of value-pluralism relates to what is often called the multidimensional nature of the capability approach. Functionings and capabilities are not 'values' in the sense of 'public values' (justice, efficiency, solidarity, ecological sustainability, etc.) but they are objects of ultimate value — things that we value as ends in themselves. Given some very minimal assumptions about human nature, it is obvious that these dimensions are multiple: human beings value the opportunity to be in good health, to engage in social interactions, to have meaningful activities, to be sheltered and safe, not be subjected to excessive levels of stress, and so forth. Of course, it is logically conceivable to say that for a particular normative exercise, we only look at one dimension. But while it may be consistent and logical, it nevertheless makes no sense — for at least two reasons.

First, the very reason why the capability approach has been offered as an alternative to other normative approaches is to add informational riches — to show which dimensions have been left out of the other types of analysis, and why adding them matters. It also makes many evaluations much more nuanced, allowing them to reflect the complexities of life as it is. For example, an African-American lawyer may be successful in her professional life in terms of her professional achievements and the material rewards she receives for her work, but she may also encounter disrespect and humiliation in a society that is sexist and racist. Being materially well-off doesn't mean that one is living a life with all the capabilities to which one should be entitled in a just society. Only multi-dimensional metrics of evaluation can capture those ambiguities and informational riches.

Second, without value pluralism, it would follow that the happiness approach is a special case of the capability approach — namely a capability theory in which only one functioning matters, namely being happy. Again, while this is strictly speaking a consistent and logical possibility, it makes no sense given that the capability approach was conceived to form an alternative to both the income metric and other resourcist approaches on the one hand, and the happiness approach and other mental metric approaches on the other. Thus, in order to make the capability approach a genuine alternative to other approaches, we need to acknowledge several functionings and capabilities, rather than just one.

2.6.8 A8: The principle of each person as an end

A final core property of each capability theory or application is that each person counts as a moral equal. Martha Nussbaum calls this principle "the principle of each person as an end". Throughout her work she has offered strong arguments in defence of this principle (Nussbaum 2000, 56):

> The account we strive for [i.e. the capability approach] should preserve liberties and opportunities for each and every person, taken one by one, respecting each of them as an end, rather than simply as the agent or supporter of the ends of others. [...] We need only notice that there is a type of focus on the individual person as such that requires no particular metaphysical position, and no bias against love or care. It arises naturally from the recognition that each person has just one life to live, not more than one. [...] If we combine this observation with the thought [...] that each person is valuable and worthy of respect as an end, we must conclude that we should look not just to the total or the average, but to the functioning of each and every person.

Nussbaum's principle of each person as an end is the same as what is also known as ethical or normative individualism in debates in philosophy of science. *Ethical individualism*, or *normative individualism*, makes a claim about who or what should count in our evaluative exercises and decisions. It postulates that individual persons, and only individual persons are the units of *ultimate* moral concern. In other words, when evaluating different social arrangements, we are only interested in the (direct and indirect) effects of those arrangements on individuals.

As will be explained in more detail in section 4.6, the idea of ethical individualism is often conflated with other notions of individualism, such as the ontological idea that human beings are individuals who can live and flourish independently of others. However, there is no such claim in the principle of ethical individualism. The claim is rather one about whose interests should count. And ethical individualism claims that only the interests of persons should count. Ultimately, we care about *each* individual person. Ethical individualism forces us to make sure we ask questions about *how the interests of each and every person are served or protected*, rather than assuming that because, for example, all the other family members are doing fine, the daughter-in-law will be doing fine too. If, as all defensible moral theories do, we argue that every human being has equal moral worth, then we must attach value to the interests of each and every one of the affected persons. Thus, my first conclusion is that ethical individualism is a *desirable* property, since it is necessary to treat people as moral equals.

But ethical individualism is not only a desirable property, it is also an *unavoidable* property. By its very nature the evaluation of functionings and capabilities is an evaluation of the wellbeing and freedom to achieve wellbeing of individual persons. Functionings are 'beings' and 'doings': these are dimensions of a human being, which is an embodied being, not merely a mind or a soul. And with the exception of the conjoined twins, and the case of the unborn child and the pregnant mother, bodies are physically separated from each other.[33] We are born as a human being with a body and future of her own, and we will die as a human being with a body and a past life narrative that is unique. This human being, that lives her life in an embodied way, thus has functionings that are related to her person, which is embodied. It is with the functionings and capabilities of these persons that the capability approach is concerned with.[34] However, as I will explain in detail in section 4.6, from this it *does not follow* that the capability approach conceptualises people in an atomistic fashion, and thus that the capability approach is 'individualistic' — meant in a negative, pejorative way. And it also does not imply that a capabilitarian evaluation could not *also* evaluate the

---

33 As Richardson (2016, 5) puts it, "all capabilities [...] are dependent on the body. Without relying on one's body there is nothing one can do or be".

34 Some have argued in favour of what they call 'collective capabilities', which I will discuss in section 3.6.

means (including social institutions, structures, and norms) as well as conversion factors, as well as non-capabilitarian elements of value — *as long as we are clear what the role or status of each of those elements is.*[35]

Note that the use of the term 'normative individualism' is deeply disputed. Some scholars see no problem at all in using that term, since they use it in a technical sense that they believe should not be conflated with any pejorative use of the term 'individualism' in daily life. Other scholars resist the term 'ethical individualism', since they cannot separate it from (a) the notions of ontological and explanatory individualism, and/or (b) from the pejorative meaning that the term 'individualism' has in daily life, which is probably close to a term such as 'egoism'. While the first group is, in my view, right, the second group conveys important information about how the capability approach will be perceived in a broader setting, including outside academia. It may therefore be recommendable to replace the term 'ethical or normative individualism' with the term 'the principle of each person as an end' whenever possible.

2.7 The B-modules: non-optional modules with optional content

I believe that the best way to understand the capability approach is by taking the *content* of the A-module as non-optional. All capability theories need to endorse the content of the A-module (ideally in an *explicit* way) or at a very minimum should not have properties that violate the content of the A-module. But there are also properties of a capability theory where the module is non-optional, yet there is choice involved in the content of the module. This doesn't mean that 'anything goes' in terms of the choice of the content, but it does mean that within each module, there is a range of options to choose from. These are the B-modules, each of which contains a range of possible content,

---

35 However, the question remains whether the capability approach is fully compatible with indigenous world views and normative frameworks, as well as thick forms of communitarianism. This is a question that doesn't allow for a straightforward answer, and requires more analysis. For some first explorations of the compatibility of indigenous world views with the capability approach, see Binder and Binder (2016); Bockstael and Watene (2016); Watene (2016).

from which the capability theorist can decide what content to adopt. However, the range of content of the B-modules must not contradict the A-module. The following table lists the non-optional B-modules with optional content.

Table 2.3 The B-modules: non-optional modules with optional content
B1: The purpose of the capability theory
B2: The selection of dimensions
B3: An account of human diversity
B4: An account of agency
B5: An account of structural constraints
B6: The choice between functionings, capabilities, or both
B7: Meta-theoretical commitments

2.7.1 B1: The purpose of the capability theory

The first module, which is itself non-optional, but where the content can be chosen, is the purpose of the theory. For example, one could use the capability approach to construct a theory of justice, to develop an international empirical comparison, to reform an educational curriculum, to develop alternative welfare economics, or to evaluate the effects of laws on people's capabilities. Questions of scope and reach also need to be addressed in this module. For example, is a theory of justice a political or a comprehensive theory? Is such a theory domestic or global? Other questions that need to be addressed involve the intended audience. Is one constructing an academic theory where great attention is given to detail and even the smallest distinctions are taken as relevant, or is one addressing policy makers or societal organisations for whom every detail does not matter and the time to think and read may be much more constrained, while the accessibility of the ideas is much more important?

Of course, one could argue that B1 is not specific to capability theories, and also holds for, say, deontological theories, or utilitarian theories, or theories that use care ethics as their basic normative foundation.

While that is true, there are two reasons to highlight B1, the purpose of the capability theory, in the account that I am developing. The first is that it will help us to be *explicit* about the purpose. There are plenty of pieces published in the capability literature in which the purpose of the application or theory is not made explicit, and as a consequence it leads to people based in different disciplines or fields talking alongside each other. Second, it seems that the need to be explicit about the purpose (including the audience) of one's capability theory or application is stronger in the capability literature than in other approaches, because in comparison to those other approaches it has a much more radically multidisciplinary uptake.

2.7.2 B2: The selection of dimensions

The second B-module is the selection of capabilities and/or functionings. We need to *specify which capabilities matter* for our particular capability theory. This is a deeply normative question, and touches the core of the difference that the capability approach can make. After all, the dimensions that one selects to analyse will determine what we will observe — and also, equally importantly, what we will not observe since the dimensions are not selected.

There is, by now, a large body of literature discussing the various ways in which one can make that selection, including some overview articles that survey the different methods for particular purposes (e.g. Alkire 2002; Robeyns 2005a; Byskov forthcoming). These methods explicitly include various participatory, deliberative and/or democratic approaches, which are widely used in capability applications.

There are two crucial factors determining which selection procedure is suitable. The first is the purpose of the capability theory (hence the choice made in B1). If we develop an account of wellbeing for thinking about how our lives are going, we are not constrained by questions such as the legitimate scope of government intervention, whereas a theory of political justice would need to take that element into account. Another example is if we would like to use the capability approach to think about what is universally demanded by moral principles, hence to develop the capability approach into a theory of morality: there the selection may be constrained by a method of moral justification for categorically binding principles, which is much more demanding than a method that justifies principles we offer to each other as rationally defensible proposals in the public realm. At the empirical and policy level, similar questions arise. For example, one could take the international human rights treaties as reflecting a given political consensus, and use those to select capabilities (Vizard 2007). Or, one's main goal may be to analyse what difference the capability approach makes for poverty or inequality analysis in comparison with income metrics, in which case one may opt for a method that makes the normativity explicit but nevertheless stays close to existing practices in the social sciences, assuming the epistemic validity of those practices (Robeyns 2003).

The second factor determining which selection procedure is suitable is the set of constraints one takes as given in the normative analysis one is making. In an ideal world, there would always be cooperation between scholars with different disciplinary expertise, who would understand each other well, and who would be able to speak the language of the other disciplines involved in developing the capability theory. In an ideal world, there would also be no time constraints on the amount of time one has to develop a capability theory, and no financial constraints on the data gathering, or social, psychological or political constraints on the types of question one can ask when conducting a survey. One would be able always to conduct one's own fieldwork if one wanted, one would have access to all the empirical knowledge one needed, and one would not be constrained in gathering the information one wanted to gather. Clearly, the methods for such an ideal world would be very different from the methods that are used in practice — where database-driven selection may be the best one can do.

Still, whichever method one uses, what always remains important, and very much in the spirit of the capability approach, is not to act in a mechanical way, or to see the question of the selection of dimensions as a technocratic exercise. Even if one cannot, for example, collect certain data, one could nevertheless still mention the dimensions that one would have wanted to include if it had been possible, and perhaps provide some reasonable informed guess of what difference the inclusion of that dimension would have made.

2.7.3 B3: Human diversity

Within the capability approach human diversity is a core characteristic, and indeed a core motivation for developing the capability approach in the first place. Yet the account of human diversity that one endorses can differ. For example, scholars with a background in structuralist sociology or Marxism often believe that the social class to which one belongs is a very important factor in human diversity, which has great influence on which options lie open to a person, but also on how a person's character and aspirations are formed. For those scholars, class interacts with, and in some cases even outweighs, all other identity aspects. For others, such as libertarians, these differences are not so important.[36] They would not attach much (normative or explanatory) importance to one's gender, ethnicity, race, social class, and so forth: everyone is, first and foremost, an individual whose personal ambitions and projects matter. Yet, whether one is a Marxist or a libertarian or one of the many other positions one can take, one always, either implicitly or explicitly, endorses a view on human nature and on human diversity. That choice should be made in capability theories, since the capability approach rejects the use of an implicit, unacknowledged account of human diversity. Hence such an account belongs to the B-modules: one has to have an account of human diversity, but, as long as one is willing to defend one's account and it survives critical analysis, there are several accounts that one can opt for.

Note that if one puts all the modules A, B and C together, a picture will emerge about the great importance attached to human diversity in the capability approach; this will be analysed in more detail in section 3.5.

2.7.4 B4: Agency

Another B-module is the acknowledgement of *agency*. As a working definition, we can use Sen's definition of an agent as "someone who acts and brings about change, and whose achievements can be judged in

---

36 For an introduction to libertarianism, see Vallentyne and Van der Vossen (2014).

terms of her own values and objectives, whether or not we assess them in terms of some external criteria as well" (Sen 1999a, 19).

Applications of the capability approach should endorse *some account* of agency, except if there are good reasons why agency should be taken to be absent, or why in a particular capability application agency is simply not relevant (for example, when one wants to investigate the correlation between an income metric and some achieved functionings).

But clearly, as with other key ethical concepts such as 'wellbeing' or 'freedom', the concept of 'agency' can be fleshed out in many different ways. The capability approach is not committed to one particular account of agency. Similar to the acknowledgement of structural constraints, there is no agreed-upon or standard claim about how much agency, or what particular type, should be assumed; the claim is minimalistic in the sense that, as with the structural constraints which will be discussed in the next section, agency cannot simply be ignored and must be accounted for. One can give agency a key role in a capability theory (e.g. Crocker 2008; Claassen 2016) or a more restricted role, perhaps also using different terminology. One can also develop the account of agency by spelling out some of its preconditions, which may include capabilities. For example, Tom de Herdt (2008) analysed the capability of not having to be subjected to public shame as a precondition of agency, and showed how this may be relevant for social policymaking by illustrating its importance in a food relief programme in Kinshasa. For empirical scholars and policy scholars, an empirically sound account of agency will be crucial; for moral philosophers, a more theoretical account of what conceptualisation of agency is morally relevant will be needed. Thus, the precise content of this B-module will differ significantly between different capability theories and applications — but, in all cases, some acknowledgement of agency will be needed.[37]

---

37 Martha Nussbaum explicitly refrains from integrating the notion of 'agency' in her capability theory (Nussbaum 2000, 14). However, this does not mean that there isn't an account of agency in her theory, since the inclusion of the capability of practical reason on her list of central human capabilities can be understood as corresponding to one particular conceptualisation of agency.

2.7.5 B5: Structural constraints

The fifth B-module is the account of structural constraints: the institutions, policies, laws, social norms and so forth, that people in different social positions face. Those differences in the structural constraints that people face can have a great influence on their conversion factors, and hence on their capability sets. For example, if relationships between people of the same sex are criminalised, then gay people may have all the means and resources they would wish, but they will still not be able to enjoy a happy family life. Or if people of colour face explicit or implicit discrimination on the labour market, then they will not be able to use the same labour-market resources (their degrees, training, experience) to generate the same levels of capabilities in the professional sphere of life, compared with groups that face no (or less) discrimination.

In addition, structural constraints also play a role in the shaping of people's capabilities that are not heavily dependent on material resources. If one group of people is, for cultural, historical or religious reasons, stigmatized as outcasts, then they will be treated with disrespect by other groups in society. The same holds for all groups that suffer from stigma, such as, for example, people with psychiatric disorders or other mental health issues. These structural constraints will also affect the capabilities that do not rely on resources directly, such as opportunities for friendships or for a healthy sense of self-confidence.

Which of those structural constraints will be important for a particular capability analysis will depend on the context. For example, in her study of the living standards of waste pickers, scavengers, and plastic recycling and scrap trading entrepreneurs in Delhi, Kaveri Gill (2010) showed that caste plays a very important role in the capability sets of different castes. For example, those at the very bottom of the hierarchical ladder of waste workers — the waste pickers — have no opportunities for upward mobility due to social norms and societal discrimination related to their caste. In this study, social norms related to caste are key as a structural constraint; in other studies, it may be the anatomy of twenty-first century capitalism, or gender norms in gender-stratified societies, or some other set of structural constraints.

In sum, structural constraints can have a very important role in shaping people's capability sets, and therefore have to be part of capability theories. Structural constraints vary depending on one's caste, class, ethnicity, age, gender, sexual orientation, (dis)abilities, and the economic system in which one lives. These structural constraints are very likely to have an influence on a person's capability set (and in most cases also *do* have that influence). Having an account of structural constraints is therefore non-optional: every capability theory has one, although sometimes this account will be very implicit. For example, I will argue in section 4.10 that part of the critique of mainstream welfare economics is that it has a very weak or minimal account of structural constraints. Heterodox welfare economists who are embracing the capability approach are not only doing so because they think the endorsement of the capability account of wellbeing is better than the preferences-based accounts that are dominant in mainstream economics, but often also because they hope that the minimal account of structural constraints in welfare economics can be replaced by a richer account that is better informed by insights from the other social sciences and from the humanities.

2.7.6 B6: The choice between functionings, capabilities, or both

In developing a capability theory, we need to decide whether we think that what matters are capabilities, functionings, or a combination of both. The core proposition that functionings and capabilities form the evaluative space (A5), was not decisive regarding the question of whether it is only functionings, or only capabilities, or a mixture of both, that form this space.

There are various arguments given in the literature defending a range of views that only capabilities matter; or that primarily secured functionings matter; or that for particular capability theories it is impossible only to focus on capabilities; or that we sometimes have good reasons to focus on functionings. These various claims and arguments will be reviewed in section 3.4; as will be argued in that section, there are good reasons why people could reasonably disagree on whether the capability analysis they are conducting should focus on functionings or capabilities or a mixture. It follows that a choice must be made, but that there are various options to choose from.

2.7.7 B7: Meta-theoretical commitments

Finally, each capability theory will embrace some meta-theoretical commitments. Yet often, these meta-theoretical commitments are shared commitments within one's discipline or one's school within that discipline, and as a graduate student one has become socialised in accepting these meta-theoretical commitments as given. As a consequence, it often happens that scholars are not even aware that there are such things as meta-theoretical commitments. For example, if one wants to conduct a measurement exercise (a choice made in the module B1) then one may be committed to the methodological principle of parsimony (to build a model with as few assumptions and as elegantly as possible) or, instead, to providing a measurement that is embedded into a rich narrative description aimed at a better understanding. Or, if one wants to construct a theory of justice (again, a choice made in the module B1), then one may aim for an ideal or non-ideal theory of justice, or for a partial or a comprehensive account of justice. Or one may espouse certain views about the status of theories of justice or meta-ethical claims related to, for example, the role that intuitions are permitted to play as a source of normativity. Some debates within the capability approach, but also between capability scholars and those working in other paradigms, would be truly enlightened if we made the meta-theoretical commitments of our theories, accounts and applications more explicit.

2.8 The C-modules: contingent modules

In addition to the compulsory content of the core A-module, and the optional content of the non-optional B-modules, a capability theory could also add a third type of module, which I will call *the contingent modules*. These are either modules that need to be taken on board due to some choices that have been made in a B-module, or else they are entirely optional, independent of what one has chosen in the B-modules. The following table gives an overview of the contingent modules.

Table 2.4 The C-modules: contingent modules

C1: Additional ontological and explanatory theories
C2: Weighing dimensions
C3: Methods for empirical analysis
C4: Additional normative principles and concerns

2.8.1 C1: Additional ontological and explanatory theories

Two capabilitarian thinkers could each aspire to make a theory of justice, yet embrace very different views on human nature and on the degree to which certain outcomes can be explained solely by people's choices or are also affected by structural constraints. This can matter a lot for the particular capability theories that one develops.

For example, in earlier work, I showed that the capability approach's answer to whether there is anything wrong with the traditional gender division of labour depends a lot on the social ontological claims related to gender that are (implicitly) endorsed as well as the explanatory views of how that division of labour came about (Robeyns 2008c). If one believes that the fact that women end up doing most of the unpaid and care work, while men end up doing most of the paid labour market work, is a result of differences in talents, dispositions and preferences, then one would judge that the different functionings outcomes that result for men and women within households provide them with maximal levels of wellbeing given the formal institutional background that they face. But if one endorses a feminist explanation of this division of labour between men and women within households, then one is likely to stress power differences, the role of societal expectations and social norms in decision making, and so forth (e.g. Okin 1989; Folbre 1994). The same observed functionings outcomes in households with a traditional gender division of labour would then be evaluated differently.

Similarly, Miriam Teschl and Laurent Derobert argue that a range of different accounts of social and personal identity are possible, and this may also impact on how we interpret a person forfeiting a capability that we would all deem valuable (Teschl and Derobert 2008). If we believe that our religious identities are a matter of rational deliberation and decision-making, then we will judge the choice to physically self-harm because of one's religion differently than if we have an account of identity where there is much less scope for choice and rational deliberation regarding our religious affiliation or other group memberships.

In short, different ontological and explanatory options are available in module C1, and they may have effects on various other elements or dimensions of the capability theory that are being constructed. However, we should be careful and not mistakenly conclude that 'anything goes' when we add additional ontological theories, since there should not be any conflicts with the propositions of the A-module — and, in addition, some ontological and explanatory accounts are much better supported by critical analysis and empirical knowledge.

2.8.2 C2: Weighing dimensions

For some capability theories, the prioritising, weighing or aggregating of dimensions (functionings and capabilities) may not be needed. For example, one may simply want to describe how a country has developed over time in terms of a number of important functionings, as a way of giving information about the evolution of the quality of life that may give different insights than the evolution of GDP (e.g. Van Zanden et al. 2014). Weighing dimensions is therefore not required for each capability theory or capability application, in contrast to the selection of dimensions, which is inevitable.

However, for some other choices that one can make in B1, the capabilitarian scholar or practitioner needs to make choices related to the weighing of the different dimensions. If that is the case, then there are different methods for how one could weigh. When considering which weighing method to use, the same factors are relevant as in the case of selecting the dimensions: the purposes of one's capability theory, and the constraints one has to take into account when choosing a method.

In contrast to the overview works that have been written on how to select dimensions (e.g. Alkire 2002; Robeyns 2005a; Byskov forthcoming), capability scholars have written much less about which methods one could use to decide on the weights given to each dimension, specifically focussing on functionings or capabilities as the dimensions. What lessons and insights can we learn from what has so far been argued in this literature on the weighing of dimensions? (Alkire 2016; Alkire et al. 2015, chapter 6; Robeyns 2006b, 356–58)

First, the selection of weights for the capability approach is structurally similar to other multidimensional metrics (in the case of evaluations) or decision-making procedures (in case one needs to decide to which capabilities to give priority in policies or collective decision making). Hence one should consult existing discussions in other debates where multidimensionality plays an important role. Let us first look at the group of applications in which the capability approach is used to make decisions about what we, collectively, ought to do. That may be in an organisation; or at the level of a community that needs to decide whether to spend tax revenues on investing more in public green spaces, or in social services for particular groups, or in taking measures to prevent crime, or in anything else that can likely be understood as leading to positive effects on our capabilities. In those cases, we can learn from social choice theory, and from theories of democratic decision making, how we could proceed.[38] Decisions could be made by voting, or by deliberation, or by deliberation and/or voting among those who are the representatives of the relevant population.

Second, the applications of the capability approach that involve a multidimensional metric of wellbeing or wellbeing freedom could use (most of) the weighing methods that have been discussed for multidimensional metrics in general. Koen Decancq and María Ana Lugo (2013) have reviewed eight different approaches to set weights for multidimensional metrics, which they categorize in three classes: data-driven weights in which the weights are a function of the distribution of the various dimensions in the population surveyed; normative approaches in which either experts decide on the weights, or the weights are equal or arbitrary; and hybrid weights that are in

---

38   In the case of democratic theory, the discussion is often about which laws to implement, but the same insights apply to policy making. Both the literature on democratic theory (e.g. Dryzek 2000; Gutmann and Thompson 2004) and social choice theory (e.g. Arrow, Sen and Suzumura 2002, 2010; Sen 1999c, 2017; Gaertner 2009) are vast and will not be further discussed here.

part data-driven but in addition depend on some normative decision. Note that in the data-driven and hybrid approaches, the selection of dimensions and the weights tends to be done through a process in which the selection of dimensions and the determination of the weights go hand in hand. One example is the proposal by Erik Schokkaert (2007) of using happiness as the master-value by which we weigh the various capabilities that together form the multidimensional account of wellbeing. In this proposal, if the functionings do not contribute to one's happiness, they are given a zero weight and hence no longer count in the wellbeing index. In methods such as this one, there are two rounds of the selections of the dimensions: the first before one collects the data, and the second when one uses econometric techniques to determine the contribution that the various functionings make to the master-value (here: life-satisfaction) and uses those as weights; those functionings that will make no contribution will receive a weight of zero, which is the same as being deleted as a dimension in the wellbeing index.

Third, for non-empirical applications, we can categorize methods to determine weights in the same way as we could categorise methods for the selection of dimensions. Morten Fibieger Byskov (forthcoming) distinguishes between ad-hoc methods (such as the data-driven methods discussed by Decancq and Lugo), procedural methods, or foundational methods. A theoretical capability application could include answers to all B-modules (including the selection of dimensions) yet decide that the weighing of those dimensions should be done in a procedural way, e.g. via a democratic decision-making process. Alternatively, one could introduce one master-value that will determine which capabilities are relevant, and also what weights they should be given. One example is the empirical work done by Erik Schokkaert (2007), which was discussed above. Another example, which is theoretical, is Rutger Claassen's capabilitarian theory of justice, in which the selection and weighing of capabilities is done based on their contribution to that person's "navigational agency" (Claassen 2016).

Note that in the case in which one has essentially a monistic theory in which there is a master-value, one may doubt whether this doesn't violate property A7 from the A-module. At first value, it seems that it does. But proponents of a monistic theory may respond that *all* theories or measures ultimately must choose one principle or value that tells us something about the relative weight of the different dimensions. In Nussbaum's work, they argue, there is also an implicit master-value, namely human dignity. It seems to me that this issue is not sufficiently analysed and the dispute not settled. One question one could raise is whether all master-values have the same function. It seems to be different whether the capabilities *constitute* the dimensions of a good life (as in the case of flourishing), or whether they *contribute* to the master-value. For the time being, we should in any case flag this as an issue to which more attention should be paid in the further development of our understanding of the capability approach.

2.8.3 C3: Methods for empirical analysis.

If in B1 one chooses an empirical study, one needs to know which methods to use. This is the task of the module C3. For example, the study could contain choices about which multivariate analysis tools to use or whether certain existing data sets are capturing functionings, capabilities, or merely rough indicators. In C3, we also make methodological choices related to empirical analysis: does a particular capability issue require quantitative analysis, qualitative analysis, or a combination? In part, the contours of the empirical analysis will be influenced by one's ambitions and goals: is one trying to measure functionings and/or capabilities directly, or is one measuring resources and conversion factors in order to infer the capability set?

For empirical capability applications, these are of course huge methodological questions that need to be answered. These empirical methods questions may be particularly challenging for the capability approach for two reasons. First, because it is a radically multidimensional approach, and multidimensional analysis is by its very nature more complicated than a one-dimensional analysis. Second, in many cases, the relevant dimensions will include dimensions on which the collection of data is difficult, or on which no data are available — such as the quality of our social networks, the degree to which we do not suffer from excessive levels of stress, or our mental health. Nevertheless, as Alkire

(2005, 129) rightly points out in her discussion on what is needed for the empirical operationalisation of the capability approach, one has to adopt the best existing empirical research (and its methods) that exists, and either master those new techniques that have been developed in other fields, or else engage in collaborations. Hick and Burchardt (2016, 88) raise the related point that there is a need for capability scholars to reach out and engage with related fields where similar themes and problems are faced. Only after that route has been travelled can we know the limits of empirical analyses of the capability approach.

2.8.4 C4: Additional normative principles and concerns

Finally, module C4 provides room for additional normative concerns or moral principles that capability scholars aim to add to their capability theory. For example, in a particular capability theory, a principle of non-discrimination may play a role or, alternatively, one may want to work out a capabilitarian theory that subscribes to the non-domination principle as it has been defended by Republican political theory (Pettit 2001, 2009). Or, if one ascribes to a rich account of empowerment that stresses the relevance of 'power' and hence strongly incorporates relational aspects (e.g. Drydyk 2013; Koggel 2013), then one may add a principle related to enhancing people's empowerment, or prioritising the empowerment of the worst-off, as an additional normative principle to be added in module C4. Again, there are several elements belonging to module C4 that could be added to a capability theory.

2.9 The modular view of the capability account: a summary

In the previous sections, we have looked at the different elements of the modular account of the capability approach, consisting of the core A-module, the compulsory B-modules with optional content, and the contingent C-modules. For an easily accessible overview, the different elements of the modular view of the capability approach are summarised in table 2.5.

Table 2.5 The modular view of the capability approach

The A-module: the non-optional core
A1: Functionings and capabilities as core concepts
A2: Functionings and capabilities are value-neutral categories
A3: Conversion factors
A4: The distinction between means and ends
A5: Functionings and/or capabilities form the evaluative space
A6: Other dimensions of ultimate value
A7: Value pluralism
A8: Valuing each person as an end

The B-modules: non-optional modules with optional content
B1: The purpose of the capability theory
B2: The selection of dimensions
B3: An account of human diversity
B4: An account of agency
B5: An account of structural constraints
B6: The choice between functionings, capabilities, or both
B7: Meta-theoretical commitments

The C-modules: contingent modules
C1: Additional ontological and explanatory theories
C2: Weighing dimensions
C3: Methods for empirical analysis
C4: Additional normative principles and concerns

What, exactly, is the status of this characterisation of the capability approach? Is this list of modules and the core properties exhaustive, and is this a proposal to change the current definitions on offer in the literature?

The answers have been given throughout the sections so far, but now that we have gone through the different modules and know their content, it is worthwhile to repeat and summarize this in a very explicit manner. The modular view is an attempt at understanding the plurality of capability theories on offer in the literature, doing justice to this plurality, yet at the same time avoiding the idea that 'anything goes'. By distinguishing between three types of modules — the A-module, the content of which one must adopt, the B-modules, which are non-optional but have optional content, and the C-modules, which are contingent — we can get a better grasp of the peculiar nature of the capability approach: not exactly a precise *theory*, but also not something that can be anything one likes it to be. I hope that this way of looking at the anatomy of the capability approach will help us to understand what the approach is, but also provide more guidance to those who want to use the general capability approach as a guiding theoretical framework to work on particular theoretical or empirical issues and problems.

The content of the A-module, the B-modules and C-modules is, as with everything in scholarship, a proposal that can be modified to accommodate new insights. If someone has convincing arguments why one element or module should be deleted, modified, or added, then that should be done. Given what we know from the history of scholarship, it is rather unlikely that no further modifications will be proposed in the future.

2.10 Hybrid theories

In the previous sections, we have seen which modules are core in a capability theory, which ones need to be addressed but have optional content, and which ones may or may not be necessary to add to a particular capability theory. One question that this modular view raises is what we should think of a theory or an application that uses the addition of normative principles that are in contradiction with a property of the A-module. For example, suppose one would want to add the normative principle that institutions and personal behaviour should honour the traditions of one's local community. There may be aspects of those traditions that are in tension with the principle of treating each person as an end, for example, because women are not given the same moral status in those traditions as men. What should we then say? Would such a theory no longer be a capability theory, even if the bulk of the theory is trying to think about the quality of life and desirable institutions in terms of the enhancement of functionings and capabilities?

I propose that we introduce the notion of a *hybrid theory* — theories or applications that use the notions of 'functionings' and 'capabilities' yet do not endorse all propositions in the A-module. Let me stress that categorizing these theories as 'hybrid' entails no value judgement, whether positive or negative; rather, it is only a matter of clarifying the possibilities of having capability theories but in addition also hybrid theories which use part of the A-module yet also insert elements from other ethical frameworks that go against some propositions in the A-module. Thus, appreciating the possibility of hybrid views enlarges the diversity of theories that are possible.

Can we give an example of such a hybrid theory? Perhaps surprisingly, an example may be Amartya Sen's theorising about justice. According to the interpretation by Antoinette Baujard and Muriel Gilardone (2017), Sen's (2006, 2009c) recent work on justice does not endorse functionings and/or capabilities as the metric of justice, but should rather be seen as a procedural or democratic account of justice, in which the idea of having functionings and capabilities as the evaluative space is merely a suggestion, which should be put to the public who eventually, in a process of public reasoning, have to decide what justice is about. If that interpretation is correct, then Sen is unwilling to commit to proposition A5 ('functionings and capabilities form the evaluative space') when theorising about justice, since that is something to be decided by a process of public reasoning.[39] Clearly, when Sen theorises about justice, he has certain meta-theoretical commitments (module B7) that make it *inconsistent* for him to endorse A5, namely the meta-theoretical commitment that the nature of justice will be decided by a democratic process. Whether that is a plausible meta-theoretical position, has been subject of debate in the capability literature (e.g. Claassen 2011; Byskov 2017) but need not concern us here. The point that is relevant for us is that Sen's theorizing about justice could be seen as a public reasoning-capability theory of justice.

---

39   Note that *for other capability applications or capability theories*, such as making quality of life assessment studies, Sen has no problem endorsing proposition A5. Moreover, one could also ask whether regarding his earlier publications on justice it would be implausible to interpret Sen's writings as an endorsement of A5. In my view (and *pace* Baujard and Gilardone's interpretation), Sen has made several statements in earlier work that could be seen as an endorsement of all propositions of module A for the case of theorizing about justice (e.g. Sen 1980, 1990a, 2000).

Other potential candidates for hybrid theories are the theories that we discussed in section 2.8.2, in which functionings and capabilities play an important role, yet in the theory or measurement construction those functionings and capabilities turn out not to be of ultimate value, but rather to be instrumental for some further end that is normatively prior to the functionings and capabilities themselves. There is, in those cases, a master-value that determines how important (if at all) those capabilities are: capabilities that we could value, but which do not contribute to the master-value, will then not be given any ultimate value. As we discussed there, it is unclear whether those theories that endorse a master-value violate module A7 (value pluralism) or not. If we conclude they do, then the best way to understand these views is to regard them as hybrid theories too.

2.11 The relevance and implications of the modular view

Understanding the capability approach as having a modular structure leads to a number of insights. Let me highlight three important ones: countering the risk of inflation, whereby we have no criteria for deciding when a theory is or is not a capability theory; appreciating the diversity of capability theories that are possible; and getting a better sense of how Sen's and Nussbaum's writings relate to each other.

First, the modular view can help us to contain the risk of *inflation*: too many things being labelled as belonging to the 'capability approach', whereas they do not meet the essential characteristics of the A-module. The modular view of the capability approach which I presented gives us a description that includes all the work in the capability approach that should legitimately be included. There are, of course, other descriptions of the capability approach available in the literature. Yet to my mind most of these descriptions (including my own previous attempts at describing the approach) were insufficiently detailed and illuminating. If a description is too vague, we run the risk of inflation.

For example, one could aim to work on multi-dimensional poverty analysis and highlight the fact that we should be interested in the combination of achievements that people are able to have. This would point at two important insights in the capability approach — namely its multidimensional character, as well as focussing on opportunity *sets* rather than on outcomes. But if the opportunities one focusses on are not capabilities, but rather opportunities to access certain bundles of commodities, then it would be an unjustified inflation to call this a capability application; rather, it would be another type of opportunity-based multidimensional inequality measure.

Second, to understand that capability theories have a modular structure is crucial in understanding the diversity of capability theories that are possible. Let me try to illustrate this. Module C4 states that additional normative principles may be part of a capability theory, and property A6 that functionings and capabilities are not necessarily all that matters in a capability theory. From this it does not follow that all capability scholars have to endorse each and every capability theory. Surely there will be capability theorists who will take issue with the normative principles that are added in module C4 by other capability theorists when they design their theory. That is perfectly fine, as long as both theorists recognise that (a) the capability approach entails the possibility to add such additional normative principles in module C4, and (b) the normative principles they have added in module C4 are not thereby required for each and every other capability theory.[40]

Take the following example. One may defend a political theory of disadvantage which states that no-one should live in poverty, no matter whether people are partly causally responsible for having ended up in that situation. Such a theory would endorse a principle (in module C4) that there should be, at the level of outcomes (and hence not at the level of opportunities) institutionally enforced solidarity via redistribution. Let us call those who endorse this principle the S-theorists (S for solidarity). This is a strong normative claim: many other normative political theories

---

40 I believe that Martha Nussbaum makes a mistake when she argues that a commitment to the normative principle of political liberalism is *essential* to the capability approach, hence to each and every capability theory. For my arguments why this is a mistake, see Robeyns (2016b). Political liberalism is an additional normative commitment that is not a property of the A-module, but rather a choice in module C4.

rather defend that everyone should have a genuine opportunity to live a decent life, but still attribute some responsibility to all persons for realising that life. Let us call these theorists the O-theorists (O for opportunity). Both the S-theorists and the O-theorists can agree that we should understand people's wellbeing in terms of functionings and capabilities. The S-theorists and the O-theorists are both capabilitarians. They have to acknowledge that the other group's theory is a capability theory, *without* having to endorse the other theory. In other words, a capability theorist can agree that the normative position or theory that someone else is defending is a capability theory, without having to endorse that specific theory. There is absolutely no inconsistency in this situation.

Thirdly, the modular view of the capability approach endorses the view that Martha Nussbaum's work on the capability approach should be understood as a capability theory, that is, a theory in which specific choices are made regarding the modules. It is not, as Nussbaum (2011) suggests in her *Creating Capabilities*, a version of the capability approach structurally on a par with Sen's more general capability approach. What Sen has tried to do in his work on the capability approach, is to carve out the general capability approach, as well as to give some more specific capability applications. Admittedly, Sen's work on the capability approach (rather than his work on a variety of capability applications) would have benefited from a more systematic description of how he saw the anatomy of the capability approach. To my mind, that has been missing from his work, and that is what I have tried to develop here and in an earlier paper (Robeyns 2016b). Yet everything put together, I agree with the understanding of Mozaffar Qizilbash, who concludes an analysis of the difference between Nussbaum's and Sen's work on the capability approach by saying that "On this reading [...] Nussbaum's capabilities approach emerges as one particular application or development of Sen's original formulation of the approach" (Qizilbash 2013, 38).

It is a mistake to understand the capability literature as a field with two major thinkers who have each proposed one version of the capability *approach*, which have then inspired the work by many other scholars. Rather, there is *only one* capability approach which is a generalisation of the work by Sen together with further developments by many others. In addition, there are many dozens capability theories — about justice, human rights, social choice theory, welfare economics, poverty measurement, relational egalitarianism, curriculum design, development project assessment, technological design, and so forth. Clearly, Nussbaum has been one of the most prolific and important contributors; she has pushed the boundaries of capabilitarian theories and has rightly advanced the agenda to achieve more clarity on the essential characteristics that any capability theory should meet. However, she has offered us a more specific capability *theory*, rather than another version of the *approach*, even if it is the capability theory that is by far the most influential capability theory among philosophers. Establishing the anatomy of the capability approach and its relation to particular capability theories is very important, because it vastly expands the scope of the capability approach, and increases the potential types of capability applications and capabilitarian theories.

In sum, there is much *pluralism within the capability approach*. Someone who considers herself a capabilitarian or capability thinker does not need to endorse all capability theories. In fact, it is impossible to endorse all capability theories, since different choices made in module C1 (ontological and explanatory theories that are endorsed) and module C4 (additional normative principles) can be in conflict with each other. It is presumably coherent to be a Marxist capabilitarian, and it is presumably also coherent to be a libertarian capabilitarian, but it is not coherent to endorse the views taken by those two positions, since they are incompatible.

2.12 A visualisation of the core conceptual elements

We have now covered enough ground in understanding the core concepts of the capability approach to construct a visualisation of these concepts. Figure 2.1 below gives a graphical representation of the different elements of the capability approach, and how they relate. Note that the arrows do not indicate *normative importance* but rather indicate which parts of this conceptual system are determinants of, or have an influence on, other parts.

Let us start our description where economists generally start (and often also end): with resources. In the capability approach, the term 'resources' is interpreted in a broader sense than the understanding of that term elsewhere in the social sciences. Economics and the quantitative empirical social sciences have traditionally focussed on material resources only: either income and wealth, or else on the consumption that these financial means (or unpaid production) generated. One important lesson learnt from feminist economics is that about half of economic production happens outside the market and the formal economy, which is the reason why the box at the far left in Figure 2.1 also includes resources created by non-market production (Folbre 2008; Folbre and Bittman 2004).

Both the resources and the consumption could be conceptualised as capability inputs: they are the means to the opportunities to be the person one wants to be, and do what one has reason to value doing. The means do not all have the same power to generate capabilities; this depends on a person's conversion factors, as well as the structural constraints that she faces. Those structural constraints can have a great influence on the conversion factors as well as on the capability sets directly.

From this visualisation, we can also see the difference between the social conversion factors and the structural constraints. The structural constraints affect a person's set of conversion factors, including the social conversion factors she faces. But recall that those conversion factors tell us something about the degree to which people can turn resources into capabilities. Conversion factors are thus, conceptually and empirically, closely related to the capability inputs — that is, the resources that are needed to generate capabilities. Structural constraints affect conversion factors, but can also affect a person's capability set without impacting on the conversion of resources in capabilities. For example, if a certain set of social norms characterizes a group in society as not having the same moral status as others, then this affects the capabilities of the members of that group directly, not merely in terms of what they can get out of their resources. A good example is gay people, a significant percentage of whom are not worse off in financial terms than straight people, but they often cannot express their sexual orientation in public, at the risk of humiliation, aggression, or even risking their jobs or their lives.

Another part of the visualisation to pay attention to is the choice that people make given the capability set they have. These choices are always constrained in some sense, and the question is which types of constraints a particular capability theory will take into account. Also, the term 'choice' is used here in a very thin (or, as philosophers say, 'weak') sense: it is not assumed that elaborate thinking and weighing is done before we decide which capabilities to use and realise into functionings. In fact, we have ample evidence from psychology that there are many other factors that influence the decisions we make, including how hungry or tired we are, the people in our company, or the amount of time we have to make a decision (Ariely 2010; Kahneman 2011). Most capability theories will have an (implicit) theory of choice: they will have views on the extent to which people's past history (which includes the structural constraints they faced in their personal past) as well as societal processes, such as preference formation mechanisms, influence the choices that we make from the opportunities that are available to us.

The last element of the visualisation is the level of satisfaction or dissatisfaction with one's functionings and capability levels each person will have. Of course, this does not mean that we need to attribute *ethical significance* to those levels of satisfaction; rather, the point in the visualisation is that satisfaction with one's functionings and capability levels is *not the same thing* as those capability sets and combination of functionings achievements themselves. For now, we will concentrate on deepening our understanding of the capability approach itself, but in section 3.8, we will engage in more depth with the question whether we should look at functionings and capabilities, rather than satisfaction, or some other mental metrics, such as happiness.

Two remarks are important. First, this is a *stylized* visualisation, and also a simplification. It is meant to help us see the different elements of the capability approach and how they relate; it is not a fine-grained and exhaustive picture of all the elements that determine a person's capability set. One important limitation is that this is not a dynamic visualisation and that many arrows, indicating relationships between

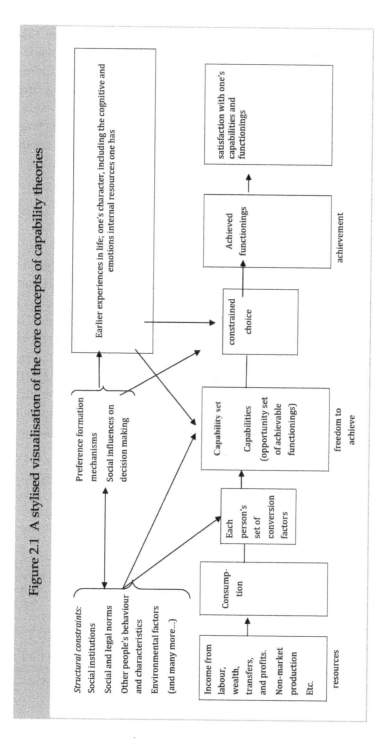

Figure 2.1 A stylised visualisation of the core concepts of capability theories

Source: Based on Robeyns (2005b), updated and expanded.

various parts, are not present.[41] In addition, the choices we make from our capability set at one point in time, will be determinants of our resources and our capability set in the future. Another important limitation of this visualisation is that it gives us only the resources, capabilities, functionings and satisfaction of one person, but, as was mentioned before, capability sets are interdependent; hence choices made from one person's capability set will lead to changes in another person's capability set.

2.13 The narrow and broad uses of the capability approach

We have now reached the end of the discussion of the modular view of the capability approach. Yet before closing this chapter, let us pause to use this modular view to clarify something that has been noted by several capability scholars, namely that the capability approach has been used and can be used in narrower or more limited ways on the one hand, and broader or richer ways on the other (e.g. Alkire, Qizilbash and Comim 2008, 4–5; Crocker and Robeyns 2009; Qizilbash 2012).[42] The distinction has been slightly differently presented by different authors, but the general gist of their analyses has been that the capability approach can either be seen as offering something limited, or else much more ambitious and wide-reaching:

> [...] several interpretations of the scope of the capability approach are used in the wider literature [...]. These can be charted between two poles: one narrow and broad, with the broad subsuming the narrow. [...] The *narrow* interpretation sees the approach primarily as identifying

---

41 In reality, almost everything is related to almost everything else in one way or another, but putting all those arrows on a visualisation would make it completely uninformative. After all, the task of scholarship is to abstract away from distracting details to see more clearly.

42 Readers who have never come across that distinction between the narrow and broad use of the capability approach may simply ignore this section and move on, since the anatomy of the capability approach that has been presented in this book covers the same terrain. In essence, this section is written for those who came across this terminology in the literature, and wonder how it relates to what has been said so far in this book.

capability and functionings as the primary informational space for certain exercises. The *broad* interpretation views the capability approach as providing a more extensive and demanding evaluative framework, for example by introducing human rights or plural principles beyond the expansion of capabilities — principles which embody other values of concerns such as equity, sustainability or responsibility. (Alkire, Qizilbash and Comim 2008, 4–5)

In the narrow way, the capability approach tells us what information we should look at if we are to judge how well someone's life is going or has gone; this kind of information is needed in any account of wellbeing or human development, or for any kind of interpersonal comparisons. Since the capability approach contends that the relevant kind of information concerns human functionings and capabilities, the approach provides part of what is needed for interpersonal comparisons of advantage.

The modular view presented in this chapter can help to make sense of this observation that there is both a narrower and a wider use of the capability approach. In the narrow use of the capability approach, the focus is often strictly on the evaluation of individual functioning levels or on both functionings and capabilities. If we look at the narrow use of the capability approach through the lens of the modular understanding of the approach, we can see that the narrow view chooses interpersonal comparisons as the purpose of the capability theory (module B1); and that it will have to make a selection of dimensions (module B2) and make a choice between functionings or capabilities (module B6); its choice for human diversity (module B3) will be reflected in the choices it makes in B2, but also in which groups (if any) it will compare. Its meta-theoretical commitments (B7) are likely related to limiting research to those things that can be measured. The narrow use of the capability approach will most likely not have much to say about agency (B4) and structural constraints (B5) but adopt the implicit theories of agency and structural constraints that are used in the empirical literatures on interpersonal comparisons. Finally, the narrower view must decide on how to weigh the dimensions (module C2) and which methods for empirical analysis (module C3) to make.

In its broad uses, the capability approach not only evaluates the lives of individuals (as in the narrow use), but also includes other considerations in its evaluations, which are 'borrowed' from other approaches or theories. For example, the broader use of the capability approach often pays attention to other normative considerations and other values than only wellbeing, such as efficiency, agency, or procedural fairness.

The broad view would, in most cases, have a more ambitious purpose for its use of the capability approach, such as societal evaluation or policy design. It would also have (either implicit or explicit) richer theories of human diversity, agency and structural constraints, and — most importantly — add several additional ontological and explanatory theories (module C1) and additional normative principles (module C4). The narrow view does not include modules C1 and C4, and this can make a huge difference to the kind of capability theory that emerges.

An example of the broad view is David Crocker's (2008) book on development ethics, in which he has extended the capability approach with accounts of agency, democratic deliberation and participation into a more detailed account of development ethics. Yet Crocker acknowledges that not all versions of the capability approach embrace agency so explicitly. The capability approach proper *need not* endorse a strong account of agency, but there are several scholars who have developed particular capability theories and applications in which agency plays a central role (e.g. Claassen and Düwell 2013; Claassen 2016; Trommlerová, Klasen and Leßmann 2015).

Why is this difference between the narrow and the broad uses of the capability approach relevant and important? There are several important reasons. First, to assess a critique of the capability approach, we need to know whether the critique addresses the capability approach in its narrow use, or rather a specific version of its broad use. Second, we need to be clear that many of the additional normative commitments in the broad use of the capability approach *are not essential* to the capability approach: rather, they are optional choices made in modules B and, especially, module C1 (additional ontological and explanatory theories) and module C4 (additional normative principles and concerns). This insight will also be important when we address the question, in section 4.9, of whether we can simply talk about 'the capability approach' and 'the human development paradigm' as the same thing.

2.14 Conclusion

The purpose of this chapter has been to give a comprehensive explanation of the capability approach: what is it trying to do, what are the many ways in which it has been used, what are the properties that all capability theories share, and what is the structure that we can detect in the construction of capability theories and applications? In order to get a helicopter view, I have deliberately put aside a number of additional distinctions and details. They will be the focus of the next chapter, whereas critiques and areas of contestation and debate will be discussed in chapter 4.

3. Clarifications

3.1 Introduction

This chapter aims to deepen our understanding of the capability approach, by analysing and clarifying a range of questions that a student of the capability approach may have. My aim has been to include the most frequently asked questions raised by students of the capability approach, as well as a few cases which, in my view, currently lead to confusion in the literature. The questions and issues which are much more a matter of debate or contestation have been collected in chapter 4. Admittedly, the distinction between questions that require clarification on the one hand, and issues of debate on the other, is not a neat one. But that should not bother us: nothing much hangs on whether a topic is included in chapter 3 or rather in chapter 4; what matters is that students of the capability approach are able to find answers to the questions they have.

In this chapter, the following topics are clarified and analysed: How do the terminologies used by Sen and Nussbaum differ, and which additional terminological refinements have been proposed in the literature? (Section 3.2) Can 'capabilities' properly be described as freedom, and if so, which types of freedom are capabilities? And is it always a good idea to speak of capabilities in terms of freedom? (Section 3.3) Which considerations should play a role in making the relevant choices in module B6 — the choice between functionings or capabilities (or both) — for one's capability theory? (Section 3.4) How exactly does the capability approach account for human diversity, and

 https://doi.org/10.11647/OBP.0130.03

why is human diversity given so much importance in the capability literature? (Section 3.5) What does the notion 'collective capability' refer to? (Section 3.6) Which notion of wellbeing does the capability approach give us? (Section 3.7) How does the capability approach differ from the happiness approach, and what are the reasons that capability scholars do not adopt the happiness approach? (Section 3.8) To what extent — and how — can the capability approach deal with adaptive preferences? (Section 3.9) Can a capability theory also be an explanatory theory, or is that not possible? (Section 3.10) Can the capability approach be used to study *all* normative questions, or is it not a suitable framework for some normative questions? (Section 3.11) The capability approach is often positioned as an alternative for resourcist theories — but what exactly is the role of resources in the capability approach? (Section 3.12) Finally, we consider how the capability approach relates to two established literatures: theories of justice and theories of human rights. Which choices in module B and module C are needed in order to construct a capability theory of justice? (Section 3.13) And how do capabilities and human rights relate to each other? (Section 3.14)

3.2 Refining the notions of 'capability' and 'functioning'

While at a very introductory level, the terms 'functionings' and 'capability' seem to be easy and straightforward, the terminology used in the literature is, alas, not always clear. There has been quite considerable confusion in the use of the terminology, although — if one takes a meta-disciplinary helicopter view — it is possible to discern that particular uses of certain terms are more dominant than others. The confusion has several sources. First, Amartya Sen and Martha Nussbaum have used the same terminology somewhat differently to each other, and since most capability scholars are more influenced either by Sen or by Nussbaum, its use in the wider literature is not standardised. Moreover, both Sen and Nussbaum have changed their use over time, without always making this explicit. Thirdly, there are differences in terminological choices that can be traced back to established differences in different disciplines, which are having their effect on the different disciplinary streams in the capability literature.

There are at least four terminological issues that need to be noted: (1) 'capability' understood as a single opportunity versus 'capability' understood as an opportunity set; (2) Nussbaum's more complex terminology; (3) the quite different meanings given in the literature to the term 'basic capabilities'; and (4) additional refinements — both some that have been proposed in the literature, as well as a proposal that I will put on the table, namely to take the robustness of a capability into account. Let's look at these four issues in turn.

3.2.1 Capability as an opportunity versus capability as an opportunity set

Let us first look at Sen's original terminology. The major constituents of the capability approach are *functionings* and *capabilities*. Functionings are the 'beings and doings' of a person, whereas a person's capability is "the various combinations of functionings that a person can achieve. Capability is thus a set of combinations of functionings, reflecting the person's freedom to lead one type of life or another" (Sen 1992a, 40). According to Sen, a person has only one capability (or capability set), which consists of a combination of possible, reachable functionings.

A person's functionings and her capability are closely related but distinct, as the following quote illustrates:

> A functioning is an achievement, whereas a capability is the ability to achieve. Functionings are, in a sense, more directly related to living conditions, since they *are* different aspects of living conditions. Capabilities, in contrast, are notions of freedom, in the positive sense: what real opportunities you have regarding the life you may lead. (Sen 1987, 36)

Sen thus used the term 'a capability' for what we could also call 'a capability set'. The advantage of each person corresponds to *one capability* (hence 'a person's overall freedom to do the things they want to do and be the person they want to be'). In the original terminology, each person had one capability, and the use of the word 'capabilities' therefore had to refer to the capabilities of various persons.

In Sen's original terminology, a person's capability consisted of a range of potential functionings, out of which a particular combination of functionings could be chosen. Functionings could therefore be either potential or achieved. This kind of language is most familiar to social choice scholars and scholars in formal welfare economics, where the focus of much of the analysis is on the opportunity set.

However, many other scholars working on the capability paradigm, including Martha Nussbaum, have labelled these potential functionings 'capabilities', and only use the term 'functioning' for an outcome. In that terminology, the capability set consists of a number of capabilities, in the same way as a person's overall freedom is made up of a number of more specific freedoms. One does not find this usage of 'capabilities' (meaning the separate elements of one person's capability set) in Sen's earlier writings, and in his later writings he (perhaps reluctantly) uses the word 'capability' in both senses interchangeably.

What, then, is the terminology that is now predominantly used? As was explained in chapter 2, a functioning is a state of one's being (such as being healthy or ill), or something one is doing (such as going on a trip or raising children). The real opportunity to accomplish such a functioning, is the corresponding capability. Hence if my sister goes on a trip and invites me along, but I decide to stay at home because I want to do something else, then I have the capability to go on a trip, but I chose not to have the corresponding outcome — the functioning. Each functioning corresponds exactly to one capability.

This plural use of capabilities is widespread in the contemporary literature on the capability approach — with the exception of those working in social choice theory, formal welfare economics and related fields. The terminology as used by the broader group of scholars working on the capability approach seems to be more straightforward and less technical, but when reading Sen's (earlier) work it is important to know that the term 'capability' started with a different definition.[1]

3.2.2 Nussbaum's terminology

In *Women and Human Development*, her first book-length work on her capabilities theory, Martha Nussbaum used the following terminology, which she still uses in her recent book on the capability approach (Nussbaum 2011, 20–25). *Human capabilities* are "what people are

---

1   For a seminal analysis of the differences between Nussbaum's and Sen's conceptual and terminological apparatus, see the twin papers by David A. Crocker (1992, 1995).

actually able to do and to be" (Nussbaum 2000, 5). From those human capabilities, Nussbaum identifies a list of ten *"central capabilities"* which have the status of rights: they "may not be infringed upon to pursue other types of social advantage" (Nussbaum 2000, 14). According to Nussbaum's minimal account of social justice, these central capabilities have to be protected up to a certain threshold level.

Nussbaum helpfully distinguishes between three further notions to unpack the concept of 'human capabilities': basic capabilities, internal capabilities, and combined capabilities (Nussbaum 2000, 84–85). The term *basic capabilities* refers to "the innate equipment of individuals that is necessary for developing the more advanced capabilities", such as the capability of speech and language, which is present in a new-born but needs to be fostered before it can develop into a true capability. *Internal capabilities* are "the matured conditions of readiness" — the internal aspect of the capability. If I have the skill and meet the physical preconditions of walking, then I may or may not be able to go for a walk — depending, for example, on whether as a woman I am legally allowed to leave the house without a male relative, or whether there is not currently a hurricane posing a real danger if I were to leave my house. If those suitable external conditions are in place, we can speak of *combined capabilities*.

Finally, a functioning is an "active realisation of one or more capabilities. [...] Functionings are beings and doings that are the outgrowths or realizations of capabilities" (Nussbaum 2011, 25). Hence, in Nussbaum's terminology, a functioning stands in relation to a capability as an outcome stands in relation to an opportunity.

While the substantive distinctions to which Nussbaum's terminology refers are very helpful, the specific words chosen may be not ideal. There are two problems. First, for many capability scholars, the reference to the term 'capability' refers to the real opportunity to do something or be the person one wants to be; 'internal capabilities' do not fit that category. They are, starting from that perspective, simply not a capability, but rather necessary elements of a capability, or a precondition for a capability. It would have been better to call 'internal capabilities' simply 'internal characteristics' or else 'skills, talents, character traits and abilities'. Such terminology would also make the link with various other behavioural and social disciplines much easier.

What Nussbaum calls 'combined capabilities' could then simply be called 'human capabilities', which consist of the presence of those skills, talents, character traits and abilities, together with suitable external conditions and circumstances. Second, Nussbaum uses the term 'basic capability' after it had already been used in two other different ways, as the next section will show. Why not simply call these 'innate human characteristics'?

3.2.3 What are 'basic capabilities'?

The way readers from different disciplines use terminology in particular ways is clearly exemplified by the various interpretations of the term 'basic capabilities'.

One interpretation is Nussbaum's. As was mentioned before, Nussbaum (2000, 84) uses the term 'basic capabilities' to refer to "the innate equipment of individuals that is necessary for developing the more advanced capabilities", such as the capability of speech and language, which is present in a new-born but needs to be fostered. Yet of the four ways in which the term 'basic capabilities' is used in the literature, this one may be the least prevalent.

Sen (1980) mentioned the term 'basic capability' as his first rough attempt to answer the 'equality of what?' question, but changed his terminology in subsequent work (what he called 'basic capability' would later become 'capability').[2] In his later writings, Sen reserved the term 'basic capabilities' to refer to a threshold level for the relevant capabilities. A basic capability is "the ability to satisfy certain elementary and crucially important functionings up to certain levels" (Sen 1992a, 45 fn 19). Basic capabilities refer to the freedom to do some basic things considered necessary for survival and to avoid or escape poverty or other serious deprivations. The relevance of basic capabilities is "not so much in ranking living standards, but in deciding on a cut-off point for the purpose of assessing poverty and deprivation" (Sen 1987, 109).

---

2   The 'equality of what?' debate was prompted by Sen's Tanner lecture with the same title (Sen 1980a), in which he argued that almost any theory of distributive justice is egalitarian, in the sense that they all advocate equality of something. The question to pose to a theory of distributive justice is therefore not whether it is egalitarian or not, but what is its answer to the 'equality of what?' question.

A third way in which the term 'basic capabilities' can be used is, as in analytical political philosophy, to refer to essential (moral and/or political) entitlements that signify a higher level of moral urgency, according to the philosopher's own normative commitments. For example, Rutger Claassen, who has been developing an agency-based capability theory of justice, has been using the term 'basic' in that sense (Claassen 2016).

A fourth way to use the term 'basic capability' has been proposed by Bernard Williams. Yet this has, to the best of my knowledge, not been taken up by anyone. Williams has argued that it is important to distinguish between the capability to choose yet another new brand of washing powder from, say, Adam Smith's often-cited capability to appear in public without shame. Williams rightly notes that "what you need, in order to appear without shame in public, differs depending on where you are, but there is an invariant capability here, namely that of appearing in public without shame. This underlying capability is more basic" (Williams 1987, 101). I agree with the need for the distinction that Williams makes, but I would rather call these underlying capabilities the *general capabilities*, so as to avoid confusion with Sen's use of basic capabilities. I will turn to the discussion of general versus specific capabilities in section 3.2.4, but first I want to ask the question: how should we interpret the term 'basic capability'?

My reading is that, within the capability literature, the most widespread (and hence dominant) use of 'basic capabilities' is Sen's use, referring to poverty or deprivation. Hence, while the notion of capabilities refers to a very broad range of opportunities, 'basic capabilities' refers to the real opportunity to avoid poverty or to meet or exceed a threshold of wellbeing. By focusing on 'basic' capabilities, we are limiting the set of all capabilities in two ways: first, by having a selection of capabilities (i.e. those that are key to capturing wellbeing, and those that are centrally important), and second, by imposing a threshold at which those capabilities will be evaluated (i.e. at a low or poverty-like level).

Basic capabilities are thus crucial for poverty analysis and in general for studying the wellbeing of large sections of the population in poor countries, or for theories of justice that endorse sufficiency as their distributive rule. In affluent countries, by contrast, wellbeing analysis often focuses on capabilities that are less necessary both for survival and the avoidance of poverty. It is important to acknowledge that the capability approach is not restricted to poverty and deprivation analysis but can also serve as a framework for, say, project or policy evaluations or inequality measurement in non-poor communities. Sen's and Nussbaum's extensive writings on the capability approach in the context of poverty alleviation and development questions have misled some of their readers into thinking that the capability approach is about poverty and development issues only. Yet as has been absolutely clear from the description and account of the capability approach presented in chapters 1 and 2, there is conceptually or normatively no reason to restrict its scope in this way. The term 'basic capabilities' is helpful since it can signal to the reader when the capability approach is specifically used in this context.

3.2.4 Conceptual and terminological refinements

Over the years, several proposals have been made to refine the notions of 'functioning' and 'capability', or to add additional qualifications which may be helpful in capability analyses.

The first refinement — which is straightforward but still very helpful — is the distinction between *general* and *specific* functionings and capabilities (Alkire 2002, 31). Suppose we are concerned with questions about what is needed for people not to be socially excluded. Sen has repeatedly referred to Adam Smith's example that, in order to be able to appear in public without shame, one needed (in the time and place Smith lived) a linen shirt. Yet in other countries one would need a sari, or a suit, or something else. We all know that in every specific time and place, there are certain types of clothes one shouldn't wear if one doesn't want to be frowned upon or be seen as inappropriately dressed. We could say that, for women in place A, being able to wear a sari is important, and for men in another place, being able to wear a suit is important, in order not to be excluded. 'Being able to wear a sari' and 'being able to wear a suit' are specific capabilities; 'being able to wear the clothes that are considered appropriate' is the more general capability. Thus, if we formulate the relevant capabilities at a higher level of generality, it will be easier to reach agreement on what those are, than if we focus on more specific capabilities (Sen 1992a, 108–09). General capabilities are thus the more generic and more abstract capabilities. The idea of general versus more specific functionings and capabilities is also entailed by Nussbaum's idea of the *multiple realisability* of capabilities that are under scrutiny: the selected capabilities "can be more concretely specified in accordance with local beliefs and circumstances" (Nussbaum 2000, 77).

A second conceptual refinement to consider is the concept of 'refined functioning'. Sen (1987, 36–37) has proposed the concept of 'refined functioning' to designate functioning that takes note of the available alternatives. Sen (1992a, 52) notes: "'fasting' as a functioning is not just starving; it is *choosing to starve when one does have other options*". The aim of this proposal is to try to bridge the choice between functionings and capabilities by a conceptual move. That is, one could focus on achieved functionings levels but — where appropriate — include the exercise of choice as one of the relevant functionings (Fleurbaey 2002). This allows us to stay within the realm of (observable) achievements, but because the act of choosing is included, one can derive from that functioning relevant information about whether one had options or not.

A third conceptual refinement — this time a qualification or property that we can attribute to a functioning or a capability — has been proposed by Avner De-Shalit and Jonathan Wolff. They have argued that what is relevant for the most disadvantaged persons is not so much whether they have any functionings, but rather whether those functionings are secure (Wolff and De-Shalit 2007, 2013). The idea here is that we are not only interested in the functionings that people can achieve, but also in the prospects that a person has to sustain that level — that is, the risk and vulnerability of losing that functionings achievement should be taken into account, even if the risk never materialises. The objective fact of risk and vulnerability itself should be seen as having an influence on how we normatively judge a functionings achievement (Wolff and De-Shalit 2007, 63–73).

Another qualification that we could add to capabilities is their *robustness* — referring to the *probability* of a capability being realisable. The standard definition of a capability is that it is a *genuine* option: if we have the capability and we choose this opportunity, then we should also enjoy the outcome — the functioning. But this presents us with a very dichotomous view of our options: either we have an option with a 100%

probability, or else, if the probability is significantly less, it is implied that we do not have the capability. That is, arguably, a rather unhelpful way of thinking about real life processes. For example, the problem with women's opportunities in advanced economies is definitely not that women have no capabilities to achieve professional success; rather, the problem is that, given a variety of mechanisms that are biased against female professionals, the robustness of the capabilities they are given is weaker. If an equally talented man and woman both want to succeed professionally, they may, in a liberal society, both have that capability — but the probability that the man will be able to succeed will be higher than the woman's. She *does* have some opportunity, but that opportunity is less robust. Probabilities of success if one were to want to exercise that capability would be a way to express this. In the above gender case, the source of the different probabilities lies in the social and environmental conversion factors. But the source of the difference in robustness could also lie in internal factors. For example, a person with a psychiatric condition may have some opportunities for finding a job, but those opportunities may be much more precarious then they would be if she didn't have those psychiatric challenges.

3.3 Are capabilities freedoms, and if so, which ones?

Amartya Sen (1990c, 460) has described capabilities as

> the freedom[s] to achieve valuable human functionings, which can vary from such elementary things as being well-nourished and avoiding escapable morbidity and mortality, to such complex achievements as having self-respect, being well-integrated in society, and so on. Capabilities thus reflect the actual freedoms that people respectively enjoy in being able to lead the kind of lives they have reason to value.

But several philosophers and social scientists have questioned the understanding (or, for philosophers: 'conceptualisation') of capabilities in terms of freedoms, asking whether capabilities could plausibly be understood as freedoms, whether Sen was not overextending the use of freedom, whether freedom is all there is to the capability approach, and whether it is wise to use the terminology of freedom for the goals of the capability approach (e.g. Cohen 1993; Gasper and Van Staveren 2003; Hill 2003; Okin 2003, 291–92). Let us therefore clarify and analyse the conceptualisation of capabilities as freedom by answering three questions. First, capabilities have been described as positive freedoms, but how should we understand that notion, and is that the best way to describe what kind of freedoms capabilities are? (Section 3.3.1) Secondly, is there a better conceptualisation of freedom that captures what capabilities are? (Section 3.3.2) Thirdly, if it is the case that capabilities can coherently be conceptualised as freedoms, are capabilities then *best* understood as freedoms, or is it better to avoid that terminology? (Section 3.3.3).

3.3.1 Capabilities as positive freedoms?

Sen has often used the distinction between positive and negative freedoms, thereby describing capabilities as positive freedoms. For example, Sen (1984b, 315) has stated that he is trying "to outline a characterization of positive freedoms in the form of capabilities of persons".[3] In some discourses, especially in the social sciences, the term 'positive freedoms' is used to refer to access to certain valuable goods, such as the freedom to affordable high quality health care or education. Positive freedoms are contrasted with negative freedoms, which refer to the absence of interference by others, such as the freedom to own a gun.[4] Yet these are by no means standard understandings of positive and negative freedom.

In making the claim that capabilities are positive freedoms, Sen often approvingly refers to Isaiah Berlin's canonical distinction between positive and negative freedom, but unfortunately doesn't explain in detail how we should read Berlin. This is potentially confusing, since Berlin's use of the term 'positive freedom' is far from crystal clear.

---

3   Other statements equating capabilities with positive freedoms can be found in Sen (1982, 6, 38–39; 1984c, 78, 86; 1985c, 201; 2008, 18 among other places). In his 1979 Tanner lecture in which Sen coined the term 'capability', he did not refer to freedoms, but did use other terms such as 'ability' and 'power'.

4   According to Sen (2009c, 282) this is the understanding of positive and negative freedom in welfare economics.

Let us start from the clearest concept in Berlin — his notion of negative freedom — which Berlin (1969, 122) defines as follows: "I am normally said to be free to the degree to which no man or body of men interferes with my activity". The opposite of having negative freedom is being coerced — the deliberate interference of other persons in an area of my life in which I could, without the interference, act freely. Negative freedom thus corresponds to freedom as non-interference, and Berlin speaks approvingly of this kind of freedom: "[...] non-interference, which is the opposite of coercion, is good as such, although it is not the only good. This is the 'negative' conception of liberty in its classical form" (1969, 128).

On positive freedom, there is much less clarity in Berlin's work. Berlin first introduces positive freedom as the freedom to be one's own master:

> I wish to be the instrument of my own, not of other men's, acts of will. I wish to be a subject, not an object; to be moved by reasons, by conscious purposes, which are my own, not by causes which affect me, as it were, from outside. I wish to be a somebody, not nobody, a doer — deciding, not being decided for; self-directed and not acted upon by external nature or by other men as if I were a thing, or an animal, or a slave incapable of playing a human role, that is, conceiving goals and policies of my own and realizing them. (Berlin 1969, 131)

Berlin argues that the metaphor of self-mastery historically developed into the idea that a person has two selves, a dominant self which is identified with reason and a 'higher nature', and a 'heteronomous self' which follows desires and passions and needs to be disciplined. Berlin continues that the first self, the 'real self', may become seen as wider than the individual,

> as a social whole of which the individual is an element or aspect: a tribe, a race, a church, a state, the great society of the living and the dead and the yet unborn. This entity is then identified as being the 'true' self which, by imposing its collective, or 'organic' single will upon its recalcitrant 'members' achieves its own, and therefore their 'higher freedom'. (Berlin 1969, 132)

Put differently, men are "coerced in the name of some goal (let us say, justice or public health) which they would if they were more enlightened, themselves pursue, but do not, because they are blind or ignorant or corrupt" (132–133). Berlin acknowledges that one could, in principle, develop the same justification of tyranny starting from the definition of negative freedom, but continues to argue that this is easier with the positive conception of freedom. The reason is that the idea of positive freedom as self-mastery entails a distinction between my 'true' self and an 'untrue self'. It is therefore possible that someone else other than you knows better what your true self is, which opens up a space for another person to coerce you in the name of your 'true self'. Berlin believes that this has historically been the case with tyrannical regimes that propagated an ideology entailing a notion of positive freedom as self-mastery, whereby everything can be justified in the name of some true or higher self that needs to master other impulses and desires.

It is not difficult to see that positive freedom in Berlin's sense is *not* the kind of freedom that capabilities represent, especially not when understood against the historically tyrannical shape that this ideal (according to Berlin) took. Capabilities are not about people's internal attitudes towards what they should do with their lives. At the political level, the capability approach would advocate that we should organise our political life in such a way as to expand people's capabilities, whereby the capability approach will judge that two persons had the same initial equal freedom if both of them had the same initial set of valuable options from which to choose. The capability approach, therefore, is not strongly perfectionist and teleological, as is the positive freedom doctrine in Berlin's sense. In sum, capabilities are very different from Berlin's notion of positive freedom, and Berlin's understanding of positive freedom is not the best way to capture the kinds of freedom that capabilities are.

In later work, Sen acknowledged the potential for confusion that his equation of capabilities with positive freedom and his references to Berlin's work had made, and provided a clearer description of his own understanding of positive freedom. In his Arrow lectures, Sen (2002a, 586) wrote:

> positive freedom has also been variously defined, varying on one side from the general freedom to achieve in general, to the particular aspect, on the other side, of freedom to achieve insofar as it relates to influences working within oneself (a use that is close to Berlin's conceptualization of positive freedom). In my own attempts in this field, I have found it more useful to see 'positive freedom' as the person's ability to do the things

in question *taking everything into account* (including external restraints as well as internal limitations). In this interpretation, a violation of negative freedom must also be — unless compensated by some other factor — a violation of positive freedom, but not vice versa. This way of seeing positive freedom is not the one preferred by Isaiah Berlin.

This quote also draws attention to another drawback of defining capabilities in terms of positive freedom. Violations of negative freedoms will, according to Sen, always lead to violations of positive freedoms; yet for Berlin this need not be the case. In a totalitarian state which espouses a doctrine of positive freedom, in which the state will help the citizens to 'liberate their true selves', a violation of a range of negative freedoms, such as the freedom of expression or of the freedom to hold property, will not violate positive freedom; on the contrary, within the parameters of that doctrine, violations of such negative freedoms may even enhance the state-aspired positive freedom.

So where does all this terminological exegesis lead us? It has often been remarked that there are many available definitions of negative and positive freedom. Berlin's conceptualisations are canonical, but his definition of positive freedom is very different from Sen's. Moreover, as Charles Taylor (1979, 175) rightly pointed out, the debate on negative and positive freedoms has been prone to polemical attacks that caricature the views of both sides. One therefore wonders what is to be gained by describing capabilities in terms of positive freedoms — at least, if one is aware of the philosophical background to this term. Perhaps it may be wiser to look further for an alternative conceptualisation that is less prone to creating misunderstandings?

3.3.2 Capabilities as opportunity or option freedoms?

Luckily, in other parts of Amartya Sen's writings we can find the answer to the question of what kind of freedoms capabilities are (if any at all). Although Sen's first descriptions of capabilities were couched exclusively in terms of positive freedoms, he soon offered an alternative description in terms of opportunities.[5] In his 1984 Dewey Lectures, Sen

---

5   In fact, even this is not entirely correct, since in his earlier work and especially in his work written for economists, Sen did not speak of 'capabilities', but rather of 'capability sets' and thus also of 'opportunity sets' (see section 3.2.1).

(1985c, 201) defended a conceptualisation of wellbeing freedom in terms of capabilities, and defined wellbeing freedom as:

> whether one person did have the opportunity of achieving the functioning vector that another actually achieved. This involves comparisons of actual opportunities that different persons have.

Similarly, in *Inequality Reexamined*, Sen (1992a, 31) writes:

> A person's position in a social arrangement can be judged in two different perspectives, viz. (1) the actual achievement, and (2) the freedom to achieve. Achievement is concerned with what we *manage* to accomplish, and freedom with the *real opportunity* that we have to accomplish what we value.

Given Sen's descriptions of the freedoms that the capability approach is concerned with in terms of opportunities, it seems a natural suggestion to investigate whether the concept of 'opportunity freedom' better captures the nature of capabilities.

Charles Taylor, in his discussion of Berlin's distinction between negative and positive freedom, has argued that beneath the distinction between positive and negative freedom lies another set of distinctions, namely between an exercise concept of freedom and an opportunity concept of freedom. The *exercise concept of freedom* refers to an agent being free "only to the extent that one has effectively determined oneself and the shape of one's life", whereas according to the *opportunity concept of freedom* "being free is a matter of what we can do, of what is open to us to do, whether or not we do anything to exercise these options" (Taylor 1979, 177). According to Taylor, theories of negative freedom can be grounded on either an exercise or an opportunity concept, but theories of positive freedom can never be grounded merely on an opportunity concept. Taylor's goal is arguing in favour of the exercise concept of freedom, and shows that the crude view of negative freedom (which, he argues, Berlin is defending) is untenable. Taylor (1979, 177) describes the opportunity concept of freedom thus: "being free is a matter of what we can do, of what it is open to us to do, whether or not we do anything to exercise these options. [...] Freedom consists just in there being no obstacle. It is a sufficient condition of one's being free that nothing stand in the way".

Is Taylor's opportunity concept of freedom the kind of freedom we are searching for in our attempt to understand the nature of capabilities? His concept comes close, but it is narrower than the conception of freedom contained in the idea of capabilities. For Taylor, only *external* obstacles count in the definition of negative freedom (Taylor 1979, 176, 193; Kukathas 2007, 688). He holds that the acknowledgement of internal obstacles to action, including the action to choose between different opportunities, merges an element of the exercise concept of freedom into the opportunity concept. The notion of opportunity in Taylor's concept of opportunity freedom thus resembles a formal notion of opportunity more closely than a substantive notion.

Here's an example to illustrate the difference between Taylor's opportunity concept of freedom and the notion of 'capabilities'. If, in a patriarchal community, men have all the power, and in a verbally aggressive manner they teach girls and remind women that their place is inside the house, then surely these women do not have the same opportunity freedom to find employment in the nearest city where women from more liberal communities are holding jobs. In formal terms, the women from both communities may be able to work outside the home since there are jobs available to women in the city, they are able-bodied and are able to commute to the city. Yet the women from the patriarchal community would face much bigger costs and would need to gather much more courage, and resist the subtle working of social norms, before they could effectively access this formal opportunity. Put in capability terms, we would say that the first group of women has a much smaller capability to work outside the home than the women living in less patriarchal communities. If the costs and burdens borne by the women from strongly patriarchal communities are excessive, we could even conclude that the capability to work in the city is virtually nonexistent.

Luckily, more recent debates in political philosophy have further developed this discussion, in a way that is helpful in answering the question of how capabilities should be understood. Philip Pettit (2003) has argued that the philosophical debate on social freedom could benefit from being clear on the distinction between option-freedom and agency-freedom. While option-freedom is a property of options, agency-freedom is a property of agents. Agency-freedom relates to the long tradition in philosophy of seeing the slave as the prime example of someone who is not free: he is subjugated to the will of others. Agency-freedom focusses on the question of how a person relates to their fellows, and is a matter of social standing or status, not of the options that they enjoy (Pettit 2003, 394–95).

Options are the alternatives that an agent is in a position to realize. Pettit argues that option freedom is a function of two aspects: the character of access to options, and the character of options themselves. First, option freedom is a function of the character of the agent's *access* to the options. Some philosophers would hold that the physical possibility of carrying out an option is sufficient for access, and thus would conclude that the agent has option freedom. Alternatively, one could defend the position that access to an option does not only depend on the physical possibility of carrying out the option, but that non-physical barriers are relevant too. Pettit distinguishes two possibilities: either an agent is objectively more burdened than another agent when trying to access an option, whether by difficulty or by penalty, or an agent is subjectively burdened in the sense that he believes that access to an option is not possible. The second aspect of option freedom is the character of the options. Here a wide range of views exist, such as the number of options that are accessible, their diversity, and whether they are objectively significant or subjectively significant (Pettit 2003, 389–92).

Capabilities are precisely this kind of option freedom. What counts in the capability approach is indeed the access that a person has to a wide range of valuable alternative options. In sum, capabilities can be understood as opportunity or option freedoms, but are broader than Taylor's rather narrow opportunity concept of freedom. We can therefore conclude that it is conceptually sound to understand capabilities as freedoms of this sort.[6]

---

6   It doesn't follow, of course, that capability theories would not be able to pay attention to agency freedom. They do — for example by including relational capabilities in the selection of relevant dimensions, or by having some ideal of agency freedom as an additional moral principle included in module C4.

3.3.3 Are capabilities best understood as freedoms?

The detailed analysis in the previous section doesn't settle all questions, though. It may well be the case that it is coherent to see capabilities as freedoms, but that there is another notion, such as human rights, basic needs, or something similar, that much better captures what capabilities are.

The answer to that question has to be contextual in the following sense. The capability approach is a deeply interdisciplinary approach, yet scholars from different disciplines will have different associations with certain terms. Philosophers may well have very different associations with the word 'freedom' than, say, anthropologists or development sociologists. Similar remarks can be made when the capability approach is being applied for policy and political purposes, since the term 'freedom' has in some countries a particular historical connotation, or is being claimed by extreme right or extreme left political parties, in the sense that if they were to come to power, they would use that power to drastically curtail the capabilities of (some sections of) the population. However, one should also not forget that the word 'capabilities' is non-existent in many languages, and may itself also lead to mistaken connotations, for example with skills or capacities in its French translation (*capacité*).

When developing a particular capability theory or capability application, should we frame the capability approach in terms of freedoms? My suggestion would be to answer this question in a pragmatic fashion. If the context in which the capability approach is applied makes it likely that the use of the term freedom will lead to the application being misunderstood, then I would suggest that one defines, describes and illustrates the word 'capabilities' and introduces that term. Yet for moral philosophers and political theorists who are eager to further develop the capability approach into a coherent political theory, a clear understanding of capabilities as option freedoms may pave the way for work that lies ahead. Pettit's analysis of option freedoms, and the established literature to which he is referring in his analysis, give the capability scholar a neat overview of the choices that need to be made if one wants to turn the underspecified capability approach into a well-specified moral or political capability theory. For the political philosopher, there is therefore less reason to be worried about being misunderstood when referring to capabilities as option freedoms, or as opportunity freedoms.

3.4 Functionings or capabilities?

We now move to examine the issue that is central to module B6: should we, when developing a capability analysis or capability theory, focus on functionings, capabilities, or a mixture of both? After all, this question is not settled. It is one of the core features of the capability approach that it uses 'functionings' and 'capabilities' as core notions (property A1, as discussed in 2.6.1) and that every capability analysis endorses the claim that functionings and/or capabilities form the evaluative space (property A5, as discussed in 2.6.5). But this still leaves the question unanswered whether we should focus on functionings, *or* on capabilities *or* on a combination of functionings and capabilities. Perhaps we have good reasons sometimes to focus on functionings, and sometimes on capabilities, for example for different types of applications, or for different groups of people?

Luckily, this question is not new to the capability literature, and there is by now a lively debate with many different types of arguments about whether the appropriate wellbeing metric should be capabilities or functionings, hence opportunities or achievements. What reasons or considerations have been argued to be relevant for this choice?[7]

The first consideration concerns *anti-paternalism*. It is a normative consideration: by focusing on capabilities rather than functionings, we do not force people into a particular account of good lives but instead aim at a range of possible ways of life from which each person can choose. Thus, it is the liberal nature of the capability approach, or an anti-paternalist commitment, that motivates a principled choice of capabilities rather than functionings. Obviously, the strength of this argument depends on how bad one takes paternalism to be. There may be good reasons to believe that some paternalism is unavoidable, or even desired (Nussbaum 2000, 51–56; Robeyns 2016b). Moreover, some

---

7 General discussions surveying different reasons to choose for functionings, capabilities or both, can also be found in Robeyns and Van der Veen (2007, 45–99, 76–78), Hick and Burchardt (2016, 79–82) and Robeyns (2016b).

scholars have argued that some element of paternalism in the capability approach may well be unavoidable. One reason is that the protection of the capacity to choose from one's capability set requires certain functionings, such as mental health and education, to be promoted as achievements, rather than merely as freedoms (Gandjour 2008). Another reason is that the protection of certain specific capabilities requires either previously certain functionings-levels, or else requires certain levels of achievement of other capabilities, or requires that enough other people have functionings achievements within those capabilities (e.g. Robeyns and Van der Veen 2007; Claassen 2014; Robeyns 2016b). Rutger Claassen has identified five different types of mechanisms in which capability protection leads to the promotion of functionings, and has concluded that "any capability theory will have to confront the issue of paternalism" (Claassen 2014, 72).

As this literature shows, there are many reasons why one can reasonably decide sometimes to promote functionings, rather than capabilities. Here, I will only give one example, namely limits to our capacities to make informed choices in a voluntary, autonomous way. Let us start with an uncontested case: infants and the severely cognitively disabled. The concept of functioning has particular relevance for our relations to those human beings who are not yet able to choose (infants), who will never be able to make complex choices (severely mentally disabled individuals), or who have lost this ability through advanced dementia or serious brain damage. Whether or not these persons can decide to be well nourished and healthy, it is generally held that we (through families, governments, or other institutions) have the moral obligation to promote or protect their nutritional and healthy functioning. All capability theorists agree that in these cases, we should focus on functionings rather than capabilities. The implicit underlying assumption in the claim that capabilities have normative priority over functionings is that we assume the presence of a sufficient level of agency in the individuals who will be given the power to make their own choices from their capability sets. If we have strong reason to believe that such agency cannot be attributed to a person, we should not let the person herself decide on which options to choose; however, we should find ways of compensating for that lack of agency — either by having a steward make the choices for her or by guiding her in the choice-making process. Thus, we will shift our normative concern from capabilities to functionings for those who are incapable of deciding for themselves. In empirical research, this implies, for example, that it is fine to study the quality of life of small children by focussing on a range of functionings (e.g. Phipps 2002).

But the paternalism claim is not limited to the case of infants and the severely cognitively disabled: one could also apply this argument — at least to some extent and in some areas — to all adults. Adults, too, often make *systematically* irrational or mistaken choices. We are often not able to choose what is best for us simply because of our psychological makeup; many of our choices are the result of the impulsive, unreflective, habit-driven part of our brain rather than the deliberative and reflective part. There is mounting empirical evidence of our systematic failures in choice-making, that we are influenced by a large number of arbitrary factors in making choices and that we often harm our own interests in non-deliberate and non-intentional ways (e.g. Ariely 2010; Kahneman 2011). It is entirely consistent for a capability theory to argue that we have strong reasons to protect people against their own systematic irrationalities, just as it is consistent for the capability approach to argue that there are stronger reasons why we should allow people to make the errors that follow from their own systematic irrationalities: both positions follow from choices made in the B-modules.

Summing up, we have here a first normative consideration that can help us to decide whether some (limited or fuller) focus on functionings rather than capabilities is acceptable, namely the question of whether there are mechanisms that justify paternalism.

A second normative consideration in the choice between capabilities and functionings stems from the importance given to *personal responsibility* in contemporary political philosophy. If one believes that the moral aim should be to establish equality of opportunity, then it follows that one should, *at least as an ideal*, favour equality of capability over equality of functionings. If equality of capability becomes the ideal, then each person should have the same real opportunity (capability), but once that is in place, each individual should be held responsible for his or her own choices. It is important to stress, however, that philosophers and social scientists working on issues of social justice do not at all agree on whether equality of opportunity (capabilities) should be the goal, rather than equality of outcome (functionings). On the one hand, the responsibility-sensitivity principle is widely endorsed not only in political philosophy but also in the mathematical models being developed in normative welfare economics. If one wants to endorse and implement this principle of responsibility-sensitivity, then specifications and applications of the capability approach should focus on capabilities, rather than functionings. On the other hand, scholars have objected to the weight given to personal responsibility, both within the highly abstract theorising about ideals and when considering more applied and practical issues. At a highly abstract theoretical level, philosophers disagree on whether we should endorse responsibility-sensitivity in developing the capability approach (Fleurbaey 2002; Vallentyne 2005; Wolff and De-Shalit 2007). Moreover, for applied work, serious epistemological hurdles may ultimately lead us to drop the responsibility-sensitivity principle for practical reasoning about the actual world: in practice, it is often impossible to know what the causal factors were that led someone to make decisions that lowered her achieved wellbeing, and hence it is difficult or even impossible to know whether the causal factors are those for which one could be held morally responsible or not.

Thirdly, there may be *institutional considerations* that have an influence on whether we choose functionings, capabilities, or a mixture (Robeyns 2016b). Take the example of a government that has, with the broad support of the population, set up a welfare state arrangement, which includes certain welfare rights. Then this government may demand from citizens who want to be part of this societal arrangement that they proactively aim to master, secure, or maintain certain functionings, such as being able to read and write, or to speak a language that does not exclude one from holding a job. A welfare state arrangement that offers citizens relatively generous welfare rights can legitimately induce or perhaps even force citizens and legal residents to choose certain functionings that are needed in order to justly participate in that welfare state arrangement. But here, again, one has to pay attention to detail and be careful, since we would want to distinguish between those who didn't exercise a functioning but had the capability versus those who didn't exercise a functioning but due to inability didn't have the capability in the first place. For example, if the political community believes that it is a fair requirement in order to enjoy the benefits of the welfare state that one learns the major dominant local language, then we have to make a distinction between those who do, those who don't but could, and those who don't but are unable. In practice, that distinction may sometimes be very hard to make. Nevertheless, the general point to take home is that an outcome-oriented theory of justice needs to be bolstered with an account of what justice requires from the institutional design for a state or coalition of states. Reasons of reciprocity, feasibility, and stability may justify a focus on functionings rather than merely on capabilities.

Fourthly, there are pervasive cases of interdependence between people's capabilities that may prompt us to look beyond the capability of a single person. One important type of case is that in which a capability is available to a person but *only* if other people do not also want to realize that capability (Basu 1987, 74). For example, two spouses may each have the capability of holding demanding jobs which are each incompatible with large caring responsibilities. However, if these spouses also have infants or relatives with extensive care needs, then at best only one of them may effectively realize that capability. Another type of case is that in which the capability of one person is only possible if enough other people have chosen to realise the corresponding functioning (Claassen 2014, 67–68). Take the example of being protected against dangerous infectious diseases such as polio or measles by way of a vaccine. In order genuinely to have that capability, one does not only need access to a vaccination, but enough other people need to choose to be vaccinated, since protection requires that a certain minimal number of people are vaccinated. In other words, my child's capability to be protected from the debilitating effects of polio or the measles depends on your choice to exercise that capability and opt for the functioning — that is, to vaccinate your children.

Since capability sets may thus include freedoms that are conditional (because they depend on the choices of other people), it might be better to focus both on the individual's capability set and also on what people have been able to realize from their own capability sets, that is, their functionings or wellbeing achievements. The question of who decides or *should* decide this sort of question highlights the importance of agency and procedural fairness, which are often additional normative commitments included in the capability theory that is developed.

Finally, note that in many empirical applications, an analysis of functionings is used as a proxy for an analysis of the capability set. In the case of comparison of inequalities between groups, it has been argued that group-inequalities in functionings should be taken to reflect group-inequalities in capabilities, *except* if a plausible reason can be offered for why the members of those groups would systematically choose differently (Robeyns 2003; Kuklys and Robeyns 2005). Tania Burchardt and Rod Hicks have stressed that if inferences about capabilities based on information about functionings are made, one should be explicit about the underlying assumptions, and that three different situations could occur, namely:

> (1) situations in which all difference in outcomes might reasonably be attributed to differences in capabilities (such as where a person is assaulted); (2) situations where differences in preferences *may* result in differences in outcomes, but where for the purposes of public policy it may be possible to assume that any differences are a result of differing levels of capabilities; and (3) situations in which additional evidence may be needed in order to determine whether differences in outcomes are genuinely a result of differences in capability. (Hick and Burchardt 2016, 80)

What is the upshot of all these considerations? In my view, there are sound reasons why one would limit oneself to capabilities, there are sound reasons why one would rather focus only on functionings, and there are sound reasons why one would prefer a mixture. The choice depends on the purpose of the capability theory, but also on the additional ontological choices one endorses (e.g. one's idea of human nature — are we fully rational or not, and what, if anything, should be the consequences for policy making and institutional design), on the normative principles one adds to the core of the capability approach when developing a capability theory (e.g. endorsement of neutrality or not), and on practical constraints one is facing. We cannot say in general that the capability approach should focus exclusively on capabilities, or exclusively on functionings. It all depends on additional theoretical choices and normative commitments, which can be made in modules B and C, when developing a capability analysis.[8]

---

8   I therefore think that Nussbaum's (2011c) claim that it is a core property of the capability approach that it focusses on capabilities rather than functionings is mistaken (Robeyns 2011, 2016b; see also Claassen 2014).

3.5 Human diversity in the capability approach

In the previous chapter, it was already highlighted that diversity among human beings is a key motivation as well as a conceptual characteristic of the capability approach (module B3). Given how central human diversity is to the approach, it is worth saying a few more words on this topic. There are two important points to make: first, the mechanisms that the capability approach has at its disposal to account for diversity, and second, the attention given to diversity within the existing capability literature.

The capability approach takes account of human diversity in at least two ways. First, by its focus on the plurality of functionings and capabilities as important evaluative spaces. By including a wide range of dimensions in the conceptualization of wellbeing and wellbeing outcomes, the approach broadens the so-called 'informational basis' of assessments, and thereby includes some dimensions that may be particularly important for some groups but less so for others. For example, in standard outcome assessments, women as a group virtually always end up being worse off than men. But if the selection of outcome dimensions is shifted to also include the quality and quantity of social relations and support, and being able to engage in hands-on care, then the normative assessment of gender inequality becomes less univocal and requires much further argument and normative analysis, including being explicit about how to aggregate different dimensions (Robeyns 2003, 2006a).

Secondly, human diversity is stressed in the capability approach by the explicit focus on personal and socio-environmental conversion factors that make possible the conversion of commodities and other resources into functionings, and on the social, institutional, and environmental contexts that affect the conversion factors and the capability set directly. Each individual has a unique profile of conversion factors, some of which are body-related, while others are shared with all people from her community, and still others are shared with people with the same social characteristics (e.g. same gender, class, caste, age, or race characteristics). In the account of the capability approach presented in chapter 2, this is made very explicit by having module A3 focus on the conversion factors, which is an important source of interpersonal variations (the other source is how structural constraints affect people differently). As

Sen (1992a, xi) has argued, interpersonal variations should be of central importance to inequality analysis:

> Investigations of equality — theoretical as well as practical — that proceed with the assumption of antecedent uniformity (including the presumption that 'all men are created equal') thus miss out on a major aspect of the problem. Human diversity is no secondary complication (to be ignored, or to be introduced 'later on'); it is a fundamental aspect of our interest in equality.

Indeed, if human beings were not diverse, then inequality in one space, say income, would more or less be identical with inequality in another space, like capabilities. The entire question of what the appropriate evaluative space should be would become obsolete if there weren't any interpersonal difference in the mapping of outcomes in one space onto another. If people were all the same and had the same needs and abilities, then the capability approach would lose much of its force and significance, since resources would be excellent proxies for our wellbeing and wellbeing freedom. But as it happens, human beings are very diverse.

However, we also need to acknowledge that there is significant scholarly dispute about the question of which dimensions and parameters of human diversity are salient, and which are not. Scholars embrace very different accounts of human diversity, which is why we have module B3 in the capability approach. One's account of human diversity can often be traced back to the ontological accounts one accepts of diversity-related factors, as well as the role of groups in explanatory accounts. An example of the former is the account of gender and race that one embraces. If one holds a theory of gender and race that regards these as rather superficial phenomena that do not have an important impact on people's behaviour and opportunities in life, then the attention given to diversity in a capability application or capability theory will be rather minimal. This is logically consistent with the structure of capability theories (as laid out in chapter 2), but it is also a view that has not been widely embraced in the capability literature. Instead, the capability approach attracts scholars who endorse accounts of dimensions of gender, race, and other dimensions of human diversity that are much richer. Presumably, these scholars recognise the ways in which the capability approach can account for human diversity, hence this may explain why most capability scholars endorse rich accounts of such diversity.

A strong acknowledgement of human diversity has therefore become a hallmark of the capability approach as that literature has developed. Its criticism of other normative approaches is often fuelled by, and based on, the claim that human diversity is insufficiently acknowledged in many normative frameworks and theories. This also explains why the capability approach is often favourably regarded by feminist scholars, and by academics concerned with global justice, race or class relations, or care and disability issues. One of the main complaints of these scholars about mainstream philosophy and economics has been precisely this issue: the relative invisibility of the fate of those people whose lives do not correspond to that of an able-bodied, non-dependent, caregiving-free individual who belongs to the dominant ethnic, racial and religious groups.

3.6 Collective capabilities

Several scholars have proposed the introduction of a category of 'collective capabilities' or 'community capabilities' (Evans 2002; Ibrahim 2006, 2009, 2017; Schlosberg and Carruthers 2010; Murphy 2014). The idea of 'collective capabilities' is used in different ways in the literature, and not always spelled out very carefully. I will try to reconstruct what 'collective capabilities' could mean, and then discuss to what extent these are different from human capabilities *tout court*.

It is instructive, first, to see in which contexts different authors introduce the idea of 'collective capability'. Here are a few typical examples from the literature. Solava Ibrahim (2006, 2009, 2017) argues for the importance of collective capabilities from the perspective of the work done by self-help groups of poor people fighting to overcome their poverty, which is an issue also discussed by Stewart (2005).[9] David Schlosberg and David Carruthers (2010) argue for the importance of the idea of collective capabilities to understand the struggles of indigenous peoples for ecological justice. And Michael Murphy (2014) argues

---

9   Self-help groups are "any informal income-generating or social activity initiated by a poor community to achieve permanent improvements in their individual and communal wellbeings" (Ibrahim 2006, 398–399).

that political self-determination (of an indigenous group) should be considered to be a collective capability which should be a central aim for development.

What is shared in those cases, and what makes the idea of 'collective capability' plausible, is that a *group or collective* is needed to engage in collective action in order to reach the capability that the members of that group find valuable.

Sen (2002b) points out that we should be careful not to confuse this with a capability that he calls "socially dependent individual capability" — a person's capability, which that person enjoys, but for which the person is dependent on others to have that capability realised. Perhaps we should not use the term 'individual capability' but rather 'personal capability', since for many defenders of 'collective capabilities' the word 'individual' evokes pejorative images of persons living by themselves on an island. There are no such human creatures; we all live interdependently, and none of us could grow up without prolonged care from others, or, as adults, have a decent chance of surviving and living a minimally adequate life. Human beings are, just as other mammals, animals who live in groups. Although philosophers are used to working with terms outside their everyday use, and most philosophers (especially those with an analytical background) will not have these pejorative connotations when they hear the term 'individual capabilities', I will proceed with the term 'personal capabilities' in order to facilitate the discussion in this section.

Now, if we are very strict in our terminological distinctions, then collective capabilities are also personal capabilities, since it is individual persons who enjoy the capabilities that are thus secured. Still, there are two justifications to proceed with the term 'collective capability' — one fundamental one, and one additional one which is especially weighty from a practical point of view.

The fundamental reason to keep and use the term 'collective capability' is that we may want to make a distinction between capabilities that are only realisable with the help of others, versus capabilities that require a group or collective to act in order to secure a capability for the members of that group. An example of the former would be learning a foreign language. It is impossible to do that without the help of others; one needs a teacher, or at the very least books and audio-tapes or internet lessons that help one with self-study. Still, that doesn't suffice to say that learning a language is a collective capability. There is no group involved, and no collective action of that group is *necessary* in order to achieve the functioning. A different case is acquiring the capability to vote in elections for groups that are not yet given suffrage. Fighting for that capability is not possible on one's own. One needs collective action — e.g. the first wave women's movement, or the civil rights movement in the US, or the anti-apartheid movement in South Africa — to act collectively so that the group is granted the capability, and all persons who belong to that group can enjoy the newly won freedom.

The second reason to accept the notion of 'collective capability' is because it is already present in the practice of certain justice movements, whose demands fit very well with the capability approach, for example because they embody claims of diversity or because they fight for a notion of the good life or of justice that goes beyond a narrow materialist or economistic view of what is valuable. Examples include the disability movement, the women's movement and indigenous struggles.

So the idea of a collective capability can be understood and can be justified. Nevertheless, two warnings are in order, which may be needed to avoid conceptual confusion as well as an overuse or inflation of the notion. The first comment is that all that has been said so far does not permit one to conclude that one has personal (individual) capabilities and collective capabilities as two mutually exclusive categories. Rather, collective capabilities are a subset of personal capabilities, namely those personal capabilities that require for their realisation action by a group or a collectivity. Secondly, we should be very careful to be clear to keep our concepts distinct and correct when developing a capability theory. The modular account of the capability approach has ample conceptual and theoretical space to account for collective processes, the social embedding of persons, the influence of social structures on our choices and opportunities, a proper acknowledgement of social processes of preference formation as well as the crucial role of social institutions and norms in shaping a person's capability set. But if we want to account for a social process, we shouldn't just jump to the claim that we have now found a collective capability. Rather, we should use the quite complex and multi-layered framework that was presented in figure 2.1, and *be clear when something is a social structure that is shaping our capabilities, rather than a capability itself.* Means to ends (capabilities) and the 'capability determinants' (the social structures, social norms, institutions, etc.) can all be part of our evaluation — we just need to keep in mind which parts of what we evaluate are the means, which are the ends and *why* we evaluate a certain dimension. In the case of the evaluation of the means, one important reason could be to see how those means have changed over time, as well as whether there is any scope to improve the contribution that those particular means can make to the increase of capability sets.

3.7 Which notion of wellbeing is used in the capability approach?

The capability approach is closely related to notions of wellbeing and the quality of life. Sometimes it is assumed that the capability approach *is* a theory of wellbeing, which cannot be quite right since the capability approach can be used for many purposes, such as the construction of a theory of justice, poverty measurement or policy evaluation. Yet on the other hand, with its proposition that interpersonal comparisons be made in terms of functionings and/or capabilities, the capability approach is clearly *also* involved in offering us an account of wellbeing (Sen 1984c, 1985c, 2009a; Alkire 2016; Qizilbash 2013). But what, exactly, is the nature of the account of wellbeing in the capability approach? I will argue in this chapter that the more precise formulation is that the capability approach entails several slightly different accounts of wellbeing, which can be used for different purposes. Different capability theories have different purposes (module B1) and different meta-theoretical commitments (module B7), and the choices made in those modules will require different accounts of wellbeing for such capability theories.

When one looks at the accounts of wellbeing in the various disciplines in which the notion of 'wellbeing' plays a central role, one quickly notices that there are a range of quite different accounts proposed in different paradigms or disciplines, and that there is very limited discussion between those fields (Gasper 2010). In particular, there is surprisingly little interaction between the very large philosophical literature on wellbeing (Crisp 2013; Fletcher 2015) and the (theoretical and empirical) literature in psychology and economics, or the uses of the term wellbeing in particular fields, such as development studies or medical care. There are a few scholars who have tried to grasp this discrepancy, as well as explain why the philosophical and theoretical literatures, as well as the debates in different disciplines, are so little connected (e.g. Alexandrova 2013; Rodogno 2015b, 2015a). This is the background against which we must try to understand the place of the capability approach in thinking about wellbeing, and try to understand the accounts of wellbeing used in capability theories. I therefore believe that it is helpful first to try to grasp that scholarly context in somewhat more detail (section 3.7.1). Then we will briefly look at the standard typology of wellbeing theories (section 3.7.2), before analysing the question of which account (or rather, accounts) of wellbeing are entailed in the capability approach (section 3.7.3).

Before we start, one further clarification may be helpful. Recall that the capability approach includes a notion of *achieved* wellbeing (focussing on functionings) as well as a notion of wellbeing *freedom*, represented by one's capability set (Sen 1985c, 1993a). The distinction between achieved wellbeing and wellbeing freedom is virtually absent from the wellbeing literature. In contemporary philosophy, most philosophical accounts focus on how well life is going for a person, hence on achieved wellbeing. But clearly, for policy purposes, we will often focus on wellbeing freedom, since other values, such as respect for personal autonomy or even human dignity, may prevent us from having a specific wellbeing outcome as a legitimate policy goal. When in the capability approach the term 'wellbeing freedom' is used, it refers to what philosophers elsewhere would call 'opportunities for wellbeing'. This notion is especially relevant in moral theories where we try to balance a concern for wellbeing with a concern for individual freedom to choose: the term 'wellbeing freedom' tries to bring together and integrate those two values.

3.7.1 The aim and context of accounts of wellbeing

Philosophical discussions of wellbeing typically start out from a rather general definition of wellbeing, stating that wellbeing is about how well the life of a person is going *for that person*. The addition 'for that person' is important, since it means that in the philosophical literature wellbeing is generally conceived as what we could call a personal value, or a first-person value, rather than an institutional value — a value that we have to consider when we think about how to organise our collective life. While this demarcates 'wellbeing' from other public values such as 'justice' or 'efficiency', this is still a very general notion that can be elaborated in many different ways. Moreover, as was already mentioned, if we look at the debates in contemporary philosophy of wellbeing, we notice that they hardly relate at all to the empirical discussions in policy studies and the social sciences (with the exception of the relatively recent boom in subjective wellbeing analysis, which will be discussed in section 3.8).

Anna Alexandrova (2013) argues that the diversity in scholarship on wellbeing can be explained by the fact that the meaning of the use of the term 'wellbeing' differs depending on the context in which it is used. If the word 'wellbeing' is used by a medical doctor, or a policy maker, or a sociologist, or an adolescent reflecting on her options for her future life, they all use the term 'wellbeing' for different purposes and in a different context. I would like to add that, in particular, the *aim* or the *purpose* of our use of the term 'wellbeing' is crucial. That is, the term 'wellbeing' is never used in a vacuum; each use of that term plays a role in either explanatory or else normative projects. Normative projects always have a purpose, that is, something to judge, evaluate or recommend, which is precisely the choice that has to be made in module B1 in the account of the capability approach presented in chapter 2. Depending on whether we use the term 'wellbeing' for policy making, or for purely descriptive work, or for deciding what we owe to each other as fellow citizens, the term wellbeing will play a different function.

Most work on wellbeing in contemporary analytical philosophy is concerned with answering the question "What would be the best for someone, or would be most in this person's interests, or would make this person's life go, for him, as well as possible?" (Parfit 1984, 493). This is especially the case for the literature since the publication of Derek Parfit's typology of theories of wellbeing. While Parfit's typology is arguably crude, it has been very influential, and still serves an important function as an influential attempt that a philosopher has made to classify accounts of wellbeing.

In the next section, we will consider how (if at all) the capability approach fits into Parfit's typology. But it is important to note that this highly abstract, very detailed and analytical strand in philosophy is only to a very limited degree concerned with (a) empirical applicability and measurement or (b) practical consequences, in the sense of action-guidance such as the establishment of normatively sound policy making or the question of which social arrangements we should want. The dominant contemporary philosophical literature on wellbeing is concerned with philosophical investigation in the sense of finding truths, and typically focussed on the entire lives of people from their own, first-person, perspective. That literature is much less concerned with wellbeing as an institutional value, with asking which account of wellbeing would be best when deciding what institutions we should implement — a question that can only be answered after taking feasibility considerations into account, or considering what would be best from the point of view of ethically sound policy making. However, as Alexandrova (2013, 311) rightly points out, "the context of an all-things-considered evaluation of life as a whole privileged by philosophers is just that: *one* of the *many* contexts in which wellbeing is in question". Since most uses of the term 'wellbeing' in other debates, e.g. in applied philosophy or other disciplines, are concerned with overall evaluations of states of affairs and/or policy making, it shouldn't surprise us that there is very little cross-fertilisation between those philosophical debates and the policy oriented and empirical literatures in other disciplines. This will have an influence on how we will, in the next section, answer the question how the capability approach fits into the standard typology of theories of wellbeing used in philosophy.

3.7.2 The standard taxonomy of philosophical wellbeing accounts

In Appendix I of his influential book *Reasons and Persons*, Parfit (1984, 493) suggests that we should make a distinction between three types of philosophical wellbeing theories.

> On *Hedonistic Theories*, what would be best for someone is what would make his life happiest. On *Desire-Fulfilment Theories*, what would be best for someone is what, throughout this life, would best fulfil his desires. On *Objective List Theories*, certain things are good or bad for us, whether or not we want to have the good things, or to avoid the bad things.

In interdisciplinary conversations, hedonistic theories are today better known under the label 'happiness theories'. Interpreted from the perspective of the capability approach, hedonistic theories (or the happiness approach) entail that the *only* functioning that matters is happiness. The capability approach stresses what people can do and be (module A1) and 'happiness' or one's hedonic state at best refers to one aspect of one's being, not the various aspects of what we can do. The capability approach and the happiness approach do share some common characteristics, such as the fact that both focus on what they take to be of ultimate value. Yet the two approaches have very different ideas of what that 'ultimate value' should be, with the happiness approach defending an exclusive choice for a mental state versus the capability approach defending the focus on a plurality of aspects of our lives. It is therefore not plausible to see the happiness approach, or hedonism, as a specific case of the capability approach. However, more can be said about the precise relation between the capability approach and hedonistic or happiness approaches, which will be done in section 3.8.

How about the desire-fulfilment theories, or the objective list theories? Can the notion of wellbeing embedded in the capability approach plausibly be understood as either of those? Let us first very briefly describe the two types of theories, and then ask how the capability approach fits in.

Desire-fulfilment theories of wellbeing claim, essentially, that wellbeing is the extent to which our desires are satisfied. These desires could be our current, unquestioned desires. In philosophy, that is a view that cannot count on many defenders, since it is very easy to think of examples of current desires that will harm us in the near future, or else desires for something that is, arguably, not good for us, such as a desire for excessive amounts of food or alcohol. Philosophers have therefore proposed more sophisticated views of desires, called 'informed desires' (e.g. Sumner 1996). Those are desires that meet additional conditions, and different proposals have been made for what those conditions should be. Examples of such additional constraints include not being ignorant of facts, but also not being deceived, or not suffering from mental adaptation — which ranges from having adapted one's aspirations to one's dire circumstances, to having adapted one's desires to one's extremely affluent circumstances, to a more general 'preference adaptation' which applies to all of us in societies with social norms and the widespread use of advertisements.

For a philosophical theory of wellbeing, which merely asks the metaphysical question *what is wellbeing for the person who is living that life*, and which has no consequences for the choice of social arrangements or policy making, the informed desire theory has a very important attraction: it gives the authority to decide what would make life better to the person whose wellbeing we are investigating. We also see this account of wellbeing being helpfully put to work in various other contexts. For example, if the daughter of a family-owned business has no interest at all in continuing that business, and argues that her strongest desire in life is to become a medical doctor, then her parents may, regretfully, decide that it is indeed better for her to study medicine, since that is what she really wants. They may perhaps urge her to talk to a friend who is a medical doctor to get a better understanding of what that profession entails (that is, to 'test' whether her preferences are properly informed). Yet in such a context, the desire-fulfilment theory of wellbeing seems apt and appropriate.

The problems with the informed desire-fulfilment theory of wellbeing are especially relevant in *other contexts* where an account of wellbeing is needed for policy making or social change. The most significant is that our desires are moulded, not fully informed, and subject to social norms and other forms of societal pressures and expectations. For example, critics of capitalism argue that advertisement by profit-seeking companies form our preferences, and make us want things we would be better off without. There are many subtle forms of manipulation possible. Students of marketing learn that the products put at eye-height are more often taken by customers shopping in a supermarket. At the macro-level, the culture of late-modern capitalism tells us to find happiness in material success and in trying to achieve higher status in the dominant social order. We are socialised into these patterns, often not even aware of their existence. But why would those desires give us the highest level of wellbeing? Another interesting case is the standards of beauty that women are expected to meet, which will make them more attractive and ultimately happier. Dominant norms of beauty put a huge pressure on women (and increasingly also on men), leading to anxieties, low self-esteem, and even unhealthy conditions and illnesses such as anorexia (Lavaque-Manty 2001). What if we could 'reset' our cultural and social norms, which would lead to less pressure, stress and fewer anxieties? Some alternative views of living, such as those advanced by deep ecology thinkers (e.g. Naess 1973, 1984), are based on the view that with a different set of desires, and a different appreciation of certain experiences and values, we would be able to live not only in an ecologically sustainable way, but also have higher levels of wellbeing. In sum, the desire-fulfilment theory is interesting and arguably plausible at the individual level, and also at the general level as a *theoretical* approach to wellbeing, which can make ample use of counterfactual and hypothetical thinking and conditions. But it is much trickier to think about wellbeing from a macro or third-person perspective in the world as it is, in which we don't have information on how each person's preferences have been formed and influenced.

How does the objective list theory fare? *Objective list theories* are accounts of wellbeing that list items that make our lives better, independent of our own view on this. The claim of objective list theories is that there is an *irreducible plurality* of issues that make up wellbeing; wellbeing is plural and cannot be reduced to a single thing. Secondly, those items are *objectively* good for us, whether or not we attach any value to (or desire) those items. Hence items such as being healthy, or having friends, or feeling well, are all good for us, whether we personally value them or not.

What are some of the main strengths and weaknesses of the objective list theories? Objective list theories are generally criticised for not respecting people's views about their own lives, and hence taking away the authority to decide the quality of those lives from the agents leading them: in other words, for being paternalistic. Who is to decide that, say, social relationships are good for us? Now, this seems a very valid critique if we use an objective list theory for purely descriptive and first-person truth-seeking purposes, as the vast literature in philosophy does. But if one uses accounts of wellbeing for policy or political purposes, the public nature of the dimensions of wellbeing is rather important. This relates to what political philosophers have called 'the publicity criterion': if wellbeing is used for purposes of institutional design or policy making, those principles used need to be capable of being known by all to be satisfied in society (Rawls 2009; Anderson 2010, 85).

Indeed, this directly relates to an advantage of objective list theories: many of the items that have been proposed by such theories have been translated into specific indicators such as health or social policy, or else overall assessments have been made that can be used for an entire population. The long-standing literature on social indicators can be situated in this tradition (Boelhouwer and Stoop 1999; Boelhouwer 2002; Hagerty et al. 2001).

3.7.3 The accounts of wellbeing in the capability approach

So how does the capability approach fit in this standard taxonomy? The capability approach is often categorised as being an objective list theory, since functionings and capabilities are plural and the selection of dimensions gives us a list of items which are judged to be valuable for persons. However, in my view there is *not merely one* wellbeing account in the capability approach, but several wellbeing accounts.

So why is there not one, but several accounts of wellbeing in the capability literature? As was mentioned in the introduction to this section, the reason is that there are a variety of capability theories in the general capability literature, and those theories need different accounts of wellbeing. If a capability theory is used for a first-person perspective, for example by an adolescent contemplating what to do with her life, she may ask herself what she really wants: to study hard and work hard and become a medical doctor? Or does she have a stronger desire to build a family and search for a job that makes it possible to spend enough time with her children? Does she want to devote her life to fighting for a good cause? In this personal deliberation, the account of wellbeing she then uses can be seen as a desire-fulfilment account in which the desires all refer to functionings.

In the design of institutions, there is also often implicitly a desire-fulfilment account, by trying to create valuable options (capabilities) for citizens, but by not forcing them into those outcomes (functionings). But policy making can't be done by trying to enlarge a non-specific general account of freedom to realise one's desires: what would that look like? In policy making, we often assume that what we owe to each other are *specific* freedoms, not a general vague notion of overall freedom (Anderson 2000b). Therefore, at the policy level we can often see that the implicit account of wellbeing is desire-fulfilment, whereby it is assumed that the desires refer to particular functionings (such as being able to enjoy higher education or leisure activities in green spaces in cities), or, alternatively, policies provide the resources (money, and sometimes time) that are inputs for a wide range of desires that people may have.

If a capability theory is made for macro-level poverty analysis, then the researchers will select a number of functionings that they have reason to believe are good for people, such as their health, educational outcomes, and the kind of shelter in which they can live. The notion of achieved wellbeing entailed in this normative exercise is an objectively good account, although one could also argue that one has reason to assume that these are dimensions of the quality of life that people would want for themselves (hence their desires) and that, given that one is working with very large numbers, it is a safe assumption to proceed this way.

There are at least two interesting things to notice. First, for policy making we often have to choose either an approach that uses resources as a proxy for wellbeing (although this cannot account for differences in conversion factors between people) or else policy makers will try to provide a range of options to us, where ideally the policy maker assumes that these options are things that many people want. Second, the often-heard view that the account of wellbeing given by the capability approach is an objective list theory doesn't seem to be true. Rather, depending on the kind of capability theory one is pursuing (in particular, the choice in B1) it is more accurate to see this as a desire-fulfilment or an objective list account.

3.8 Happiness and the capability approach

In section 3.7.2, we encountered hedonist theories of wellbeing as an important subgroup of theories of wellbeing. The debates about hedonism and the happiness approach are closely related. Hedonism is the philosophical view that wellbeing can be captured by the balance of pleasures over pains. The core aspect is the exclusive focus on mental states, and on a person's subjective assessments of their own mental state. In recent decades, this approach has been revitalised in 'the happiness approach', although empirical scholars prefer the term 'subjective wellbeing' (SWB). The happiness and SWB literatures have in recent years gone through a revival.

On the empirical front, significant progress has been made in the last few decades by an international network of economists and psychologists, such as Andrew Clark, Ed Diener, Ada Ferrer-i-Carbonell, Bruno Frey, Richard Layard, Andrew Oswald, David Schkade, Bernard van Praag and Ruut Veenhoven.[10] Many of these scholars have concluded that sufficient scientific progress has been made for public policies to focus on subjective wellbeing. The measures of subjective wellbeing have been tested and refined, and much is supposedly known about the determinants of happiness that the government can influence. The happiness and SWB approaches are strongly focussed on empirical analysis and policy design, and this is also, therefore, the main lens that will be used in the comparison with the capability approach, although we will very briefly discuss the comparison between the theoretical happiness approach and the capability approach.

From the perspective of the capability approach, the happiness approach raises three questions: First, what is the happiness approach, exactly? Second, what are its strengths and weaknesses? Third, what role can happiness play in the capability approach?[11]

3.8.1 What is the happiness approach?

The happiness approach is based on the assumption that wellbeing (or quality of life) is constituted by the subjective experiences of a person, expressed in terms of utility, happiness, or satisfaction. Satisfaction can be expressed in terms of *overall satisfaction with life*, or satisfaction within particular domains, such as income, health, family relationships, labour, and so forth.

---

10 See, for example, Veenhoven (1996); Kahneman et al. (2006); Schkade and Kahneman (1998); Diener and Seligman (2004); Van Praag and Ferrer-i-Carbonell (2004); Ferrer-i-Carbonell (2005); Ferrer-i-Carbonell and Gowdy (2007); Frey and Stutzer (2002).

11 This section draws on, yet also modifies and expands, the analysis presented in Robeyns and Van der Veen (2007, 33–42).

In the happiness approach, life satisfaction is understood as a concept that combines two components: how we normally feel in everyday life — the *affective* or 'hedonistic' component — and how we judge the degree to which our preferences and aspirations in life have been realised — the *cognitive* component. In order to find out how 'happy' a person is, respondents are asked, for example, to rate how satisfied they are with their life on a scale from 1 to 10 (to measure the cognitive component) and to report their mood at particular moments of the day, sometimes even with the aid of a buzzer set to go off at random times (to measure the affective component). In another method, the respondents are asked to imagine the worst possible life and to give that life a value of 0, to imagine the best possible life and give that a value of 10, and then to rate their own life on a scale from 0 to 10.

The view in the happiness literature is that overall life satisfaction should be adopted as the official 'policy guide', and the task of the government is to aim for the highest possible average level of life satisfaction (Hagerty et al. 2001; Layard 2011). For comparisons in the long term, Ruut Veenhoven also proposes to measure the quality of life based on 'happy life expectancy'. This is an index obtained from multiplying life expectancy in a country with average overall life satisfaction (Veenhoven 1996).

Is the happiness approach, or the SWB approach, the best basis for thinking about wellbeing and the quality of life, especially against the background of policy design? The happiness approach certainly has a number of attractive features. Firstly, it puts the human being centre stage, rather than focusing on the means that human beings use to improve their quality of life. Hence the approach satisfies the core criterion from module A that means and ends should not be conceptually confused. Secondly, in considering the means to happiness, the subjective approach is not limited to material means, which is the major shortcoming of the dominant economic empirical methods. Income has only a limited (but not unimportant) role to play in generating happiness.

In conclusion, the happiness approach does have some significant strengths, but it also gives rise to some concerns. We will briefly discuss the main theoretical problem, and then look in more detail at the worries raised for empirical research and policy making.

3.8.2 The ontological objection

The theoretical worry is an ontological worry, that is, it asks what wellbeing *is*, and questions whether this can be captured by mental states only. This objection was forcefully made by Robert Nozick (1974, 42–45) when he introduced the 'experience machine' thought experiment. Nozick ask us to imagine that we are invited to be plugged into a machine, which would stimulate our brain and make us feel as if we were having a range of experiences that we could choose beforehand; all the time, we would be floating in a tank with electrodes attached to our brain. Would we choose such a life? Nozick claims we would not, and interestingly enough the arguments he gives to justify this claim refer to our functionings and capabilities.[12] According to Nozick, three things matter to us in addition to our experiences. First, we do not only want to have the experience of doing certain things (which we could have by sitting and taking drugs) but we also want to *do* certain things. Second, "we want to *be* a certain way, to be a certain sort of person" (Nozick 1974, 43). Third, we don't want to limit our experiences to a man-made reality (the experience machine) but also to have the opportunity to be in contact with deeper significance. The insight from Nozick's thought experiment is thus that a good life cannot be reduced to mental states, but must also contain some genuine activities and states of being. According to Nozick (1974, 43), "someone floating in a tank is an indeterminate blob", not a human being to whom we can describe human wellbeing. There is thus more to human wellbeing then merely feeling happy. If decent labour, knowledge, appreciating art and culture, and intimate relationships are to be valued only, or even primarily, because of their contribution to overall or specific life satisfaction, then we could say this is a misrecognition of the contribution they make to how well our lives progress. Phenomenologically speaking, this is an implausible account of wellbeing.

---

12 Obviously, Nozick didn't use the terminology of the capability approach, but his account of what is valuable in life could nevertheless be seen as capabilitarian.

3.8.3 Mental adaptation and social comparisons

How about the worries related to empirical research and policy making? The first worry at this level is raised by processes of mental adaptation and social comparisons. Our satisfaction is to some extent influenced by mental adaptation issues that emerge from comparisons with the situations of others. This can have problematic implications for public policies aiming at the highest happiness for the greatest number. Take the mental adaptation processes first. How do these emerge? First of all, there can be shocks in our lives that have a major effect on our wellbeing, such as immobility after an accident. People confronted with a major setback in health and mobility through such an impairment will first experience a strong deterioration of their subjective wellbeing, but after a while this effect will weaken. Obviously, this adaptation to circumstances is good, since a disabled person will not remain deeply unhappy for the rest of her life due to her limited abilities to move around without pain. However, the question is what this implies for policy. A utilitarian will say that the government has to limit itself to creating provisions such that a disabled person can return to an acceptable level of life satisfaction, taking into account the corresponding welfare costs for others.[13] A utilitarian would even say that there is no reason to invest in prevention if this is more expensive than rehabilitation. But one could also argue that a cost-sensitive policy has to try to reach an acceptable level of functioning for a disabled person, even if this makes little difference to her subjective judgement about her wellbeing after adapting to the accident. Subjective indicators focus automatically on the first goal, but this may imply that the quality aspects that relate to the things a person still can do after the accident remain out of sight.

Secondly, people can adapt to an objective disadvantage that is not caused by an external shock, but that shows a more stable pattern. This is the problem of 'adaptive preferences', which is particularly relevant for

---

13   A more fine-grained analysis than that presented in this section would need to make the distinction between act-utilitarianism and rule-utilitarianism, and ask whether both are vulnerable to these critiques to the same extent. I am assuming here that the critiques apply to both types of utilitarianism to such a degree that it leads to worrying consequences.

the happiness approach.[14] Amartya Sen has pointed out repeatedly that people living at the very bottom of the social ladder (such as 'exploited labourers' or 'oppressed housewives') adapt to their situation and come to suffer less intensely. Another example is the effect of racism. If a society becomes gradually less tolerant towards cultural minorities and increasingly accepts racist practices, then cultural minorities might get used to a racist social climate. Perhaps they will change their behaviour, in order to avoid contact with openly racist people. By changing their behaviour and mentally preparing for racist practices, it is possible that after a while the negative wellbeing effect of racism on minority groups will be partially wiped out. However, a policy that anticipates such adaptation processes is morally and politically problematic: racism should not be tolerated in society, even if it were not to have a significant impact on the subjective wellbeing of its victims. In order to judge that racism is not morally permissible and hence that policies should try to minimize racism, we don't first need to investigate whether racism makes its victims less happy: that's simply beside the point. Even if the victims of racism acted stoically and didn't let racism affect their happiness levels, that wouldn't make racism any less undesirable.

Another form of mental adaptation which is relevant for the government is the adjustment response to income changes. Subjective wellbeing judgements about income have been shown to adapt asymmetrically to income changes. Income increases go together with higher aspirations for the future, with only one third of the increase being reflected by improvements of subjective wellbeing (Frey and Stutzer 2002). Panel-analysis over a period of ten years shows that we adapt strongly to an increase in income, but much less so to a drop in income (Burchardt 2005). Thus, if people change positions in an income distribution which itself remains unchanged, then aggregate satisfaction of the population will decrease. The people who move up the ladder will be more satisfied for a short time, but quickly adapt to the new situation, whereas people who move downwards experience a larger drop in satisfaction — and this effect lasts longer as well. Tania Burchardt (2006) argues that due to similar phenomena of adaptation, people's positions in the distribution of income, health and marital

---

14   Yet the phenomenon of 'adaptive preferences' can also potentially create problems for some capability theories, as we will analyse in section 3.9.

status should preferably remain immobile, according to utilitarianism. Clearly this is a policy conclusion that goes against the principle that people should receive equal opportunities, even if the effect of one person's upward social mobility is not compensated by the effect of another person's downward social mobility.

How serious are these problems of mental adaptation for the subjective approach? In part, the response to this question depends on our normative judgements about the counter-intuitive and sometimes perverse implications of a policy that single-mindedly aims to promote maximal average utility. It also depends, however, on the empirical question of how strong these mental adaptation processes are in reality. According to Veenhoven, overall life satisfaction is primarily determined by the affective component, and therefore it is much less vulnerable to the effects of mental adaptation than satisfaction in particular domains, which he judges to be much more vulnerable to adaptation. However, the work of Kahneman and Krueger (2006, 17–18) shows that mental adaptation processes are clearly present even when predominantly affective measures of overall happiness experiences are adopted.

There are additional concerns related to the subjective wellbeing findings in particular domains, such as income or education. Recall the literature reporting on the findings that subjective wellbeing is also strongly influenced by social comparisons with reference groups. In particular, the wellbeing effect of income, but also of education, is affected by the levels reached by members of the reference groups to which individuals compare their own situation. As a consequence, increases in income, or additional educational credentials, contribute less to satisfaction in these domains, the more income or educational progress is achieved within the reference groups. Apparently, these resources have a stronger positional component than other resources do, in particular leisure time, where the comparison effect appears to have a much weaker impact on wellbeing obtained from an additional unit of free time.

In conclusion, there seems to be little consensus in the subjective wellbeing literature on the question of whether, and to what extent, phenomena of mental adaptation and reference groups cause problems for the measurement of overall life satisfaction. However, all researchers do acknowledge that satisfaction in some domains is susceptible to these phenomena, and this may result in the counter-intuitive policy implications we mentioned earlier.

3.8.4 Comparing groups

The second worry about the happiness or SWB approach concerns the effect of group differences, which will be a problem if we need an account of wellbeing to compare wellbeing levels between groups. The subjective wellbeing approach focuses on the affective and cognitive responses of people to their lives overall, or in particular domains. If groups differ on average in their responses to a situation, then this may cause problems for policies, if those differences correlate with the objective circumstances that one would intuitively judge as important. There are two symmetric possibilities: (1) groups who are in the same objective situation have different levels of life satisfaction, or (2) groups with the same level of life satisfaction are in different situations, whereby it is clear that one situation is worse than the other independently of subjective wellbeing.

Research has indeed shown that the average level of life satisfaction between demographic groups differs systematically. In other words, if we control for the relevant factors, then some groups are significantly less satisfied with their lives than others. For example, recent Australian research (Cummins et al. 2003) shows that women report a higher level of overall life satisfaction than men, after taking a number of control-variables into account.[15] The researchers cannot pinpoint the exact causes of this finding, but they do not exclude the possibility that women are 'constitutionally' more satisfied than men. This may have a biological explanation, but it may also be the consequence of processes of adaptation that men and women experience differently over their lifetimes.

If the aim of the account of wellbeing is to inform public policy, then the question is how government should deal with these findings. From a utilitarian perspective, it would be efficient to develop a policy that is advantageous to men. For example, if due to unemployment men experience a larger drop in happiness than women, as reported by Frey

---

15 A similar strong and significant gender effect has been found by Eriksson, Rice and Goodin (2007).

and Stutzer (2002, 419), then a policy that gives men priority on the labour market will minimise the average wellbeing damage in terms of happiness. But the fact that one demographic group (women, the worst off, the elderly, and so forth) are made less unhappy due to a certain event than other groups can cause perverse policy implications if life satisfaction is declared to be the guideline for policies. Fundamental political principles such as non-discrimination and equality of opportunities for all citizens are thereby put into jeopardy. This would also be true in the symmetric case where the average level of life satisfaction of discriminated or marginalised groups does not differ significantly from the average level of a group that is not faced with these disadvantages. I do not want to claim here that the subjective wellbeing approach will always lead to such injustices. But I do think that a central focus on subjective wellbeing will make policies less sensitive to signalling and combating these injustices. Hence Burchardt (2005, 94) is right in pointing out that "satisfaction — the best proxy we have for the concept of utility — is unsuitable for assessing current wellbeing, justice or equality".

3.8.5 Macro analysis

A third worry concerns the applicability of the subjective wellbeing approach at the national or regional levels of policy making. One may agree that the happiness approach can be very helpful when it can offer persons with low affect (negative moods and feelings) concrete strategies to change that, such as engaging in mindfulness training and practice. Yet what about policy making? Are the happiness indicators sufficiently refined and sensitive for policy at lower levels of aggregation than the level of a country? In their discussion of the criteria that an index of the quality of life should meet, Hagerty and his co-authors (2001, 2) include the criterion that the index must help policy makers to develop and evaluate policies at all levels of aggregation. Thus, the index should not only be useful for the national government, but also for governments in cities, communities, and regions. As Robert van der Veen and I argued in earlier work, overall life satisfaction does not satisfactorily meet this criterion (Robeyns and Van der Veen 2007); it is too crude for these purposes. It is even less suitable for the evaluation of specific policy interventions (Cummins et al. 2003). The effect of one policy measure such as improved child care facilities will be reflected hardly or not at all in reported overall life satisfaction, even if such policies have significant effects on the real opportunities of parents to organise their lives as they think best — hence on their capabilities. Overall 'happy life expectancy' is, by contrast, well-suited for comparing the effects of fundamental political and economic institutions on subjective wellbeing. This emerges clearly from the work of Veenhoven (1996), which concentrates on studies whereby the unit of analysis is the country. In other words, Veenhoven mainly uses happy life expectancy as an indicator for *macro-analysis*. The variables that emerge as the determinants of happy life expectancy are therefore typically system variables such as the degree of political freedom, or the presence of rule of law. But the quality of life in a micro-situation (say, living in a particular community or neighbourhood) is also influenced by many other variables.

3.8.6 The place of happiness in the capability approach

The previous sections argued that happiness can't be taken to represent a person's wellbeing for many purposes, including policy purposes. Yet it would also be deeply counter-intuitive to say that happiness doesn't matter at all. It may be the right concept of wellbeing for other aims. How, then, can happiness be given a proper place within the capability approach?

The first possibility is to see happiness, or some more specific capabilities that are closely related to the affective component of subjective wellbeing, as *one* important dimension to be selected. In fact, Amartya Sen has for many years argued that we could take 'feeling happy' as *one of* the functionings to be selected. For example, Sen (2008, 26) wrote:

> happiness, however, is extremely important, since being happy is a momentous achievement in itself. Happiness cannot be the only thing that we have reason to value, nor the only metric for measuring other things that we value, but on its own, happiness is an important human functioning. The capability to be happy is, similarly, a major aspect of the freedom that we have good reason to treasure. The perspective of happiness illuminates one critically important element of human living.

Indicators of happiness are already included, for example, by incorporating dimensions of mental health into capability applications. Certain specific functionings, which make up an overall 'mental health' functioning, already contain such affective items: whether, over the last week, the respondent has felt down or worthless, for example, or whether one is free from worry.

Second, we can try to capture the cognitive aspect of happiness, that is, a person's satisfaction with her capability set, or with particular options from that set. We can then compare that person's level of satisfaction with her capabilities, which should allow us to compare the objective situation with a person's satisfaction with that situation. For example, the absence of criminality is a valuable functioning.[16] But there is a long-standing finding in criminology that there are discrepancies between the objective incidence of being safe versus the subjective feeling of being in danger of becoming a victim of crime. For example, even if the incidence and impact of criminality goes down, it can still be the case that the population is more worried about crime than before and feels less safe. The discrepancy between objective outcomes and subjective perception is instructive here; it may imply, for example, that the government should communicate more effectively about its success in reducing crime, so as to make the subjective perception more in line with the objective reality, or it should work directly on factors that impact on the subjective experience of safety feelings.

Third, capability scholars would, of course, hope that an enlarging of people's functionings and capabilities would, as a further effect, increase their feelings of happiness and satisfaction, and serve as a (sometimes rough) indicator of people's satisfaction with their functionings and capabilities (Sen 2008, 26–27). Not all functionings will lead to people becoming happier, yet their lives may still be better: more flourishing, or more meaningful, or with a higher quality of life, or with a greater degree of freedom that could be realised. An interesting example is the case of writing a PhD dissertation. Very few PhD students would say that this is what makes them happy in the sense outlined above. So why, then, do so many graduates want to earn a doctoral degree, and give some of the best years of their lives to what often becomes a stressful time? It is hard to understand this, if one doesn't take into account the *meaning* it

---

16   Perhaps criminals would disagree.

brings to their lives. The capability approach can capture this — taking on a difficult and challenging project such as writing a PhD dissertation can plausibly be conceptualised as a general functioning (consisting of a set of more specific functionings) that we may want to include in our capability analyses, including in our capabilitarian theories of wellbeing for public policies.

I would thus defend the position that various roles for happiness are potentially possible within capability theories, and that it depends on the exact purpose and scope of the capability theory or application, as well as the aim that wellbeing plays in that capability theory, what the best role (if any) for both the affective and cognitive aspects of happiness would be.

3.9 The capability approach and adaptive preferences

As we saw in the previous section, a widely-voiced reason offered for rejecting the happiness approach as an account of wellbeing is the phenomenon of adaptive preferences, which has been widely discussed in the literature (e.g. Elster 1983; Sen 1985c, 3, 1992a; Nussbaum 2000; Teschl and Comim 2005; Burchardt 2009; Khader 2009, 2011, 2012, 2013; Conradie and Robeyns 2013). Phenomena of mental adaption are a problem if we take happiness or desire-satisfaction to be our account of wellbeing. Yet we also concluded in section 3.7.3 that the capability approach sometimes boils down to a desire-fulfilment account of wellbeing. Hence we need to ask: how do processes of adaptation affect the desire-fulfilment view of wellbeing, and what are the implications for the capability approach?

In the most general terms, preferences formation or adaptation is the phenomenon whereby the subjective assessment of one's wellbeing is out of line with the objective situation. Two persons who find themselves in the same objective situation will have a very different subjective assessment, because one is happy with small amounts of 'objective goods', whereas the other is much more demanding. In the capability literature, the general concern is with deprived persons who, over time, adapt to their objectively poor circumstances, and report a level of subjective wellbeing which is higher than the objective circumstances warrant.

The idea of adaptation can take different forms. Jon Elster (1983) referred to one particular type of adaptation, in which being unable to fulfil a preference or realise an aspiration leads one to reject that preference or aspiration. This phenomenon is known as 'sour grapes': the fox who cannot pick the grapes, because they are hanging too high for him, starts telling himself that they are sour anyway, and no longer desires to eat them. On Elster's account, adaptation occurs at a non-conscious level, as a reaction to the painful process of cognitive dissonance that a person who can't fulfil her unreachable desires or aspirations feels. Elster's notion of adaptive preferences only refers to a process, and makes no reference to an objective notion of wellbeing. These psychological aspects of adaptation are echoed in Sen's reference to this phenomenon, when he writes that "considerations of 'feasibility' and of 'practical possibility' enter into what we dare to desire and what we are pained not to get" (Sen 1985a, 15). Adaptive preferences are a reason for Sen to reject a focus on mental metrics, such as utility or happiness, as the metric of wellbeing. After all, someone who is in an objectively dire situation may have adapted to that situation and learnt to be pleased with little. As Sen (1985c, 21) puts it, "A person who is ill-fed, undernourished, unsheltered and ill can still be high up in the scale of happiness or desire-fulfilment if he or she has learned to have 'realistic' desires and to take pleasure in small mercies".

Serene Khader (2011) has argued that not all cases that we tend to consider as cases of adaptive preferences fit Elster's conceptualisation. Khader believes that an account of adaptive preferences must make reference to an objective notion of flourishing, even if that notion remains vague and only focusses on basic flourishing (since there is more intercultural agreement on what basic flourishing entails). She develops the following definition:

> An adaptive preference is a preference that (1) is inconsistent with a person's basic flourishing, (2) was formed under conditions nonconducive to her basic flourishing, and (3) that we do not think a person would have formed under conditions conductive to basic flourishing. (Khader 2011, 51)

A similarly perfectionist, but much less systematically developed account of adaptive preferences can be found in Martha Nussbaum's work. She understands adaptive preferences as the preferences of people who do not want to have items of her list of capabilities, whereby these preferences are deformed due to injustices, oppression, ignorance and unreflective habit (Nussbaum 2000, 114).

What questions do adaptive preferences raise for the capability approach? At the very minimum, they raise the following questions: first, why would adaptive preferences pose a problem for capability theories? Second, do we have any evidence about the prevalence of adaptive preferences? And third, how can capability scholars deal with adaptive preferences in their capability theories and applications?

Let us start with the first of these questions: why would adaptive preferences pose a problem for capability theories? There are at least two reasons. The first lies in module B2, the selection of dimensions. If that selection is done in a participatory or democratic way, then it may be vulnerable to adaptive preferences. A group that is systematically socialised to have low aspirations and ambitions will perhaps not put certain capabilities on its list, thereby telling themselves that they are unachievable, whereas objectively speaking they *are* achievable, albeit perhaps only after some social changes have taken place. The second reason is that a person with adaptive preferences may objectively have access to a certain capability, but may believe that either this capability is not available to her, or else that she should not choose it, and hence she may pick from her capabilities set a suboptimal combination of functionings. If we then assume that this person (or group) has non-adaptive preferences, then we will wrongly interpret the choice not to exercise certain capabilities as a matter of personal agency, which a capability theory that focusses on capabilities rather than functionings, should respect. The capability approach by default regards adults as agents rather than patients, but this may be problematic in the case of adaptive preferences.

So we can conclude that adaptive preferences can pose a problem for capability theories in which the choice of dimensions is made democratic, or in which we focus on capabilities rather than functionings. But a critic may raise the question: do we have any evidence about the prevalence of adaptive preferences? Is this not a theoretical problem invented by philosophers who like complex puzzles, or by western scholars who pity the lives of poor people in the Global South?

There are at least two answers to be given to this question. The first is that there are indeed good reasons to be very careful with the conclusions we draw when studying adaptive preferences, especially in a context with which one is not familiar. Serene Khader (2011, 55–60) provides a nuanced and convincing discussion of the various mistakes that can be made when we try to identify whether a person or group of persons living under unjust conditions expresses adaptive preferences. There are at least three 'occupational hazards' that those trying to identify adaptive preferences may make: we run the risk of psychologizing structural constraints, of misidentifying possible trade-offs between various dimensions of wellbeing that a person makes, or we may be unable to recognise forms of flourishing in very different culture or class settings. All this shows that thinking about adaptive preferences needs to be done with great attention to contextual details and in a very careful manner; it is not an analysis that can easily be done by applying a rigid formula. Scholars should therefore be very cautious before concluding that someone or a group shows adaptive preferences, and carefully investigate alternative interpretations of what they observe, since otherwise they run the risk of seeing adaptive preferences where there are none.

Having said this, it is clear from the literature that adaptive preferences are a genuine phenomenon. For example, Serene Khader (2011) discusses real cases of groups of women who had adaptive preferences. Tania Burchardt analysed the 1970 British Cohort Study and found that "among those able to formulate agency goals, the aspirations expressed are conditioned by their socio-economic background and experience" (Burchardt 2009, 13). She also found evidence that adaptation may play a role in the selection of functionings from one's capability set, since among the sixteen-year-olds who have the capability to continue full-time education, the choice whether or not to do so is highly influenced by past deprivation and experiences of inequality. Burchardt rightly concludes that if the influence on people's choices is so systematically related to previous experiences of disadvantage, that this is a case of injustice. Hence the need, for capability theorists and not just for those endorsing the happiness approach or the desire-fulfilment theory of wellbeing, to take processes of adapted preferences and adapted aspirations seriously. On the other hand, as David Clark (2009, 32) argued in the context of development studies, adaptive preferences may not be as widespread as some capability theorists make it out to be: "the available evidence only provides limited support for the adaptation argument and is not always easy to interpret". Given the "occupational hazards" that those trying to identify adaptive preferences face (Khader 2011, 55–60), it is important not to 'see' adaptive preferences where there are none. In conclusion, the capability scholar will have to balance the tricky tasks of neither ignoring processes of adaption, nor making the adaptation problem bigger than it really is.

This brings us to the last question: can the capability approach deal with these issues? Given that capability theories and applications can be very diverse, we will need different methods to handle the issue of adaptive preferences for different capability theories and applications.

In the context of action-research, small-scale projects and grassroots strategies, what is required above all is *deliberation and interaction* with people of whom one may be worried that their preferences may show signs of adaption, as exemplified by Ina Conradie in her project with women in a South African township (Conradie 2013; Conradie and Robeyns 2013). Khader (2011) has developed 'a deliberative perfectionist approach to adaptive preference intervention', in which a practitioner who suspects that a group of people has adaptive preferences will first attempt to understand how the suspected preferences affect their basic flourishing. This must be done via deliberative processes — a strategy that we also see in Conradie's research. If the practitioner has good reasons to suspect that some of the preferences are adapted, she can involve those with the alleged adaptive preference in a discussion and together search for a strategy for change. Note that there is an interesting parallel here with the grassroots-based development model that has been proposed by Solava Ibrahim (2017), in which 'a conscientization process' is an integral part of the development process. In this process, a person reflects critically on her life, develops aspirations for better living conditions, and makes a plan of action to bring about the desired change (Ibrahim 2017, 206). While, as Ibrahim rightly notes, adaptive preferences and aspirations may provide a challenge for this conscientization process, they are also very likely to be challenged and hence changed via such a process.

What about capability applications that involve the empirical analysis of large-scale datasets? How can adaptation be dealt with in those applications? Here, the capability approach needs to use insights from the disciplines that have built most expertise in large-scale adaptation processes, such as sociology and social policy studies. Based on the insights from those disciplines, we know the likely candidates to be dimensions of adaptation — such as social class, caste or gender. We can then use indicators of those dimensions to study whether preferences and aspirations systematically differ, as in the earlier mentioned study by Tania Burchardt (2009). But it is clear that this can only help us to identify adapted preferences or adapted aspirations; it will not always tell us whether for each application it is possible to 'launder' the data so as to clean them from processes of unjust adaptations.

3.10 Can the capability approach be an explanatory theory?

In almost all capability applications and theories, the capability approach is developed for conceptual and normative purposes, rather than for explanations. If it is used for conceptual work, then capability theories do not *explain* poverty, inequality, or wellbeing, but rather help us to conceptualize these notions. If capability analyses are used for normative work, then they help to evaluate states of affairs and prescribe recommendations for intervention and change.

Nevertheless, the notions of functionings and capabilities in themselves can be employed as elements in explanations of social phenomena, or one can use these notions in descriptions of poverty, inequality, quality of life and social change. In those cases, the properties A1 to A4 from module A would still hold, but characteristics A5 (functionings and capabilities as the evaluative space), A6 (other dimensions of intrinsic values can be important for normative analyses) and A7 (normative individualism) are not applicable.

To the best of my knowledge, few scholars use the capability approach in this way. Probably this should not be surprising, since the capability approach may not make a significant difference to this type of work. Still, there are parallels with existing studies. For example, there is a large literature on the social determinants of health (e.g. Marmot 2005; Wilkinson and Marmot 2003; Marmot et al. 2008). The goal here is to establish a set of functionings related to the general functioning of being healthy, and the determinants are investigated so that social interventions are possible. The same is done for other functionings — not surprisingly, since explaining the determinants of valuable social states is one of the main aims of social scientists.

This raises the question of whether the capability approach should aspire to do this kind of explanatory capabilitarian analysis. The answer depends on a further question: whether the capability approach would have any *added value* in conducting explanatory capability analyses. If not, then it is unclear why this should be part of the capability approach, since there seems to be very little value in doing what others are already doing successfully.

But this pessimistic dismissal of the potential of explanatory capability analyses may be too quick. Perhaps the capability approach has a role to play in *synthesising* and *connecting* these field-specific lines of explanatory research; since it is a strongly interdisciplinary approach, it may perhaps also have a role to play in bringing different disciplines within the social and behavioural sciences together. Another very important task of the capability approach is to reach out to those disciplines in order to make bridges between the normative and the explanatory analyses — one valuable element of the truly post-disciplinary agenda to which the capability approach aims to contribute.

3.11 A suitable theory for *all* normative questions?

The capability approach is primarily a normative theory, but are there also restrictions on which normative questions it can help to address? Or is it suitable for *all* normative questions?

In order to answer this, it is helpful to remind us of the key distinction in philosophical ethics between the right and the good. Questions about the good focus on what makes life valuable and include discussions about wellbeing, autonomy, freedom, and love. Questions about the right focus on how we should act in order for that action to be morally sound, as well as discussions about how institutions and policies should be designed so as not to violate universal moral rules. Here, the central issues concern fairness, respect and the avoidance of harm. Different moral theories give different answers to the question of how the good and the right relate to each other.

In philosophical ethics, if we say that an issue is a moral issue, this implies that we have duties to comply with the moral norm, no matter how we feel about it. These are very stringent and universal duties. An example is: do not kill an innocent person; or: respect the human dignity of all persons. Normative questions are much broader, and can also entail other values, such as prudential value (wellbeing). Questions about the right are questions about morality, whereas for most ethical frameworks questions about the good are questions about other areas of normativity, but not morality straight.[17]

The modular view that has been presented in chapter 2 has in the core module A only normative properties related to the good. Properties A1 and A2 define functionings and capabilities, and property A5 claims that a person's advantage should focus on functionings and capabilities: this gives the capability approach the core of its theory of the good. The complete theory of the good may be extended by additional choices made in module C4.

What does the core of the capability approach (module A) have to say about the right? The only property related to the right is normative individualism. There are no additional claims related to the right included in module A. Hence, the only conclusion we can draw is that the capability approach would claim that, *if and whenever* rightness involves a notion of the good, one should use the theory of the good as entailed by the core characteristics of the capability approach. Hence, if we believe that the right thing to do is to prioritise the lives of the worst-off, then a capabilitarian version of this claim would say that we should prioritise the functionings and/or capabilities of the worst-off rather than their happiness or their command over resources.

Yet many claims concerning the right make no reference to an account of the good. The core of the capabilities approach is, thus, orthogonal to other aspects of the theory of the right, except for ethical individualism, which is only a very small part of a theory of the right. The fact that the capability approach has, at its very core, more to offer in terms of the theory of the good than in terms of the theory of the right has an important implication, namely that *the capability approach is*

---

17   An influential exception are utilitarians and other consequentialists, who define the morally right as that which maximizes the (non-moral) good (Driver 2014; Sinnott-Armstrong 2015).

not very suitable for ethical issues that only concern questions about the right. For example, the capability approach is not a very helpful theory when analysing the morality of abortion since so much of that ethical debate is about issues of the right rather than about issues of the good. That is, most of the philosophical debates on the ethics of abortion concern the moral status of the foetus, notions of personhood, or questions about the autonomy and self-ownership of the pregnant woman — issues on which the capability approach remains mute.[18] It is therefore not surprising that the capability approach is more useful and more widely used as a theory analysing socio-economic policies where there is a consensus on those aspects that are questions about the right or where the questions about the right are much less weighty than those about the good. Examples include debates about poverty alleviation, distributive justice, environmental ethics and disability ethics. In sum, the capability approach is not a very helpful (or the most illuminating) framework for normative analyses in which elements regarding deontological duties and rights, which are not conceptually closely related to notions of wellbeing, play the most important role — that is, where aspects of the right are crucial in addressing the normative questions.

3.12 The role of resources in the capability approach

In section 2.6.4 we discussed property A4, which stresses the importance of the difference between means and ends in the capabilities approach. In section 2.6.5, we discussed property A5, which claims that in the capability approach functionings and capabilities form the evaluative space. From these two core properties from module A, some may draw the conclusion that resources are no longer important in the capability approach. This is a mistake. Resources are important, although in an instrumental manner.

Firstly, a focus on functionings and capabilities does not necessarily imply that a capability analysis would not pay any attention to resources,

---

18 Philosophical arguments on the moral permissibility of abortion come to widely divergent conclusions (e.g. Thomson 1971; Tooley 1972; English 1975; Marquis 1989).

or to the evaluation of social institutions, economic growth, technical advancement, and so forth. While functionings and capabilities are of ultimate concern, other dimensions can be important as well, but in an instrumental way, or as indicators for what ultimately matters. For example, in their evaluation of development in India, Drèze and Sen have stressed that working within the capability approach in no way excludes the integration of an analysis of resources:

> It should be clear that we have tended to judge development by the expansion of substantive human freedoms — not just by economic growth (for example, of the gross national product), or technical progress, or social modernization. This is not to deny, in any way, that advances in the latter fields can be very important, depending on circumstances, as 'instruments' for the enhancement of human freedom. But they have to be appraised precisely in that light — in terms of their actual effectiveness in enriching the lives and liberties of people — rather than taking them to be valuable in themselves. (Drèze and Sen 2002, 3)

Second, once we have decided which capabilities are relevant, we need to investigate the determinants of those capabilities — the factors which affect their emergence, size and robustness. As figure 2.1 illustrates, these determinants include resources, a person's set of conversion factors and structural constraints. Hence if we want to expand the capabilities of a person or a group, these are the levels at which we could intervene. Resources are not the only things that matter, and for some capabilities that we try to expand or try to equalise, resources may not be the most effective factor of intervention. At the same time, it is also clear that resources are very important for most capabilities and there are hardly any capabilities where resources play no role at all. Being able to buy presents enhances the capability of affiliation and social interaction; being able to get the best medical care enhances the capability of health; and being able to afford time off and time to travel enhances the capability to enjoy nature. Hence even those capabilities that could be seen as non-material dimensions of advantage are nevertheless also aided by the availability of resources, albeit probably not in a linear way, and perhaps only up to a certain threshold level. If a capability analysis is aimed at making an intervention, then the exact relationship between resources and functionings needs to be studied for each capability analysis, rather than being assumed to have a certain shape.

Third, in empirical research there are often data constraints that force scholars to work with resources as proxies for valuable functionings. There is nothing inconsistent in taking that path, as long as one is careful in the conclusions that one draws from an analysis of resources. Moreover, if one uses multiple resources, such as *a combination of* income, time, and human and social capital (e.g. Burchardt 2010), then the informational riches of the analysis increases, compared to a one-dimensional monetary analysis.

3.13 The capability approach and theories of justice

Discussions about inequality and justice are very important within the capability literature. In fact, they are so important that many philosophers studying the capability approach have made the mistake of believing that it *is* a theory of equality, or a theory of justice. But as the descriptions of the capability approach in chapter 2 have shown, that is not the case. Here, too, we need to make use of the distinction between the general capability approach and more specific capability theories: theorizing justice is only one among many different purposes that capability theories can have, that is, one of the possible choices we can make in module B1.[19] Still, given that the capability approach offers a distinct view on interpersonal comparisons of advantage, it should not surprise us that the capability approach has been widely used in thinking about inequality and justice.

The literature that develops the relevance of the capability approach in theories of justice falls primarily within the domain of normative political philosophy, but there is some overlap with the work done by welfare economists and other scholars. In order to get a grip on what the capability approach does in the literature on distributive justice, or, vice versa, what thinking goes on about theories of distributive justice within the capability literature, let us start with a brief primer on the theoretical literature on justice in the next section. Then, in section 3.13.2, I pose the question of what is required for the construction of a complete capability theory of justice. The final section, 3.13.3, explores the implications of a capability-based approach to justice in practice.

---

19   In particular, see the overview of different types of capability study in section 2.4.

3.13.1 A brief description of the literature on theories of justice

Justice is an essentially contested concept: there is no generally accepted definition of justice, and thus no consensus on what the appropriate subject matter of theories of justice is or should be. Of course, it does not follow that nothing at all can be said about the notion of justice. David Miller's description of social justice is a good starting point. He claims that when arguing about justice, we are discussing:

> how the good and bad things in life should be distributed among the members of a human society. When, more concretely, we attack some policy or some state of affairs as socially unjust, we are claiming that a person, or more usually a category of persons, enjoys fewer advantages than that person or group of persons ought to enjoy (or bears more of the burdens than they ought to bear), given how other members of the society in question are faring. (Miller 1999, 1)

Theories of justice do not cover the entire spectrum of moral issues. Social justice theorists generally agree that parts of morality fall *outside* the scope of justice. Charity is such a case: you may not have a duty of justice to help a frail, elderly neighbour, but you may nevertheless decide to help that person as an act of charity and compassion. Another example is morally laudable behaviour, such as being a volunteer for social activities in your neighbourhood. Such behaviour may be morally praiseworthy, but it may at the same time not be required as a matter of justice. Hence, justice is not all that matters, if we consider how to make the world morally better.

Can we describe justice, and theories of justice, by their properties, as philosophers often do? First, justice is a property that has been ascribed to both individuals and institutions: justice is a virtue of individuals in their interactions with others, and justice is also a virtue of social institutions (Barry and Matravers 2011). Thus, we can say that a certain society is more or less just, or we can say that the behaviour of some persons is just or unjust. Theorists of justice tend primarily to discuss the justice of social arrangements, that is, of social institutions broadly defined; justice as an individual virtue is sometimes regarded as a matter of ethics rather than of political philosophy (although not every political philosopher would agree with this way of demarcating justice from ethics). Moreover, an increasing number of theorists define social institutions more broadly so as to include societal structures related to class or caste, as well as social norms; under such broad definitions, conceptualising justice as a virtue of institutions touches upon many of the same aspects we would discuss if we were to see justice as a virtue of persons. For example, if a society has widely shared racist social norms, such as the disapproval of interracial love relationships, then a person who shows her disapproval of an interracial love relationship is acting upon an unjust social norm, but also showing non-virtuous behaviour.

Second, while sometimes the terms 'social justice' and 'distributive justice' are used as synonyms, it makes sense to understand 'social justice' as somewhat broader than 'distributive justice'. Distributive justice always deals with an analysis of who gets what, whereas social justice may also relate to questions of respect or recognition, or the attitudes that a certain institution expresses. The capability approach is mainly discussed in theories of distributive justice, although it is to some extent able to integrate the concerns of theorists of recognition about what they conceive to be the narrow or mistaken focus of theories of distributive justice.[20]

A third point to note about the literature on justice is that there are several different schools within social justice theories. According to Brian Barry and Matt Matravers, it is helpful to classify theories of social justice according to four types: conventionalism, teleology, justice as mutual advantage and egalitarian justice. *Conventionalism* is the view that issues of justice can be resolved by examining how local conventions, institutions, traditions and systems of law determine the divisions of burdens and benefits. Barry and Matravers rightly point out that this approach, which has been defended by Michael Walzer (1983), can lead to the acceptance of grossly unjust practices because they are generally endorsed by certain communities, even if they may be seen as unjust if judged on the basis of values and ideas not currently present (or dominant) in that society. *Teleology* is the view that social arrangements should be justified by referring to some good they are aiming for. Some examples are utilitarianism, natural law theory or Aquinas' Christian

---

20 It doesn't follow that all concerns of theorists of recognition are *best* expressed by using the capability approach. I doubt that this is the case, but will not pursue this issue here further.

philosophy. For teleological theories, what justice is follows from an account of the good, and thus the account of justice depends on the account of the social good itself. A criticism of teleological theories is that they *necessarily* rely on an external source (to specify what 'the good' is), such as utility, the natural law or God's authority. Teleological accounts of justice therefore necessarily depend on notions of the ultimate good. However, in pluralistic societies characterised by a variety of religious and non-religious worldviews, it is hard to see how justice can be derived from notions of the good that are not endorsed by all. Many contemporary political philosophers therefore argue that teleological theories cannot be defended since people have competing ideas of the good, and we cannot call upon a generally-accepted external source that will tell us which idea of the good should be imposed on all.

The third and fourth schools of social justice, in comparison, share a commitment to some form of liberalism that recognizes the diversity of views of the good life, which a just society should respect. These schools experienced a major revival after the publication of John Rawls's *A Theory of Justice* in 1971, which is generally regarded as the single most important work on social justice written in the last century.[21] Rawls turned to *the social contract tradition*, in which justice is understood as the fair distribution of benefits of social cooperation. The core idea is that rules of justice are ultimately more beneficial to everyone than if each were to pursue their own advantage by themselves. Some of these theories (though not Rawls's!) take the relative power or bargaining strength of every individual in society *as given*, and one may therefore question whether in situations of unequal bargaining power, justice will be done (Nussbaum 2006b). The other liberal school of justice is *egalitarian justice*, which is premised on the idea that people should be treated with equal respect and concern (Dworkin 2000). The most basic claim of those theories is that people are morally equal: each person should be treated as a being of equal moral worth. However, that

---

21   There is a large literature on the differences and complementarities between the capability approach to justice (that is, capabilitarian theories of justice) and Rawls's theory of justice (see e.g. Sen 1980, 195–200; Rawls 1988; Sen 1992a, 82–83; Pogge 2002; Nussbaum 2006b; Robeyns 2008b, 2009; and the contributions to Brighouse and Robeyns 2010).

general and abstract claim can be further developed in many different ways, and it is in specifying these further details that philosophers disagree. Distributive justice requires equality of something, but not necessarily equality of outcome in material terms (in fact, plain equality of resources is a claim very few theorists of justice would be willing to defend, since people have different needs, are confronted with different circumstances and, if given the same opportunities, are likely to make different use of them). Hence, Rawls's theory of justice can be seen as an egalitarian theory of justice, but so are theories that come to very different substantive conclusions, such as Robert Nozick's (1974) entitlement theory. Other major contemporary theorists of justice who can be labelled 'liberal egalitarian' are Brian Barry (1995), Philippe Van Parijs (1995), and Ronald Dworkin (2000), among many others.

Of those four schools, it is primarily liberal egalitarian theories that are discussed in relation to the capability approach. While there is internal diversity within this group of liberal egalitarian theories, these theories share the commitment to the principle that there should be considerable (although by no means absolute) scope for individuals to determine their own life plan and notion of the good, as well as a commitment to a notion of equal moral consideration, which is another way to put the principle of each person as an end, or normative individualism (see section 2.6.8).

Of the four schools of social justice, only the last two regard justice and equality as being closely related values. Under conventionalism, justice is guided by existing traditions, conventions and institutions, even if those existing practices do not treat people as equals in a plausible sense. Teleological theories also do not understand justice as entailing some notion of equality; instead, the idea of the good is more important, even if it implies that people are not treated as moral equals. In some theories of conventionalism and teleology, social justice *could be* consistent with a notion of equality, but this is not necessarily the case for all these theories. The social contract tradition and liberal egalitarianism, in contrast, derive their principles of social justice from a fundamental idea of people as moral equals. However, the notion of equal moral worth does not necessarily lead to the notion of equality of resources or another type of equality of outcome, as will be explained in what follows. Social justice and equality are related in these theories, but not always at the level of material inequality, but rather at a more fundamental level of treating people as moral equals or with equal respect and concern.

For a proper understanding of mainstream philosophical literature on theories of justice, it is helpful to know that the literature itself is highly abstract, and often rather detached from questions about policy design or political feasibility. Sen (2006, 2009c) has recently criticised such theories, and in particular Rawls's work, for being overly "transcendental". Such ideal theories give an account of the perfectly just society, but do not tell us what needs to be done to get closer to that very ideal, how we can make the world less unjust and which of two situations might be more unjust than the other. Another critique of contemporary theories of justice is that they are often based on so-called idealisations or strong assumptions, which may introduce significant biases or exclude certain groups of people from the theory. For example, Dworkin (2000) sets his egalitarian theory against a set of background assumptions that rule out racist and sexist attitudes and behaviours, as well as the adaptation of preferences to unfair circumstances (Pierik and Robeyns 2007). Certain assumptions and meta-theoretical as well as methodological choices also put philosophical theories of justice at risk of being too far removed from practical applicability. When we try to apply contemporary theories of justice to the actual reality of our chaotic and often messy world, there are all sorts of complications that need to be taken into account, such as trade-offs between different values, power imbalances between different social groups, unintended consequences of justice-enhancing interventions and policies, or interests of individuals and groups that may conflict with concerns for justice (e.g. a desire for re-election on the part of government administrations).

Debates about the practical relevance of contemporary philosophical theories of justice have gained momentum in the last decade. It remains unclear whether the outcome will change the way theories of justice are constructed in the future. It may well be that we will see a turn towards more non-ideal, empirically-informed, 'directly useful' theories that are easier to translate into practice. In any case, it is fair to say that most capability theorists working on justice are among those who strongly advocate this turn to make theories of justice more relevant to practice.

3.13.2 What do we need for a capability theory of justice?

In the previous section I gave a very brief account of the philosophical literature on theories of justice. What contribution can the capability approach make to this field? The first thing to note is that Martha Nussbaum has written at great length developing a capabilities theory of justice (e.g. Nussbaum 1988, 1992, Nussbaum 2000, 2002a; Nussbaum 2006b). Her capabilities theory is the most detailed capability theory of justice that has been developed up till now. Her theory is comprehensive, in the sense that it is not limited to an account of political justice, or to liberal democracies. Her account holds for all human beings on earth, independently of whether they are living in a liberal democratic regime, or of whether they are severely disabled. However, Nussbaum's theory of social justice doesn't amount to a *full* theory of social justice. The main demarcation of Nussbaum's account is that it provides only "a partial and minimal account of social justice" (Nussbaum 2006b, 71) by specifying thresholds of a list of capabilities that governments in all nations should guarantee to their citizens. Nussbaum's theory focuses on thresholds, but this does not imply that reaching these thresholds is all that matters for social justice; rather, her theory is partial and simply doesn't discuss the question of what social justice requires once those thresholds are met. Not discussing certain things is not necessarily a flaw of a theory: this may be theoretical work that Nussbaum will do in the future, or it may be work that will be done by other scholars. Moreover, it is quite possible that Nussbaum's account of partial justice is consistent with several accounts of what justice requires above the thresholds.

Yet, while Nussbaum's theory of justice has been worked out in great detail and has received a lot of attention, it would be a grave mistake to think that there can be only one capability theory of justice. On the contrary, the open nature of the capability framework allows for the development of a family of capability theories of justice. This then prompts the question: what is needed if we want to create such a capability theory of justice?[22]

---

22 I have presented this overview of steps that need to be taken in earlier publications (e.g. Robeyns 2016d).

First, a theory of justice needs to explain on what basis it justifies its principles or claims of justice. For example, Rawls uses the method of reflective equilibrium, including the thought experiment of the original position.[23] Dworkin's egalitarian justice theory starts from the meta-principle of equal respect and concern, which he then develops in the principles that the distribution of burdens and benefits should be sensitive to the ambitions that people have but should not reflect the unequal natural endowments with which individuals are born (Dworkin 1981, 2000). One could also develop a capability theory of justice arguing that the ultimate driving force is a concern with agency (Claassen and Düwell 2013; Claassen 2016) or with human dignity (Nussbaum 2000; Nussbaum 2006b). If capability scholars want to develop a full theory of justice, they will also need to explain on what bases they justify their principles or claims. As mentioned earlier, Nussbaum starts from a notion of human dignity, whereas the Senian strand in the capability approach stresses the importance of what people have reason to value, hence an account of public reasoning. However, little work has been done so far to flesh out this embryonic idea of 'having reason to value', and it therefore remains unclear whether the capability approach has a solid unified rationale on the basis of which a full account of justice could be developed.

Second, as indicated above, in developing a capability theory of justice we must decide whether we want it to be an outcome or an opportunity theory; that is, whether we think that we should assess injustices in terms of functionings, or rather in terms of capabilities, or a mixture. At the level of theory and principles, most theorists of justice endorse the view that justice is done if all have equal genuine opportunities, or if all reach a minimal threshold of capability levels. Translated to the capability language, this would imply that at the level of theory and principles, capabilities are the relevant metric of justice, and not functionings. However, among theorists of justice, not everyone subscribes to this view. Anne Phillips (2004) has been a prominent voice arguing for equality of outcome, rather than opportunities. In the capability literature, Marc Fleurbaey (2002) has argued against an approach that takes only capabilities into account and has defended a

---

23 An accessible explanation of the method of reflective equilibrium can be found in Knight (2017).

focus on 'refined functionings' (being the combination of functionings and capabilities).

A third issue which needs to be solved if one hopes to develop a capability theory of justice is to decide and justify which capabilities matter the most. There are at least two ways of answering this question: either through procedural approaches, such as using criteria from which the relevant capabilities are derived, or by defending a specific list of capabilities. This selection of relevant capabilities for the purpose of justice can be done at the level of ideal theory (without taking issues of practical feasibility and implementation into account), at the level of abstract principles (Anderson 1999; Nussbaum 2006b; Claassen 2016) or at an applied theoretical level, which is useful for practical assessments of unjust inequalities (e.g. Robeyns 2003; Wolff and De-Shalit 2007).

Fourth, a capability theory of justice may need to engage in a comparison with other 'metrics of justice'. In the literature on social justice there are several terms used to indicate what precisely we are assessing or measuring: the metric of advantage, the currency of justice, or the informational basis for the interpersonal comparisons for the purpose of justice. Within theories of justice, the main arguments are with Rawlsian resourcists[24] and with defenders of Dworkinian resourcism.[25] Other possible metrics are basic needs or the many different types of subjective welfare or preference satisfaction. A full capability theory of justice would need to show why it serves better as a metric of justice than these other metrics.

Fifth, a capability theory of justice needs to take a position on the "distributive rule" (Anderson 2010, 81) that it will endorse: will it argue for plain equality, or for sufficiency, or for prioritarianism, or for some other (mixed) distributive rule? Both Martha Nussbaum's and Elizabeth Anderson's theories are sufficiency accounts, but from this it does not follow, as one sometimes reads in the secondary literature, that the capability approach entails a sufficiency rule. Sen may have given the (wrong) impression of defending straight equality as a distributive rule,

---

24 An analysis of this comparison between social primary goods and capabilities was made by the various contributions to the volume edited by Brighouse and Robeyns (2010).

25 For comparisons of the capability view with Dworkin's egalitarian theory, see Sen (1984b, 321–23, 2009c, 264–68); Dworkin (2000, 299–303); Williams (2002); Browne and Stears (2005); Kaufman (2006); Pierik and Robeyns (2007).

by asking the question "Equality of what?" (Sen 1980), though a careful reading shows that he was merely asking the question "*If* we want to be defending equality of something, then what would that be?" In fact, Sen has remained uncommitted to one single distributive rule, which probably can be explained by the fact that he is averse to building a well-defined theory of justice but rather prefers to investigate how real-life unjust situations can be turned into more just situations, even if perfect justice is unattainable (Sen 2006, 2009c). The capability approach clearly plays a role in Sen's work on justice, since when assessing a situation, he will investigate inequalities in people's capabilities and analyse the processes that led to those inequalities. Yet Sen has an eclectic approach to theorizing, and hence other notions and theories (such as human rights or more formal discussions on freedoms from social choice theory) also play a role in his work on justice. The presence and importance of the capability approach in Sen's work is thus undeniable, but should not be seen as the only defining feature.

Sixth, a capability theory of justice needs to specify where the line between individual and collective responsibility is drawn, or how this will be decided, and by whom. There is a remarkable absence of any discussion about issues of responsibility in the capability literature, in sharp contrast to political philosophy and welfare economics where this is one of the most important lines of debate, certainly since the publication of Dworkin's (1981, 2000) work on justice and equality which led to what Anderson (1999) has called "luck-egalitarianism". Nevertheless, whether one wants to discuss it explicitly or not, *any* concrete capability policy proposal can be analysed in terms of the division between personal and collective responsibility, but this terminology is largely absent from the capability literature. In part, this might be explained by the fact that much of the work on capabilities deals with global poverty, where issues of individual responsibility seem to be less relevant since it would seem outrageous to suggest that the world's most destitute people are personally responsible for the situation they are in. That doesn't mean that the responsibility question is not important: it is indeed of utmost importance to ask who is responsible for global poverty reduction or the fulfilling of international development targets, such as the Sustainable Development Goals on which political philosophers have written a great deal (Singer 2004,

2010; Pogge 2008). The point is rather that philosophical puzzles, such as the issue of expensive tastes (for expensive wine, caviar, fast cars, or you name it), are simply beyond the radar of the child labourer or the poor peasant. However, while this may perhaps justify the absence of any discussion about personal responsibility among capability scholars concerned with poverty, it does not absolve theorists of justice who deal with justice in affluent societies (or affluent sections of poor societies) from discussing the just division between personal and collective responsibility (Pierik and Robeyns 2007, 148–49).

This brings us to a related issue: a theory of justice generally specifies rights, but also duties. However, capability theorists have remained largely silent on the question of whose duty it is to expand the selected capabilities. Nussbaum passionately advocates that all people all over the world should be entitled, as a matter of justice, to threshold levels of all the capabilities on her list, but apart from mentioning that it is the governments' duty to guarantee these entitlements (Nussbaum 2006b, 70), she remains silent on the question of who precisely should bear the burdens and responsibilities for realizing these capabilities. Yet as Onora O'Neill (1996, 122–53) has argued, questions of obligations and responsibilities should be central to any account of justice.

This section makes clear that a capability theory of justice is theoretically much more demanding than the basic presupposition of the capability approach that 'functionings' and 'capabilities' are the best metric for most kinds of interpersonal evaluations. While much has been written on the capability approach in recent years by an increasing number of scholars, including philosophers, much of the philosophical work needed for turning the open-ended capability approach into a specific theory of justice remains to be done.

Note, however, that not all capability theorists working on issues of justice believe that such a fully worked-out theory is required. Sen (2009c) himself has argued at length that we don't need a theory that describes a utopian ideal, but rather we need theorising to help us with making comparisons of injustice, and to guide us towards a less unjust society. Similarly, Jay Drydyk (2012) has argued that the capability approach to justice should focus on reducing capability shortfalls, for which a utopian account of perfect justice is not needed. Some capability theorists may want to work out a full theory of justice by addressing the various specifications outlined above, while others may want to change the very nature of theorising about justice, moving it more to applied, non-ideal or grounded theories (Watene and Drydyk 2016).

3.13.3 From theories of justice to just practices and policies

Before closing this section on capabilitarian theorizing about justice, let us briefly shift from theory to practice. Since theories of justice are mainly developed at a highly abstract level, often entailing ideals of perfect justice, we may wonder whether the capability approach to social justice and equality is of any use in telling us what justice-enhancing strategies and policies to develop. Indeed, this has sometimes been phrased as a serious concern, namely, that theories of justice are too abstract and do not help us with social justice struggles on the ground. One may well argue that we roughly know what is going wrong and we need political action rather than more and more detailed theorising. Moreover, some think that in the real world the subtleties of theories of justice are easily abused in order to justify gross inequalities, as may have been the case with philosophical discussions on individual responsibility. For example, Brian Barry's (2005) later work exemplified this concern with the direct application of theories of justice to political change and the reform of the welfare state, rather than with further philosophical refinements of theories of justice. Related charges have been aimed at the capability approach as well. For instance, it has been argued that not enough attention has been paid to issues of social power in the capability writings on justice, and Feldman and Gellert (2006) have underscored the importance of recognising the struggles and negotiations by dominated and disadvantaged groups if social justice is ever to be realised. Such questions of power politics, effective social criticism, successful collective action, historical and cultural sensitivities, and the negotiation of competing interests are indeed largely absent from the philosophical literature on theories of justice. These ideal theories develop *standards* of a just society, but often do not tell us what institutions or policies are necessary if just societies are to be constructed, nor do they tell us what social and political processes will help advocates implement these social changes in concrete ways.

But the capability approach *can* be linked to more concrete justice-enhancing policy proposals that have been developed. For one thing, the Millennium Development Goals could be understood as being a practical (albeit specific and also limited) translation of the capability approach in practice, and their successors, the Sustainable Development Goals, can also be seen as influenced by the capability approach.[26] In fact, at the level of severe global poverty, any concrete poverty-reduction strategy which conceptualises poverty in a capability sense is, for most accounts of justice, a concrete justice-enhancing strategy, since these theories would include the absence of severe poverty as a principle of justice.

If we move from the area of poverty-reduction strategies to the question of just social policies in countries or regions with higher levels of affluence, we observe that there are much fewer actual examples of justice-enhancing policies that have been explicitly grounded in, or associated with, the capability approach. Yet many concrete policies and interventions could be interpreted as such, or are consistent with the capability perspective itself. One example relates to a policy of providing, regulating and/or subsidising child-care facilities. This can arguably be justified as a prerequisite for gender justice in capabilities since, due to gender norms, women will in effect not be able to develop themselves professionally if they are not supported in their need for decent quality-regulated (and possibly subsidised) child-care facilities. Mothers at home may be materially well-off if their husbands earn a good income but, if they do not have the genuine opportunity to hold jobs, then their capability sets are severely constrained and gender justice in capabilities cannot be achieved. An income metric which assumes equal sharing in the household may not detect any moral problem, but a capability metric will claim that women have more limited freedoms than men, since the provisions are not there to ensure that both parents can hold jobs, and gender norms and other gendered social mechanisms make it highly unlikely that men will volunteer to stay at home with their children. At the same time, men are also losing out since they have a very limited capability to spend time with their newborn babies.

26　See http://www.un.org/sustainabledevelopment/sustainable-development-goals/

A slightly different example concerns a justice-enhancing intervention that can be found in the form of adult volunteers who visit disadvantaged families to read to the children in order to enhance their language skills.[27] It is well-known that many children of immigrants are disadvantaged at school since they are very likely to enter school with weaker knowledge of the language of instruction than non-immigrant children. For this reason, in several cities there are networks of volunteers to read books to small immigrant children in their own homes. In this way, they effectively reduce the gap in educational opportunity between immigrant children and non-immigrant children. This example also illustrates that justice-enhancing strategies are not confined to public policy, but can also be initiated by persons and groups at the grassroots. The government is not the only agent of justice; we can all do our part.

3.14 Capabilities and human rights

Several capability theories are closely related to accounts of human rights. Within the capability literature, some scholars have developed capability theories that they regard as a human rights theory. In the human rights literature, scholars have examined to what extent the capability approach can help to develop stronger theories of human rights. The same topics (e.g. provision of or right to basic health or basic education) are defended based on both approaches, or are defended appealing both to human rights and capabilities (e.g. Osmani 2000). Amartya Sen has in several of his publications analysed the relationship between human rights and capabilities (e.g. Sen 2004b, 2005). In addition, Martha Nussbaum has claimed that her capabilities theory is a version of human rights theory, which has drawn much attention to the question about the relationship between capabilities and human rights.

It should not be surprising that there are so many scholars and practitioners interested in both the human rights framework and the capability approach, since they share some important aspects. First, they are both widely endorsed ethical frameworks. Second, they seem to share an underlying motivation, namely to protect and enhance

---

27   In the Netherlands, this volunteer organisation is called *De Voorleesexpress* (https://voorleesexpress.nl) but similar initiatives must exist around the world.

people's freedoms. Third, they are both used for global as well as domestic questions. Fourth, both frameworks want to build strong links between theory and practice: they are studied and used by scholars but also used by practitioners (political parties, activists, policy makers, etc.). Finally, both discourses are strongly interdisciplinary in nature.

All this raises some questions. What is the relationship between human rights and capabilities? Can we say that capabilities are the objects of human rights? If so, do human rights theories and analyses have something to gain by developing capabilities-based human rights theories? Can the capability approach deliver all that is important in human rights theories? And what should we make of the alleged disadvantages of using the capability approach in thinking about human rights?

3.14.1 What are human rights?

Human rights are rights each human being is entitled to in order to protect her from severe harms that could be inflicted by others — either by deliberate actions, or else by the failure to protect human rights caused by institutional design. They are norms aimed at protecting people from severe social, political and legal abuse (Nickel 2014, 1). Examples of human rights are the right to life, the right to food, the right to freedom of assembly, the right to freedom of religion, the right to a fair trial when charged with a crime, the right not to be tortured, and the right to privacy.

Human rights are not *all* the rights that people have. As Sen (2004b, 329) writes, "there have to be some 'threshold conditions' of (i) importance and (ii) social influenceability for a freedom to figure within the interpersonal and interactive spectrum of human rights". Take the 'importance threshold' first. Here is an example of a right that is *not* a human right, because it does not meet the threshold condition of importance: the right to parental leave. In many European countries, parents who are employed have a right to paid parental leave upon the birth of their child or when they adopt a child. While many have argued that such a right would help meet our duties towards children and parents as well as advance gender justice (e.g. Gheaus and Robeyns 2011), it is not at all plausible to argue that this should be seen as a *human* right. It has a much weaker moral urgency than the right to a fair trial, let alone the right to life. Human rights thus correspond to a subset of the domain of justice, and focus on those questions that are of utter importance, the protection of which should have a greater urgency than the support of other normative claims. The second threshold — social influenceability — implies that even if something valuable is hugely important, as long as there is no or very limited social influenceability, its protection cannot be a human right. For example, it makes no sense to speak of a human right to be protected from volcano eruptions, or a human right to be protected from cancer. However, one can say that there is a human right to be warned about volcano eruptions if the government has the relevant information. To the extent that there is more social influenceability, the scope to speak coherently of human rights increases.

Human rights have corresponding duties. But on whom do those duties fall and what kind of duties are they? A broad, inclusive account of duties is given by Pablo Gilabert (2009, 673) who writes:

> [Human rights impose] a duty of the highest priority for individuals and governments to identify ways to protect certain important interests through (a) specific rights and entitlements, but also, when these are insufficient or not presently feasible, through (b) urgent goals of institution-building.

Note that this definition does not limit the duty to protect human rights to governments only, and that it does include institution-building as an important path towards protecting human rights.[28]

3.14.2 The interdisciplinary scholarship on human rights

The human rights literature is, just like the capability approach, deeply multidisciplinary and interdisciplinary. The *philosophy* of human rights "addresses questions about the existence, content, nature, universality, justification, and legal status of human rights" (Nickel 2014, 1). How can human rights exist in the first place? What should be the content of

---

28 This relates to a complex discussion in legal and political philosophy on whether human rights can be protected by so-called 'imperfect duties' or 'imperfect obligations' which is beyond the scope of this book. See, amongst others, Polly Vizard (2006, 84–91) and Frances Kamm (2011) for further discussion.

human rights, that is, what kinds of harms or abuses should they protect us from? What kind of rights are human rights — are they moral claims, or legal claims, or political claims, or something else? The question of justification asks: on what grounds can we say that people have human rights? Is it because humans have rational capacities or agency? If so, does that mean that newborn babies do not have human rights? All these questions are studied in the vast philosophical literature on human rights.

Note that while the relationship between normative political philosophy, justice and human rights is not entirely disputed, the dominant view in the contemporary literature is that the domain of human rights is a subset of the domain of justice, which in turn is a subset of the domain of morality. The reason is that "[n]ot everything that is desirable to be realized in politics is a matter of human rights, and not everything that is a matter of justice is a matter of human rights. Human rights constitute the most urgent demand of basic global justice" (Gilabert 2009, 676).

Legal scholars are interested in questions related to the treaties and constitutions in which human rights are codified. The idea of human rights gained momentum with the 1948 adoption of the Universal Declaration of Human Rights (UDHR), which over time received a canonical status in legal and political debates. The UDHR subsequently served as a template for human rights instruments that are legally binding, such as the International Covenant on Civil and Political Rights, the International Covenant on Economic, Social and Cultural Rights, the European Convention on Human Rights, the American Convention on Human Rights and the African Charter of Human and People's Rights. One question this raises is to what extent national constitutions are consistent with those legally binding treaties, or with the UDHR. Another question frequently asked by legal scholars is to what extent national jurisprudence can be in tension with — and violate — a human right that is part of an international treaty to which that particular nation signed up. For example, in the famous 'Lautsi case', the question emerged whether the Italian state's policy to have a compulsory crucifix in the classroom of public schools was in violation of the human right to the freedom of religion as codified in the European Convention on Human Rights (Weiler 2010; Pierik 2012; Pierik and van der Burg 2011).

In the social sciences and international relations, questions are asked about what role human rights play in politics. How do countries differ in the degree in which they protect human rights? What are the effective instruments that support human rights in countries in which they are not violated? Is it effective to condemn human rights violations in other countries, or is silent support for grassroots human rights activists a more effective strategy?

Of course, human rights are hugely important for human right activists, who are working on actual human rights protections. Other activists, such as those focusing on the empowerment of disadvantaged groups, often take a more instrumental attitude towards human rights, and ask whether such rights are effective instruments to reach their goals of inclusion, development and combatting forms of injustice and oppression.

3.14.3 Why a capability-based account of human rights?

After this brief sketch of the huge literature on human rights, we can now explore the relation between human rights and capabilities. The first question that needs to be asked is: why would we be at all interested in a capabilities-based theory of human rights? What could be gained by theorizing human rights, or trying to protect human rights, by referring to capabilities?

The first reason is philosophical, and concerns the justification of human rights. Human rights are norms or instruments to protect certain valuable things (which are called 'the *objects* of human rights'). But every time we claim an object is so important its protection must be enshrined as a human right, we must argue why that object has this special importance. Part of the philosophical literature on capabilities does precisely that — to *justify* why we need to protect certain valuable personal states. Both Sen (2004b, 2005) and Nussbaum (1997, 2011a) have argued that human rights can be seen as entitlements to certain capabilities. However, Sen's views are more qualified, since he has argued that the object of some but not necessarily all human rights can be viewed as capabilities. There are plausibly also other objects of human rights, such as process freedoms and liberties.

The second reason builds on the first. If some human rights can be understood in terms of capabilities, and poverty can also be conceptualized in terms of the denial of capabilities, then poverty can be conceptualized as a human rights violation (Osmani 2005). This is important for various reasons, including the strong rhetorical force that a human rights violation has in comparison with other claims, and also because socio-economic human rights have sometimes been regarded as more in need of conceptual foundations, in comparison with the civic and political human rights whose status as human rights has been less contested.

This relates to the third reason why it can be helpful to conceptualise human rights in terms of capabilities, which is the often-stated worry that the protection of human rights, especially social and economic rights, is *infeasible* (Gilabert 2009). To counter that pessimism, we need greater clarity on the chain of steps that are involved in socio-economic human rights protection. Capabilities are the objects of our rights, and we know, from our understanding of how capabilities relate to resources and social structures, which parameters can influence the capabilities that people enjoy (see the figure in section 2.12). Hence, if we want to protect human rights, in particular socio-economic rights, which sceptics believe cannot effectively be protected, the capability approach helps us see that "promoting socioeconomic rights may require attention to specific parameters that affect the capabilities of people" (Gilabert 2009, 666). In sum, the language of the capability approach helps us to respond and address the feasibility worry of socio-economic rights.

Fourthly, we are unsure whether some things we want to protect meet the threshold condition of importance that human rights should meet. If one is unsure about whether a certain freedom should be a right, let alone a *human* right, one could already start to protect or enhance it if one sees it as a capability. One does not need to wait until the discussion about the threshold is settled before one starts to protect something that everyone agrees is in any case important.

A final reason is more practical or political. In some countries, the terminology of 'human rights' is regarded with suspicion, as it is seen as stemming from a colonial era, and, as a consequence, is regarded as an instrument of western domination. This makes it hard for both local and global advocates of human rights to advance their cause. By using the terminology of capabilities, which is not linked to a particular colonial era or western power, instead of the language of human rights, these same valuable rights can be argued for.

3.14.4 Are capabilities sufficient to construct a theory of human rights?

There is quite a lot of interest among capability scholars and those working in the human development paradigm to try to bring the best of the capability approach and the human rights approach together (e.g. Vizard 2006, 2007; Vizard, Fukuda-Parr and Elson 2011; Fukuda-Parr 2011; Gilabert 2009, 2013). One important question, though, is how much the capability approach can offer if one is interested in constructing a powerful human rights theory. Is the notion of capabilities sufficient for such a theory?

The answer clearly must be negative. A theory of human rights needs other elements, such as a discussion of the scope of, and, importantly, the justification for, human rights. Yet, by making use of the distinction between the capability approach and capability theories that was introduced in section 2.3, we can see that it is not at all an embarrassment for the capability approach that, by itself, it cannot deliver a theory of human rights. Instead, that should be the task of a specific capability theory, for which, in the various modules, additional elements that are needed for a human rights theory can be added.

This raises the next question: what would have to be added, then? One important thing that may need to be added (in A6 — other dimensions of ultimate value) are process freedoms. Sen (2004b) argues that we should make a distinction between freedoms as substantive opportunities and the process aspect of freedom (procedural aspects). Both are, in his view, relevant when thinking about human rights, but only the opportunity aspect of freedom is captured by the notion of 'capabilities'. Linda Barclay (2016) makes a similar point, by saying that rights that concern *equitable processes* are very important for human rights, and cannot be captured by the notion of capabilities. Clearly, procedural characteristics, for example those that guarantee a free trial, may not necessarily best be understood as capabilities, but perhaps rather more as elements of institutional design. Yet as proposition A6 emphasizes, not everything that is of crucial importance is a capability. Recall that proposition A6 allows us to include other elements of ultimate value, and this could incorporate what Sen calls process freedoms.[29] In short, by

---

29   The example that Barclay gives is the right not to be discriminated against. Barclay believes that "to be protected from discrimination" is a very important human

seeing a capability-based human rights theory as a capability *theory*, for which various theoretical additions and choices are possible, it becomes clear that more is needed than the mere reference to 'capabilities'.

Note also that we can, of course, ask the question the other way around — what is needed to make a capability theory? — and use the human rights framework as the theory of value that is used to make the selection of capabilities. This route has been developed by Polly Vizard, and has led to the "human rights based capability set" (Vizard 2006, 2007).

3.14.5 The disadvantages

Finally, we need to ask whether there are any disadvantages in using the capability approach to further our thinking, policy making and activism on human rights, and — ultimately — in letting a capabilities-based human rights theory compete with the existing human rights accounts.

The first thing to note is that there is a long-standing human rights discourse that is used by activists all over the world, and often very effectively so. Clearly there are costs involved for these activists to become familiarized with the capability language. If the human rights discourse delivers to them what they need, why would we change it?

Second, there is a worry about legitimacy. The current human rights declarations and treaties have been the result of *actual* political processes, and the treaties were drafted by a large number of people, drawn from all over the world. For the capability approach, this is different. Given the prominence of Amartya Sen and Martha Nussbaum, and also the many publications that (wrongly) reduce the capability approach to the work by, primarily, Sen and Nussbaum,[30] the capability approach is much more associated with specific individuals. A capability-based human rights theory that is the work of one thinker can never have the political leverage that the existing human rights framework has. For the

---

right, but cannot plausibly be conceptualized as a capability, since one does not have a choice to be discriminated against or not. However, not being discriminated against is a functioning, and it is a mistake to think that the capability approach holds that we should only focus on capabilities and never on functionings, as was argued in section 3.4.

30 Unfortunately, Nussbaum's (2011c) account of the capability approach only adds to that reductive and misleading portrayal of the capability literature (Robeyns 2011, 2016b; Unterhalter 2013).

various practices in which human rights are used (creating laws, making policy and activism) a capability-based human rights framework can therefore never replace the existing human rights framework.

However, there is, of course, a more fruitful relationship possible, and that is to see the two frameworks as complementary rather than competitive (Nussbaum 2011a). Note, however, that any merging of the two frameworks has to be between a particular capability *theory* and human rights thinking, rather than between the general capability approach and human rights thinking.[31] A good example of such practical work is the UK's Equality and Human Rights Framework. Tania Burchardt and Polly Vizard (2011) used insights from both the capability approach and the existing work on human rights to create a framework that is used for the monitoring undertaken by the Equality and Human Rights Commission in order to meet its legal mandate.[32]

3.15 Conclusion

The aim of this chapter has been to deepen our understanding of the capability approach, by analysing some questions of clarification that are often posed, and by reconstructing and synthesizing some developments that have taken place in the capability literature over time.

The next chapter will focus on a range of critiques that have been put to the capability approach. Of course, it is not always entirely clear whether a certain question or debate is purely a matter of clarification, or rather a matter of debate and dispute; put differently, there is no neat demarcation between the main focus of this chapter and that of the next. Still, in this chapter I have tried to be as neutral and even-handed as possible in describing the literature, whereas in the next chapter I will take a more active role in arguing for or against certain views or claims.

---

31 Hence, when Nussbaum (2011a, 24) writes "the CA is a type of human rights approach", we should read this as "Martha Nussbaum's capability theory is a type of human rights approach". Many other capability theories are, evidently, not human rights approaches, and hence the capability approach, as the overarching framework, cannot be either.

32 See https://www.equalityhumanrights.com/en

4. Critiques and Debates

4.1 Introduction

In chapter 2 I gave an account of the capability approach that gave us a better sense of its necessary core and its scope, as well as describing the structure of a capability theory or capability analysis. While that account has aimed to be precise and comprehensive, it nevertheless raises some further issues.

Hence, this chapter is focussed on investigating those further questions and debates. We will look into the following issues. Section 4.2 asks whether everything that has been called a capability in the literature is genuinely so. Section 4.3 addresses a dispute that has kept capability theorists busy for quite a while over the last two decades, namely whether a capability theorist should endorse a specific list of capabilities. For many years, this was debated under the banner 'the question of the list' and was seen as the major criticism that Martha Nussbaum had of Amartya Sen's work on the capability approach. Section 4.4 investigates the relationship between the basic needs approach and philosophical theories of needs, and argues that the capability scholars may be able to engage more fruitfully with theories of needs. Section 4.5 asks whether, as Nussbaum suggests, we should understand the capability approach as a theory that addresses the government; I will argue that we should reject that suggestion and also take other 'agents of change' into account. Section 4.6 analyses a debate that has generated much controversy, namely whether the capability approach can be said to be too individualistic. The next section, 4.7, focuses on a closely related issue: the scope

　　https://doi.org/10.11647/OBP.0130.04

for the inclusion of 'power' into the capability approach. Should the capability approach pay much more attention to political economy? Section 4.8 asks whether the capability approach is a liberal theory, and whether it can be anything other than a liberal theory. Section 4.9 argues that, despite the many references to 'the human development and capability approaches', these are not the same thing. Finally, section 4.10 discusses the potential and problems of a capabilitarian welfare economics.

4.2 Is everything that's called a capability genuinely a capability?

Since this chapter is the place to collect critiques and debates, let me start with a very basic point of criticism: not everything that is called 'a capability' in the capability literature is, upon closer examination, genuinely a capability. The main criticism that I want to offer in this brief section is that we should be very careful in our choices of terms and concepts: not everything that is important is a capability, and it is conceptually confusing (and hence wrong) to call everything that is important a capability. As an interdisciplinary language used in many different disciplines, the capability approach already suffers from sloppy use of terms because of interdisciplinary differences in their usage, and we should avoid contributing to this conceptual confusion. Let me give one example to illustrate the critique.

In her book *Allocating the Earth* as well as in earlier work, Breena Holland (2008, 2014) argues that the role of the environment in making capabilities possible is so important and central that we should conceptualize environmental ecological functioning (that is, the ecosystem services that the environment offers to human beings) as a *meta-capability* that underlies all other capabilities. As Holland puts it, "the environment's ecological functioning is a meta-capability in the sense that it is a precondition of all the capabilities that Nussbaum defines as necessary for living a good human life" (2014, 112). By using this terminology, Holland wants to stress that protecting the ecosystem is not just one way among many equally good ways to contribute to human wellbeing — rather, it is a *crucial* and *non-substitutable* precondition for living. Yet one could question whether conceptualizing it as a "meta-capability" is correct. As I have argued elsewhere (Robeyns 2016a), the environment is not a capability, since capabilities are real opportunities for beings and doings. The environment and the services that its ecosystems give to human beings are absolutely necessary for human life to be possible in the first place, but that doesn't warrant giving it the conceptual status of a 'capability'. It would have been better, in my view, to introduce a term showing that there are substitutable and non-substitutable preconditions for each capability, and that there are absolutely necessary (or crucial) versus less central preconditions. An environment that is able to deliver a minimal level of ecosystem services to life on our planet is both a non-substitutable as well as an absolutely necessary precondition for human wellbeing understood in terms of capabilities. There are many other preconditions for human wellbeing, but a minimum level of sustainable ecosystem services is one of the very few — perhaps even the only one — that is both non-substitutable and absolutely necessary. That makes it hugely important — perhaps even more important than some capabilities (which could be accommodated by including it in proposition A6), but the absolute priority it should receive does not warrant us to call it a capability.

4.3 Should we commit to a specific list of capabilities?

At an earlier stage of the development of the capability approach, a rather heated debate took place on whether or not it was necessary for Sen to list the capabilities he felt were relevant for the issue under consideration. This 'question of the list' debate wasn't always very helpful, since participants were not making the distinction between capability theories and the capability approach, which, as I will show in this section, is crucial to answer this question. Several scholars have criticized Sen for not having specified which capabilities matter or for not giving us some guidelines on how the selection of capabilities could be conducted (e.g. Sugden 1993; Roemer 1996; Nussbaum 2003a). As is well known, Sen has explicitly refrained from committing himself to one particular list of capabilities. But *should* Sen (or anyone else) do so?

In order to answer that question, it is important to keep the distinction in mind between the general capability approach, and particular capability theories. As Mozaffar Qizilbash (2012) rightly points out, Sen has written on the capability approach in general and he has developed particular capability applications, critiques, and theories. When asking whether Sen (or anyone else) should commit to a particular list of capabilities, we have to keep that distinction firmly in mind — since it is relevant to our answer.

It is obvious that there cannot be one list that applies to all the different purposes for which the capability approach can be used — that is, one list that applies to more specific capability theories and applications. Hence insofar as it is argued that Sen (or any other capability scholar) should endorse a particular list of capabilities when discussing the capability *approach*, rather than more specific capability *theories*, this critique misfires. This is part of the answer that Sen has given to his critics. Each application or theory based on the capability approach will always require a selection of valuable functionings that fits the purpose of the theory or application. Hence the capability approach as such is deliberately too underspecified to endorse just one single list that could be used for all capability analyses (Sen 1993, 2004). It is quite likely that those who have criticised Sen, or the capability approach in general, for not entailing a specific list of capabilities, have not sufficiently appreciated the distinction between the capability approach in general and more specific capability theories.

But what then about specific capability theories, applications and analyses? Should these always commit to a particular list of capabilities? It is possible to distinguish between two types of critique addressing capability theories, which I labelled the weak and strong critiques (Robeyns 2005a). The strong critique entails that there must be a clear list of capabilities that we can use for all capability theories and their application.

The strong critique is most clearly voiced by Nussbaum, who has proposed a list of ten "central human capabilities" that specify the political principles that every person should be entitled to as a matter of justice.[1] Nussbaum's capabilities theory differs in a number of ways from Sen's version. Nussbaum (1988, 2003) not only argues that these ten capabilities are the relevant ones, but in addition claims that if

---

1   These ten capabilities are: Life; Bodily health; Bodily integrity; Senses, imagination and thought; Emotions; Practical reason; Affiliation; Other species; Play; and Control over one's environment. For more details, see Nussbaum (2006b, 76–78).

Sen wants his version of the capability approach to have any bite for addressing issues of social justice, he has to endorse one specific and well-defined list of capabilities.

Sen does not accept the stronger critique as it applies to particular capability theories. The reason is the importance he attaches to agency, the process of choice, and the freedom to reason with respect to the selection of relevant capabilities. He argues that theory on its own is not capable of making such a final list of capabilities (Sen 2004). Instead, Sen argues that we must leave it to democratic processes and social choice procedures to define the distributive policies. In other words, when the capability approach is used for policy work, it is the people who will be affected by the policies who should decide on what will count as valuable capabilities for the policy in question. This immediately makes clear that in order to be operational for (small-scale) policy implementation, the capability approach needs to engage with theories of deliberative democracy and public deliberation and participation.

Sen's response to the strong critique can be better understood by highlighting his meta-theoretical views on the construction of theories, and theories of justice in particular. One should not forget that Sen is predominantly a prominent scholar in social choice theory, which is the discipline that studies how individual preferences and interests can be combined to reach collective decisions, and how these processes affect the distribution and levels of welfare and freedom. Sen published ground-breaking work in social choice theory before he started working on the capability approach, and he has never ceased to be interested in and to contribute to social choice theory.[2] Sen's passion for social choice theory is also a very likely explanation for his critique of the dominant forms of contemporary theories of justice, which, he argues, focus on describing a utopian situation of perfect justice, rather than giving us tools to detect injustices and decide how to move forward to a less unjust society (Sen 2006, 2009c).

According to my reading of Sen's work on capability theories and applications, he is not against the selection of dimensions in general, but rather (a) against one list that would apply to all capability theories and

---

2   Sen was also awarded the Nobel Memorial Prize for his contributions to social choice theory and welfare economics. For some of his work on social choice theory, see Sen (1970a, 1970b, 1976, 1977b, 1979, 1983, 1986, 1992c, 1999c, 2017).

applications, and (b) as far as those capability theories and applications are concerned, in favour of seriously considering procedural methods to decide which capabilities matter.

However, even if we all accept that view, it doesn't settle all disputes. Even if we agree that a selection of capabilities for, say, a poverty evaluation should differ from the selection of capabilities for a theory of justice, this still allows for different views on how that selection should be made. Some scholars have argued that it should be based on normative grounds, in other words based on philosophical reasoning and argumentation (Nussbaum 2000; 2006b; Claassen 2016). Others have argued for a selection based on a procedural method (Byskov 2017). For empirical applications, it has been argued that the selection of dimensions should be made in a way that minimises biases in the selection (Robeyns 2003). For policy-relevant applications, it has been argued that the freedoms listed in the Universal Declaration of Human Rights could provide a good starting point, and should plausibly be playing a larger role in the selection of capabilities (Vizard 2007; Burchardt and Vizard 2011). There are by now various overviews published on how to select functionings and capabilities but, interestingly, they almost always are limited to a certain type of capability theory, such as wellbeing for policy making (Hick and Burchardt 2016; Alkire 2016), multidimensional poverty measurement (Alkire 2016; Alkire et al. 2015), human development projects and policies (Alkire 2002; Byskov forthcoming) and theories of justice (Robeyns 2016d). Thus, there are a range of arguments pointing out that the selection of capabilities for particular capability theories needs to be sensitive to the purpose of the theory in question, hence selection is a matter to be decided at the level of the individual capability *theories*, rather than at the more general and abstract level of the capability approach (see also Sen 2004a).

4.4 Why not use the notion of needs?

By introducing the concepts of 'functionings' and 'capabilities', the capability approach offers some specific notions of 'advantage' and provides an ethical framework to guide our actions and institutional design. It is also a theoretical framework with clear commitments to practice and policy making in the world as it is, not just in some hypothetical world or in a stylized model. However, the same can be said of the (basic) needs approach, which was introduced and developed much earlier in the landscape of ethical approaches related to wellbeing and poverty. Hence, the obvious question to ask is: why not use the notion of needs for our theoretical work, and the basic needs approach for work on development?

To answer that question, it makes sense to make a distinction between the basic needs approach as it has been used by development scholars and policy makers, and the philosophical theories of basic needs. Let us look at the basic needs approach first. This is a practice and policy oriented approach "that gives priority to meeting people's basic needs — to ensuring that there are sufficiently, appropriately distributed basic need goods and services to sustain all human lives at a minimally decent level" (Stewart 2006, 14). The basic needs approach was a reaction to the development policies that many countries in the Global South pursued after independence from colonial rule, and that led to a dualistic pattern of development, with a small modern sector that allowed some people to flourish while at the same time leaving many other people in poverty and unemployment. The fundamental claim of the basic needs approach was that the poor not only need a monetary income but also some very basic goods and services such as clean water, enough food, health services, and education. Given the urgency of these needs, the hope was that the requirement to supply them would be more readily accepted by governments in both the Global South and North than theoretical arguments about inequality (Stewart 2006, 15).

In the 1980s, the basic needs approach lost support because development donors shifted their attention to the goals of stability and adjustment, but when they again started to pay attention to the poor, adopting the capability approach, and especially the more policy oriented human development paradigm, seemed more attractive. However, according to Frances Stewart (2006, 18), when applied to the concern of reducing poverty in the Global South, the capability approach and the basic needs approach are very similar in terms of the actions they recommend.

Why, then, would anyone consider the capability approach over the basic needs approach? The first reason is that the capability approach seems to have a more elegant philosophical foundation (Stewart 2006, 18). However, while its seeming elegance might have been perceived by the basic needs practitioners as a reason for its adoption, the question is whether this is true, given that there have always been the philosophical theories of needs, to which we turn below. Perhaps the answer is pragmatic and points to an advantage of the interdisciplinary nature of the capability approach: Sen did not only lay out its theoretical foundations, but also, via his empirical work and his contributions to the Human Development Reports, translated those philosophical ideas into practice. Perhaps it is the case that a philosophical theory needs some charismatic thinker who translates it into practice, since otherwise it is not picked up by policy makers. In the case of the capability approach, Sen did both the philosophical work and the policy translation.

Another reason mentioned by Stewart is that the capability approach focuses more on the situation of individuals than the basic needs approach (Stewart 2006, 18). The capability approach doesn't recommend the delivery of the same basic goods to everyone, but rather that we take human diversity as much as possible into account. The basic needs approach was more broad-brush than the capability approach, which stresses the additional resources needed by some people, such as the disabled. A third reason is that the capability approach applies to all human beings, hence also to the rich, whereas the basic needs approach has generally been perceived as focused on poor people in poor countries (Streeten 1995, ix). The more inclusive scope of the capability approach, which applies to all human beings, resonates with an increasing acknowledgement that countries in the Global North also include people with low levels of wellbeing, and that ideas of development, social progress and prosperity apply to *all* countries. This is very well captured in the case of the Sustainable Development Goals, which are goals applicable to all countries.

Many of the earlier key advocates of the basic need approach are pursuing their goals now under the umbrella of the human development paradigm. Hence the pragmatic and policy oriented basic needs approach has joined the human development paradigm, which has become much stronger politically. For policy making, the influence of frameworks at a particular point in time is one of the relevant considerations whether one should adopt one framework rather than another, and hence there is a good reason why, given their pragmatic goals, the basic needs advocates have contributed to a joint endeavour with capability scholars to set up the human development paradigm.

But what about the philosophical theories of basic needs? Are there reasons why we should favour them rather than the capability approach? The arguments that were given for the pragmatic basic needs approach apply also to some extent to the questions of the complementarities and differences between the theories. There are, theoretically, close similarities between theories of needs and capabilities, and Soran Reader (2006) has argued that many of the objections that capability scholars have to theories of needs are unwarranted and based on implausibly reductionist readings of theories of needs. According to Reader, theories of needs and capability theories have much more in common than capability scholars have been willing to see.

Still, Sen has been notorious in arguing that the capability approach is superior to the basic needs approach, a critique he has reaffirmed in his latest book (Sen 2017, 25). In his paper 'Goods and people', Sen (1984a, 513–15) criticised the basic needs approach for being too focussed on commodities, and seeing human beings as passive and needy. Those criticisms were rebutted by Alkire (2002, 166–74), who believed they were based on misinterpretations. However, Alkire did argue that the other two claims by Sen were correct. First, that the basic needs approach confines our attention to the most desperate situations, and is therefore only useful to developing countries. Alkire, however, sees this as potentially a strength of the basic needs approach; one could argue that it helps us to focus our attention on the worst off. Sen's final criticism was, according to Alkire, the one with most theoretical bite: that the basic needs approach does not have solid philosophical foundations.

However, the question is whether that is true. A set of recent papers by basic needs scholars (Brock and Reader 2002; Reader and Brock 2004; Reader 2006) make clear that the philosophical theory of basic needs is sophisticated; moreover, several philosophically highly sophisticated theories of needs have been proposed in the past, both in the Aristotelian tradition but also more recently by contemporary philosophers (e.g. Doyal and Gough 1991; Wiggins 1998). Instead, a more plausible explanation for the basic needs approach losing ground in comparison to the capability approach seems to me that in the case of the basic needs approach, there was less interaction between empirical scholars and policy makers on the one hand, and philosophers on the other. It is hard to find evidence of a clear synergy between basic needs philosophers and basic needs development scholars and policy advisors — an interaction that is very present in the capability literature. This may explain why the basic needs approach has been seen as lacking solid conceptual foundations.

Yet despite these hypotheses, which may help us understand why the capability approach to a large extent replaced the focus on needs in the practical field and in empirical research, some genuine differences remain. The first difference requires the capability approach to adopt some basic distinctions that are fundamental to philosophical needs theory, and for which the capability approach in itself does not have the resources: the distinction between non-contingent needs on the one hand, and contingent needs, desires, wants, etc. on the other hand. Non-contingent needs are cases in which "the needing being simply cannot go on unless its need is met" (Reader and Brock 2004, 252). This relates to a more common-sense distinction between 'needs' and 'wants', that has an important relevance to our everyday ethical life and to policy making, but that has no equivalent in the capability approach. For some applications of the capability approach, such as those related to prioritising in conditions of extreme scarcity of resources (whether these resources are money, food, water, the right to emit greenhouse gasses, etc.) theories of needs can provide tools to guide our moral priorities that are lacking in the capability approach. Right now, preferences dominate in public decision making, but the concept of preferences cannot make a distinction between a preference for minimal amounts of water, food, safety, and social interaction, versus a preference for wine and a jacuzzi. The preferences-based approach, which has become very dominant in ethical theory as well as policy analysis by economists, doesn't have the theoretical resources to make such a distinction, whereas it is central to some of our intuitions of how to prioritise our actions in cases of scarcity (e.g. J. O'Neill 2011; Robeyns 2017a).

The second difference follows from the first. The distinction in theories of needs between the morally required (meeting non-contingent or basic needs) and the morally laudable but not required (the other needs, wants, desires, etc.) implies that the needs approach may have a smaller scope than the capability approach. The modular view of the capability approach presented in chapter 2 makes clear that the capability approach can be used for a wide variety of capabilitarian theories and applications. The basic needs approach is more focussed on situations in which we need to prioritise — but the domain of ethical questions is broader than that.

In conclusion, the basic needs approach in practice is, for pragmatic and political reasons, now part of the human development paradigm. At the theoretical level, though, capability scholars neglect to take the philosophy of needs seriously or to draw on the theoretical resources of those theories to strengthen particular capabilitarian theories and applications.

4.5 Does the capability approach only address the government?

Some capability scholars believe that the capability approach is a theory about public policy or state action. For example, Nussbaum (2011, 19) writes that it is an essential element of the (general) capability approach that it ascribes an urgent task to *government and public policy*. In her own capabilities theory of justice, Nussbaum makes very clear that she sees the government as the actor of change. But is it right to see the government as the only agent of change or of justice in the capability approach? I think the literature offers ample evidence that this is not the case.

The first thing to note is that, while the dominant view is that the capability approach is related to public policy and assumes the government as the main or only agent of change, and while Nussbaum highlights the government as the actor of change in her account of the capability approach in *Creating Capabilities*, not all capability scholars endorse this focus on the government. For example, as Frances Stewart (2005, 189) writes:

> Given that improvements in the position of the poor rarely happen solely through the benevolence of governments, and are more likely to occur because of political and economic pressures, organisation of groups among the poor is important — even essential — to achieve significant improvements.

The view that the capability approach is government-focussed may thus be reinforced by the fact that Nussbaum makes this claim, but other capability scholars are developing theories or applications that address other agents of change. A prominent example is the work of Solava

Ibrahim (2006, 2009) who has shown how self-help initiatives can play a crucial role in promoting the capabilities of the poor, by enhancing their ownership of development projects, and "overcoming their helplessness by changing their perceptions of their own capabilities" (Ibrahim 2009, 236). Similar research has been conducted in more informal settings in Khayelitsha, a South African township, by Ina Conradie (2013). These are just two studies that have been published in widely read scholarly journals — but there is a broad range of capability theories and capability applications that do not, or do not primarily, address the government. In conclusion, the first observation is that some of the capability literature does not address the government. But can we in addition also find *reasons* for not restricting the agents of change in the capability approach to the government?

The first reason relates to the distinction between the capability approach and capability theories and applications, which was introduced in section 2.3. As far as we are looking at the capability approach, rather than particular capability theories or applications, an exclusive focus on the government is clearly unwarranted. There is nothing in module A that forces us to see the government as the addressee of our capability theory, and module B1 (the purpose of the capability theory) gives us the choice between any addressee we would like to pick. One could also use the capability approach to analyse what neighbours, in a particular street or neighbourhood in a well-functioning democratic state, could do for each other and in their common interests, in order to improve the quality of life in their neighbourhood. The neighbours may prefer to keep the initiative for themselves, and not ask the government to solve their local problems.

Another example of a capability application in which the government is not involved at all is the case of parents deciding to which school to send their child (assuming they have options to choose from, which globally is not the case for many parents). Suppose that parents have the choice between two schools. The first school focusses more on making pupils ready to excel in their future professional life, endorsing a human capital understanding of education. In the other school, there is more attention paid to creative expression, learning the virtues of cooperating, taking responsibility for oneself, for others and for the environment, and a concern with the flourishing of the child as he or she is now, not just as a future adult. Clearly there is a different ideal of education in these two school. The parents may sit down and write two lists of the pros and cons of the different schools — and many items on that list will be functionings or capabilities. Parents choosing between these two schools will choose different future capability sets for their children. Although the terminology may not be used, capabilities are at work in this decision; yet very few people would argue that it is a task for the government to decide whether children should be sent to schools focussing on human capital training, or rather on human flourishing. The scholarship focussing on curriculum design using the capability approach, or on making us understand the difference between human capital and human capabilities is doing precisely all of this (Brighouse 2006; Robeyns 2006c; Wigley and Akkoyunlu-Wigley 2006; Walker 2008, 2010, 2012b).

Of course, one could respond to these examples by saying that there may be capability applications or theories that belong to the private sphere and that therefore the government is not the (only) agent of change — yet that capabilitarian *political theories*, such as theories of justice, should address the government.

But this response will not do either. As several political theorists have argued, the question of who should be the agents of justice is one that needs to be properly discussed and analysed, and it is not at all obvious that the primary or only agents of justice should be the government (O. O'Neill 2001; Weinberg 2009; Deveaux 2015). There are at least three reasons one could give for not giving the government the main role as agent of change, or indeed any role at all. The first reason is one's general ideological commitment as regards political systems. Anarchism and (right-)libertarian political theories would either give the government no agency at all, or else only insofar as property rights need to be protected (Nozick 1974). There is nothing in the structure of anarchist or libertarian political theories that rules out their adoption of functionings and capabilities as (part of) the metric of quality of life that should guide the social and economic institutions that we choose for our societies. People have very different views on the question of what can realistically be expected from a government. Just as we need to take people as they are, we should not work with an unrealistic utopian account of government. It may be that the capabilitarian ideal society is better reached by a coordinated commitment to individual action or by relying on market mechanisms. Adherents of public choice theory would stress that giving the government the power to deliver those goods will have many unintended but foreseeable negative consequences, which are much more important than the positive contributions the government could make.[3]

A second reason why capabilitarian political theories may not see the government as the only, or primary, agent of justice, relates to the distinction between ideal theories of justice (which describe those normative principles that would be met in a just world, and the institutions that would meet those principles) versus non-ideal theory (which describes what is needed to reduce injustices in the world in which we live).[4] In several areas of the world, governmental agents are involved in the creation of (severe) economic and social injustice, either internationally or against some of its own minorities, or — in highly repressive states — against the vast majority of the population (e.g. Hochschild 1999; Roy 2014). The government is then more part of the problem than part of the solution, and some would argue that it is very naive to construct capabilitarian political theories that simply assume that the government will be a force for the good (Menon 2002). Similarly, some political philosophers have argued that in cases of injustice in which the government doesn't take sufficient action, as in the case of harms done by climate change, duties fall on others who are in a position to 'take up the slack' or make a difference (Karnein 2014; Caney 2016).

The third reason why capabilitarian political theories may not see the government as the only, or primary, agent of justice, relates to the question of how we decide to allocate the responsibility for being the agent of change.[5] As Monique Devaux points out, we can attribute moral and political agency derived from our responsibility in creating the injustice (a position advocated by Thomas Pogge (2008) in his work on global poverty) or because of the greater capacities and powers that

---

3   For an introduction to the public choice literature, see Mueller (2003).
4   On the distinction between ideal and non-ideal theories of justice, see e.g. Swift (2008); Stemplowska (2008); Robeyns (2008a); Valentini (2012).
5   The second and third reasons may sometimes both be at work in an argument to attribute agency to a particular group or institutions.

agents have, as Onora O'Neill (2001) has advocated. Devaux (2015, 127–28) argues that in the case of justice related to global poverty, the moral agency of the poor stems from their experience of living in poverty. This may not only make them more effective as political agents in some contexts, but it might also lead to the poor endorsing a different political agenda, often focussing on empowerment, rather than merely reducing poverty understood in material terms. This is in tune with the earlier-mentioned research by Ibrahim (2006, 2009) and Conradie (2013) on self-organisation by the poor.

It has not been my aim in this section to defend a particular way to answer the question of who should be the agent(s) of justice. Rather, my goal has been much more limited — namely, to show that it is not at all self-evident that a capabilitarian political theory, let alone another type of capabilitarian theory or application, would always posit the government as the only agent of change, or the primary agent of change. *Pace* what Nussbaum (2011) claims on this issue, there is no reason why this should be the case, and there are many good reasons why we should regard our answer to this question as one that requires careful reasoning and consideration — and ultimately a choice that is made in module B and module C, rather than a fixed given in module A.

4.6 Is the capability approach too individualistic?

At the beginning of this century, an often-heard critique at academic meetings on the capability approach was that "the capability approach is too individualistic". This critique has been especially widespread among those who endorse communitarian philosophies, or social scientists who argue that neoclassical economics is too individualistic, and believe that the same applies to the capability approach (e.g. Gore 1997; Evans 2002; Deneulin and Stewart 2002; Stewart 2005). The main claim would be that any theory should regard individuals as part of their social environment, and hence agents should be recognised as socially embedded and connected to others, and not as atomised individuals. Very few scholars have directly argued that the capability approach is too individualistic, but a few have stated it explicitly. Séverine Deneulin and Frances Stewart (2002, 66) write that "the [capability] approach is an example of methodological individualism" and also add "the individualism of the [capability] approach leads us [...] to a belief that there are autonomous individuals whose choices are somehow independent of the society in which they live". But is this critique correct? What are we to make of the argument that the capability approach is "too individualistic"?[6]

4.6.1 Different forms of individualism

To scrutinise the allegedly individualistic character of the capability approach, we should distinguish between ethical or normative individualism on the one hand and methodological and ontological individualism on the other. As we already saw in section 2.6.8, *ethical individualism*, or *normative individualism*, makes a claim about who or what should count in our evaluative exercises and decisions. It postulates that individuals, and only individuals, are the units of *ultimate* moral concern. In other words, when evaluating different states of affairs, we are only interested in the (direct and indirect) effects of those states on individuals. *Methodological* and *ontological individualism* are somewhat more difficult to describe, as the debate on methodological individualism has suffered from confusion and much obscurity. Nevertheless, at its core is the claim that "all social phenomena are to be explained wholly and exclusively in terms of individuals and their properties" (Bhargava 1992, 19). It is a doctrine that includes semantic, ontological and explanatory individualism. The last is probably the most important of these doctrines, and this can also explain why many people reduce methodological individualism to explanatory individualism. *Ontological individualism* states that only individuals and their properties exist, and that all social entities and properties can be identified by reducing them to individuals and their properties. Ontological individualism hence makes a claim about the nature of human beings, about the way they

---

6   Amartya Sen has responded to their critique by stating that "I fear I do not see at all the basis of their diagnosis" (Sen 2002b, 80). As my arguments in this section will show, I think Sen is right, because Deneulin's and Stewart's critique fails to distinguish properly between different types of individualism, including methodological individualism (which the capability approach is not) and normative individualism (which the capability approach meets, and, as I have argued in section 2.6.8, *should* meet).

live their lives and about their relation to society. In this view, society is built up from individuals only, and hence is nothing more than the sum of individuals and their properties. Similarly, *explanatory individualism* is the doctrine that all social phenomena can in principle be explained in terms of individuals and their properties.

The crucial issue here is that a commitment to normative individualism is not incompatible with an ontology that recognises the connections between people, their social relations, and their social embedment. Similarly, a social policy focussing on and targeting certain groups or communities can be perfectly compatible with normative individualism.

As I argued in section 2.6.8, the capability approach embraces normative individualism — and this is, for reasons given there, a desirable property. However, it also follows from the discussion on the importance of structural constraints (section 2.7.5) that the capability approach does *not* rely on ontological individualism.

Clearly, scholars have divergent (implicit) social theories, and hence some attach more importance to social structures than others do. Nevertheless, I fail to see how the capability approach can be understood to be methodologically or ontologically individualistic, especially since Sen himself has analysed some processes that are profoundly collective, such as his analysis of households as sites of cooperative conflict (1990a). In later work too, he acknowledged persons as socially embedded, as the following quote from his joint work illustrates:

> The [capability] approach used in this study is much concerned with the opportunities that people have to improve the quality of their lives. It is essentially a 'people-centered' approach, which puts human agency (rather than organizations such as markets or governments) at the centre of the stage. The crucial role of social opportunities is to expand the realm of human agency and freedom, both as an end in itself and as a means of further expansion of freedom. The word 'social' in the expression 'social opportunity' [...] is a useful reminder not to view individuals and their opportunities in isolated terms. The options that a person has depend greatly on relations with others and on what the state and other institutions do. We shall be particularly concerned with those opportunities that are strongly influenced by social circumstances and public policy [...]. (Drèze and Sen 2002: 6)

Of course, the critique is not only (and also not primarily) about Sen's work, but about the capability approach in general, or about capability theories. But the work done by other scholars similarly doesn't meet the criteria for being plausibly considered to be methodologically or ontologically individualistic. In general, we can say that the capability approach acknowledges some non-individual structures, and for the various more specific capability theories, the degree to which they move away from methodological or ontological individualism depends on the choices made in modules B and C. But whatever those choices are, there are already some features in module A that prevent capability theories from being methodologically or ontologically individualistic.

4.6.2 Does the capability approach pay sufficient attention to groups?

The critique that the capability approach should focus more on groups is often related to the critique that the focus of the capability approach is too individualistic, but it is nevertheless a distinct critique. A clear example can be found in the work of Frances Stewart (2005), who argues that in order to understand processes that affect the lives of people, such as violent conflict, one has to look at group capabilities — which she defines as the average of the individual capabilities of all the individuals in the selected group. The reason we need to focus on these 'group capabilities' is because they are a central source of group conflict. They are thus crucial to *understand* processes such as violent conflict.

We will return to Stewart's specific complaint below, but first unpack the general critique that the capability approach doesn't pay enough attention to groups. To properly judge the critique that the capability approach does not pay sufficient attention to groups, we need to distinguish between a weaker and a stronger version of that claim.

A stronger version of that claim would be that the capability approach *cannot* pay sufficient attention to groups — that there is something in the conceptual apparatus of the capability approach that makes it *impossible* for the capability approach to pay attention to groups. But that claim is obviously false, because there exists a large literature of research analysing the average capabilities of one group compared to another, e.g. women and men (Kynch and Sen 1983; Nussbaum 2000; Robeyns 2003, 2006a) or the disabled versus those without disabilities (Kuklys 2005; Zaidi and Burchardt 2005). Capability theorists have also written on the importance of groups for people's wellbeing, like Nussbaum's discussion of women's collectives in India. Several lists of capabilities that have been proposed in the literature include capabilities related to community membership: Nussbaum stresses affiliation as an architectonic capability, Alkire (2002) discusses relationships and participation, and in earlier work I have included social relationships (Robeyns 2003). The UNDP (1995, 2004) has produced Human Development Reports on both gender and culture, thus policy reports based on the capability approach focus on groups.

The weaker claim states that the present state of the literature on the capability approach does not pay *sufficient* attention to groups. I agree that contemporary mainstream economics is very badly equipped to account for group membership on people's wellbeing. But is this also the case for the capability approach? While some capability theorists have a great faith in people's abilities to be rational and to resist social and moral pressure stemming from groups (e.g. Sen 1999b, 2009b), other writers on the capability approach pay much more attention to the influence of social norms and other group-based processes on our choices and, ultimately, on our wellbeing (e.g. Alkire 2002; Nussbaum 2000; Iversen 2003; Robeyns 2003a). There is thus no reason why the capability approach would not be able to take the normative and constitutive importance of groups fully into account. Admittedly, however, this is a theoretical choice that needs to be made when making scholarly decisions in modules B3, B5 and C1, hence we may not agree with the assumptions about groups in each and every capability theory.

If we return to the reasons Stewart gave for a focus on group capabilities, we notice that the main reason stated is that analysis of group capabilities is needed to *understand* outcomes. Yet that is precisely what the just mentioned capability applications do (since they do not only measure group inequalities in capabilities but also try to understand them). Those applications also investigate how group identities constrain groups to different degrees, or which privileges they ensure for certain groups. In my reading of the literature, many capability scholars do precisely this kind of work, and to the extent that they do not do so, one important reason is that they are engaging in documenting and measuring inequalities, rather than in explaining them. The complaint should then be that capability analysis should be less concerned with documenting and measuring inequalities, and should spend more time on understanding how inequalities emerge, are sustained, and can be decreased — but that is *another* complaint.

Still, I do think that a consideration of the role of groups in the capability approach gives us a warning. To fully understand the importance of groups, capability theories should engage more intensively in a dialogue with disciplines such as sociology, anthropology, history, and gender and cultural studies. This will make the choices of the account of human diversity (module B3), the account of structural constraints (module B5), and of ontological and explanatory theories (module C1) more accurate. Disciplinary boundaries and structures make these kinds of dialogues difficult, but there is no inherent reason why this could not be done.

4.6.3 Social structures, norms and institutions in the capability approach

The critique that the capability approach is too individualistic is sometimes also put in another way, namely that the capability approach should pay more attention to collective features, such as social structures, social norms, and institutions. How can the capability approach account for such collective aspects of human living?

At the theoretical level, the capability approach does account for social relations and the constraints and opportunities of societal structures and institutions on individuals in two ways. First, by recognising the social and environmental factors which influence the conversions of commodities into functionings. For example, suppose that Jaap and Joseph both have the same individual conversion factors and possess the same commodities. But Jaap is living in a town with cycle lanes and low criminality rates, whereas Joseph is living in a city with poor infrastructure for cyclists, and with high levels of criminality and theft. Whereas Jaap can use his bike to cycle anywhere he wants, at any moment of the day, Joseph will be faced with a much higher chance that his bike will be stolen. Hence, the same commodity (a bike) leads to different levels of the functioning 'to transport oneself safely', due to characteristics of the society in which one lives (its public infrastructure, crime levels etc).

The second way in which the capability approach accounts for societal structures and constraints is by theoretically distinguishing functionings from capabilities. More precisely, moving from capabilities to achieved functionings requires an act of choice. Now, it is perfectly possible to take into account the influence of societal structures and constraints on those choices, by choosing a nuanced and rich account of agency (module B4 — account of agency) and of societal structures (module B5 — account of structural constraints). For example, suppose Sarah and Sigal both have the same intellectual capacities and human capital at the age of six, and live in a country where education is free and children from poorer families receive scholarships. Sarah was born in a class in which little attention was paid to intellectual achievement and studying, whereas Sigal's parents are both graduates pursuing intellectual careers. The social environment in which Sarah and Sigal live will greatly influence and shape their preferences for studying. In other words, while initially Sarah and Sigal have the same capability set, the social structures and constraints that influence and shape their preferences will influence the choice they will make to pick one bundle of functionings. The capability approach *allows* us to take those structures and constraints on choices into account, but whether a particular capability theory will take that into account depends on the choices made in the various modules, especially modules B4 and B5. Yet it is clear that the choices made in modules B and C will have ultimately far reaching consequences for our capabilitarian evaluations.

Summing up, one could, plausibly, complain that a certain capability theory doesn't pay sufficient attention to social structures or collective features of human life. This may well be a very valid critique of a particular capability theory in which the additional theories of human diversity, social structures, and other social theories more generally, are very minimal (that is, the explanatory and ontological theories added in C1 do not properly account for many collective features of life). But I have argued that it is not a valid critique against the capability *approach* in general.

4.7 What about power and political economy?

In section 4.6, I analysed the critique that the capability approach is too individualistic, and argued that this charge is based on a misunderstanding of different distinct types of individualism, as well as a flawed (and unduly limited) understanding of the potential for capability theories to include social structures as factors that explain varying levels of advantage between different people. However, there are two closely related critiques that must be addressed briefly: first, that the capability approach downplays power and social structures, and second, that capability theories divert our attention from the political economy of poverty and inequality, which is much more important than the measurement and evaluation of poverty and inequality. Let us analyse these two critiques in turn.

4.7.1 Which account of power and choice?

The first worry is that the capability approach is insufficiently critical of social constraints on people's actions, and does not pay due attention to "global forces of power and local systems of oppression" (Koggel 2003). Put differently, the worry is that the capability approach does not pay sufficient attention to inequalities in power (Hill 2003). Similarly, there is also a worry that the capability approach could be used in combination with a stripped-down version of human choice. For example, despite Sen's repeated criticism of choice as revealed preference, one could in principle make interpersonal comparisons of functionings that assume revealed preference theory: a person will choose from their option set what is best for them. But this ignores the fact that our choices are heavily influenced by patterns of expectations and social norms,[7] as well as commitments we have to certain interests that do not necessarily affect our own advantage.[8] Depending on the choice theory one adopts, the capability approach could lead to widely divergent normative conclusions (Robeyns 2000; 2001). Standard economics pays very little attention to the *social* and *cultural* constraints that impinge on people's

---

7   On the importance of social norms in explaining a person's choice and behaviour, see e.g. Elster (1989); Anderson (2000a).

8   On commitment, see e.g. Sen (1977a, 1985b); Cudd (2014).

choices, in contrast to sociology, gender studies and cultural studies, among other disciplines. In political philosophy, one sees a similar split between the core of Anglo-American political philosophy, in which the concept of the self that is endorsed is that of a rational, autonomous agent whose own plans take precedence over things he finds as 'given' in his life, versus other traditions in philosophy that pay more attention to relations and the social embedding of individuals, including unjust structures in which one finds oneself, as well as mechanisms that reproduce power differences. The consequence is that it is possible to use functionings and capabilities as the evaluative space in combination with many different normative accounts of choice, with a widely divergent critical content.

Take as an example the choices made by men versus women between paid (labour market) or unpaid (care and household) work. In all societies women do much more household and care work, whereas men do much more paid work. Both kinds of work can generate a number of different functionings so that the largest capability set might perhaps be reached only by giving everyone the opportunity to combine both types of work. However, I would argue that in the world today, in which hardly any society allows people to combine market work and non-market work without having to make significant compromises when it comes to the quality of at least one of them, the labour market enables more (and more important) functionings than care work. These include psychological functionings like increased self-esteem; social functionings like having a social network; material functionings like being financially independent and securing one's financial needs for one's old age or in the event of divorce.[9] Many schools in political philosophy and normative welfare economics have typically seen the gender division of labour as ethically unproblematic, in the sense that this division is seen as the result of men's and women's *voluntary* choices, which reflect their preferences. However, this is an inadequate way of explaining and evaluating this division, because gender-related structures and constraints convert this choice from an individual choice under perfect information into a collective decision under socially constructed constraints with imperfect information and asymmetrical risks. Moreover, evaluating the gender

---

9   As is also suggested by the empirical findings of Enrica Chiappero-Martinetti (2000) who measured achieved functioning levels for Italy.

division of labour can only be done if we scrutinise the constraints on choice, and these may turn out to be very different for men and women.[10] What is crucial for the discussion here is that both positive theories of the gender division of labour (which are choices made in modules B3, B4, and B5) bear different normative implications. If a housewife is held fully responsible for the fact that she works at home then the logical consequence would be that she had the capability to work in the labour market. However, if we embrace a theory of choice that focuses on gender specific constraints, then we will not hold the housewife fully responsible for her choice but acknowledge that her capability set was smaller and did not contain the possibility for a genuine choice to work in the labour market. It seems, thus, that it is perfectly possible to apply the capability approach in combination with different accounts of gender-specific constraints on choices.

By giving choice such a central position and making its place in wellbeing and social justice evaluations more explicit, the capability approach opens up a space for discussions of how certain choices are constrained by gender-related societal mechanisms and expectations. But again, the capability approach provides no guarantee for this: it depends on the choices made in modules B and C. For example, conservatives will want to integrate a conservative theory of gender relations within the capability approach, whereas for critical scholars it will be crucial to integrate a feminist account of gender relations, which includes an account of power. No doubt the two exercises will reach very different normative conclusions. In short, for scholars who defend a theory of human agency and social reality that challenges the status quo, one of the important tasks will be to negotiate which additional theories will be integrated in further specifications of the capability approach, especially the choices made in module C1.

The conclusion is that the core characteristics of the capability approach (as listed in module A) do not *necessarily* have significant implications for the role of power in capability theories and applications, which can include widely divergent views on social realities and interpersonal relations. Indeed, the fact that the capability approach

---

10   The seminal work in this area is Susan Okin's book *Justice, Gender and the Family* (Okin 1989). On the gendered nature of the constraints on choice, see also Nancy Folbre (1994).

interests both scholars who work in the libertarian tradition, as well as scholars who work in more critical traditions, illustrate this conclusion. My own personal conviction is that there is ample reason why we should not adopt a stripped-down view of the roles of social categories and social structures, and hence include a rich account of power that is supported by research in anthropology, sociology and other social sciences. But for everyone advancing a capability theory or application, it holds that they should *defend* their implicit social theories, and be willing to scrutinize them critically.

4.7.2 Should we prioritise analysing the political economy?

Capability scholars have been criticised for having the wrong priorities: by focusing so much on the metric of justice and on human diversity in the conversion of resources into capabilities, their approach draws attention away from huge inequalities in terms of resources (income, wealth) and therefore helps to preserve the (unjust) status quo. Thomas Pogge (2002) has specifically argued that the capability approach — Sen's work in particular — overemphasises the role of national and local governments, thereby neglecting the huge injustices created by the global economic system and its institutional structures, such as global trade rules. Similarly, Alison Jaggar (2002, 2006) has argued that western philosophers, and Martha Nussbaum's work on the capability approach in particular, should not prioritise the analysis of cultural factors constraining poor women's lives, or listing what an ideal account of flourishing and justice would look like, but rather focus on the global economic order and other processes by which the rich countries are responsible for global poverty.

Pogge and Jaggar may have a point in their charge that capability theorists have paid insufficient attention to these issues, which have been discussed at length in the philosophical literature on global justice. But one might also argue that this is orthogonal to the issues about which the capability approach to social justice is most concerned, namely, how to make interpersonal comparisons of advantage for the purposes of social justice. One could, quite plausibly, hold the view that, since most capability theorists are concerned with human wellbeing, they should invest their energies in addressing the most urgent cases of injustice, investigate their underlying causal processes and mechanisms, and concentrate on the development of solutions. Using the modular view of the capability approach, this critique boils down to the view that we should concentrate on modules outside the core, namely those that explain certain unjust structures.

This is not, however, a valid critique of the capability *approach* as a general framework, nor does it recognise the role that capability *theories* can play in substantive debates about global justice and inequality. Rather, the critique should be reformulated to say that the most urgent issues of justice do not require theories of justice, but rather a political and economic analysis of unjust structures. But then we are no longer facing a critique of the capability approach, but rather a critique of our research priorities, which goes beyond the scope of this book.[11] It is clear that the capability approach will not solve all the world's problems, and that we should regard it as a tool to help us in analysing cases that need our attention, rather than an intellectual project that has become an end in itself for academics. However, it doesn't follow therefore that all scholars developing the capability approach should become political economists — or malaria researchers, for that matter.

4.8 Is the capability approach a liberal theory?

Students of the capability approach often ask whether it is a liberal theory — something those who ask that question seem to think is a bad thing. Given the various audiences and disciplines that engage with the capability approach, there is a very high risk of misunderstandings of discipline-specific terms, such as 'liberal'. Hence, let us answer the question: is the capability approach a liberal theory, and if so, in what sense?

In many capability theories and applications, including the work by Amartya Sen and Martha Nussbaum, there is a great stress on capabilities rather than functionings, as well as on agency and the power of people to

---

11 Serene Khader (2011, 24–30) faces similar critiques in her study of adaptive preferences (rather than the global economic order), and provides a sensible response to those worries.

shape their own destinies.[12] What is ultimately important is that people have the freedoms (capabilities) to lead the kind of lives they want to lead, to do what they want to do and be the person they want to be. Once they have these freedoms, they can choose to act on them in line with their own ideas of the kind of life they want to live. For example, every person should have the opportunity to be part of a community and to practice a religion, but if someone prefers to be a hermit or an atheist, they should also have this option. Now, it is certainly true that individual freedoms and agency are a hallmark of liberalism. But is this enough to conclude that the capability approach, in contrast to specific capability theories, is a liberal framework?[13]

First, given the interdisciplinary context in which the capability approach is operating, it is very important that the word 'liberal' is not confused with the word 'liberal' in daily life. In ordinary language, 'liberal' has different political meanings in different countries, and can cover both the political right or left. In addition it is often used to refer to (neo)liberal economic policies that prioritise free markets and the privatization of public companies such as water suppliers or the railways. In contrast, philosophical liberalism is neither necessarily left or right, nor does it *a priori* advocate any social or economic policies.

The first misunderstanding to get out the way is that capabilities as freedoms refer exclusively to the 'free market' and thus that the capability approach would always lead to an endorsement of (unfettered) markets as the institutions that are capabilities-enhancing. Sen does argue that people have reason to value the freedom or liberty to produce, buy, and sell in markets. This point, however, is part of his more general work on development, and it is very different to the highly disputed question in economics and politics regarding the benefits and limits of the market as a system of economic production and distribution. Functionings and capabilities are conceptualizations of wellbeing achievements and wellbeing freedoms, and the question of which economic institutions are the best institutional means to foster functionings and capabilities

---

12 Sen's work on identity testifies to the great faith he puts in people's power to choose whether or not to adopt certain group memberships and identities. See e.g. Sen (2009b).

13 In earlier work, I argued that on those grounds we could conclude that the capability approach is a liberal theory. I now think this conclusion was premature.

is both analytically and politically a question that can only be settled after we first agree what economic outcomes we should be aiming for: a question to which the capability approach gives a (partial) answer.

The question of what are the appropriate institutions to lead to capability expansions is a separate one, which cannot be answered by the capability approach in itself; it must be coupled with a political economy analysis. However, there is nothing in the (limited) literature that has undertaken this task so far to suggest that a capability analysis would recommend unfettered markets — quite the contrary, as the work by Rutger Claassen (2009, 2015) shows: capabilities theories give reasons for regulating markets, and for constraining property rights. In sum, if the word 'liberal' is used to refer to 'neoliberalism' or to 'economic liberalization policies', then neither the capability approach in general, nor Sen and Nussbaum's more specific theories, are liberal in that sense.

Yet I believe it is correct to say that Sen and Nussbaum's writings on the capability approach are liberal in the philosophical sense, which refers to a philosophical tradition that values individual autonomy and freedom.[14] However, even philosophical liberalism is a very broad church, and Sen and Nussbaum's theories arguably participate in a critical strand within it, since the explanatory theories that they use in their capability theories (that is, the choices they make in module C1), are in various ways aware of social structures.

Third, while the particular capability theories advocated by Sen and Nussbaum aspire to be liberal, it is possible to construct capability theories that are much less so. Take a capability theory that opts in module C1 for (1) a highly structuralist account of social conditions, and (2) theories of bounded rationality, that place great emphasis on people's structural irrationalities in decision-making. In module C4, the theory accepts some degree of paternalism due to the acknowledgement of bounded rationality in decision-making. Similarly, one could have a capability theory of social justice that argues that the guiding principle in institutional design should be the protection of the vulnerable, rather

---

14   Nussbaum (2011b, 2014) has written explicitly on the type of liberalism that her capabilities approach endorses: political liberalism. For arguments that Nussbaum's capability approach is, upon closer scrutiny, not politically liberal but rather perfectionist liberal, see Barclay (2003), and Nussbaum (2003b) for a response.

than the maximal accommodation of the development of people's agency. Such theories would already be much less liberal.

Is it possible for capability theories to be *non-liberal*? This would probably depend on where exactly one draws the line between a liberal and a non-liberal theory, or, formulated differently, which properties we take to be *necessary* properties of a theory in order for that theory to qualify as 'liberal'. The capability approach draws a clear line at the principle of each person as an end, that is, in the endorsement of normative individualism. The principle of normative individualism is clearly a core principle of liberal theories. Yet it is also a core principle of some non-liberal theories that do not give higher priority to agency or autonomy (e.g. capability theories that merge insights from care ethics, and which give moral priority to protecting the vulnerable over enhancing and protecting agency). However, if a theory endorses functionings and/or capabilities as the relevant normative metric, yet violates the principle of each person as an end, it would not only not qualify as a liberal theory, but it would also not qualify as a capability theory. At best, it would qualify as e.g. a hybrid capabilitarian-communitarian theory.

4.9 Why 'human development' is not the same idea

Some believe that the terms 'human development approach' and 'the capability approach' are synonymous, or else scholars talk about the 'capability and human development approach'. Although I will argue that this usage is misleading, the equation of 'human development' with 'capability approach' is often made. Why is this the case? And is that equation a good thing?

First, the Human Development Reports and their best-known index, the Human Development Index, have been vastly influential in making the case for the capability approach, and in spreading the idea of 'functionings' and 'capabilities' both inside and outside academia (UNDP 1990). In other words, one of the main series of publications within the human development approach, and the corresponding analyses and indexes, is arguably one of the most politically successful applications of the capability approach. However, it doesn't follow from this that they are the same thing.

A second possible explanation for this misleading equation is that both the international association and the current name of the main journal in the field have merged both terms: the Human Development and Capability Association (HDCA) and the *Journal of Human Development and Capabilities*. This seems to suggest that 'human development' and 'capabilities' necessarily go together. But this need not be the case: the use of a particular title doesn't make the two things the same (and in a moment, I will give a few examples in which this *isn't* the case).

Thirdly and most importantly, the equation of 'human development approach' and 'capability approach' shouldn't be surprising because human development aims to shift the focus of our evaluation of the quality of life and the desirability of social arrangements, from material resources or mental states to people's functionings and capabilities. The capability approach is thus a central and indispensable element of the human development paradigm.

Finally, one may believe that the two terms are equivalent given that some influential authors in the capability literature equate the two terms, or merge them into one idea (Alkire and Deneulin 2009a, 2009b; Fukuda-Parr 2009; Nussbaum 2011). Let me highlight two examples. Sabina Alkire and Séverine Deneulin (2009a, 2009b) do not distinguish between the reach of the capability approach and the human development approach; instead, they merge them into one term, "the human development and capability approach". More recently, Martha Nussbaum (2011) has written on the distinction in her *Creating Capabilities*. Nussbaum has suggested that 'human development approach' is mainly associated, historically, with the Human Development Reports, and that the term 'capability approach' is more commonly used in academia. Nussbaum prefers the term 'capabilities approach' since she also likes to include non-human animals in her account. However, for those of us, like me, who are using the capability approach to analyse and evaluate the quality of life as well as the living arrangements of *human* beings, this is not a valid reason to make the distinction between 'the human development approach', and 'the capability approach'.

So, should we use 'human development approach' and 'capability approach' as synonyms, and merge them together into 'the human development and capability approach'? I believe we shouldn't. I think there are at least four valid reasons why we should make a distinction between the two ideas.

The first reason is historical: while the capability approach has been very important in the development of the human development paradigm, the human development paradigm has derived insights and concepts from several other theories and frameworks. Human development has been defined as "an expansion of human capabilities, a widening of choices, an enhancement of freedoms and a fulfilment of human rights" (Fukuda-Parr and Kumar 2003, xxi). There are important historical ideas in the human development paradigm that are to a significant extent based on Sen's capability approach. And Sen was closely involved in the development of the Human Development Reports that have been key in the maturing of the human development paradigm. Yet as some key contributors to this paradigm have rightly pointed out, it had *other* intellectual roots too, such as the basic needs approach (Streeten 1995; Fukuda-Parr 2003; Sen 2003a).

The second reason is intellectual. The capability approach is used for a very wide range of purposes, as the account I presented in chapter 2 makes amply clear. These include purposes that are only tangentially, or very indirectly, related to human development concerns. For example, the philosopher Martin van Hees (2013) is interested in the structural properties of capabilities, especially how the formal analysis of rights fits into the capability concept. This research allows us to see how capabilities, as a concept, would fit in, and relate to, the existing literature on the structure of rights. But it would be a big stretch to say that this is also a contribution to the human development literature; in fact, I would find such a statement an implausible inflation of what we understand by 'human development'. Rather, it is much more plausible to say that the study by Van Hees is a contribution to the capability literature, but not to the human development literature. If we were wrongly to equate the capability approach with the human development paradigm, this would create problems for understanding such a study as part of the capability approach.

The third reason is practical. Those who have written about the human development paradigm stress that 'development' is about all people and all countries, and not only about countries which are often called 'developing countries', that is, countries with a much higher incidence of absolute poverty, and often with a less developed economic infrastructure. For example, Paul Streeten (1995, viii) writes:

> We defined human development as widening the range of people's choices. Human development is a concern not only for poor countries and poor people, but everywhere. In the high-income countries, indicators of shortfalls in human development should be looked for in homelessness, drug addiction, crime, unemployment, urban squalor; environmental degradation, personal insecurity and social disintegration.

The inclusion of all human beings within the scope of 'human development thinking' is widely endorsed within human development scholarship and policy reports. However, it is also a matter of fact that most people, including policy makers, associate the term 'development' *not* with improvements to the lives of people living in high-income countries. This is unfortunate, but it is a fact one needs to reckon with. In high-income countries, some of the terms often used for what could also be called 'human development interventions' are 'policies', 'institutional design', or 'social transformations'. While it is laudable to deconstruct the term 'development', at the same time we should be careful about using words that would lead to scholars and policy makers in high-income countries to neglect the capability approach if they (mistakenly) believe that it is a framework only suitable for 'developing countries' (as they would use the term).

The final reason is political. There are many capability scholars who would like to develop an alternative to neoliberalism, or, more specifically when it concerns development policies, to the 'Washington consensus'. While more sophisticated analyses of both doctrines have been put forward, both doctrines focus on private property rights; the primacy of markets as an allocation mechanism; the focus in macro-economic policies on controlling inflation and reducing fiscal deficits; economic liberalisation with regard to free trade and capital flows; and, overall, restricted and reduced involvement of governments in the domestic economy, such as markets in labour, land and capital (the so-called 'factor markets') (Gore 2000; Fukuda-Parr 2003; McCleery and De Paolis 2008). The 'Washington consensus' refers to the development policy views propagated by the World Bank and the International Monetary Fund (two international institutions based in Washington, D.C., hence its name). The ideas of the Washington consensus spread in the 1980s and were endorsed as the consensus view by the IMF and the World Bank by 1990, and they dominated for at least two decades. Over the last decade, neoliberalism and the Washington consensus have been heavily criticised from many different corners, and there is a renewed recognition of the importance of considering the historical, cultural and institutional specificity of countries when deciding what good development policies look like; but it seems too early to conclude that any of those alternative views is now more influential then neoliberalism and the Washington consensus. Many citizens, scholars, policy makers and politicians are searching for alternatives, and some hope that the capability approach can offer such an alternative.

My suggestion would be that if one's goal is to develop a powerful alternative to neoliberalism and the Washington consensus, one has to look at the human development paradigm, rather than the capability approach. The human development paradigm includes many specific explanatory theories that stress the importance of historical paths and local cultural and social norms in understanding development outcomes and options in a particular country. The human development paradigm is, therefore, much more powerful than the capability approach *for this specific purpose.*

Recall the modular view of the capability approach that I presented in chapter 2. The human development paradigm is a capabilitarian theory or capability application, because it endorses all the elements from module A. In addition, it has made particular choices in modules B, such as a strong notion of agency (B3) as well as an elaborate account of social structures (B4), and, importantly, it has chosen anti-neoliberal ontological accounts of human nature and explanatory theories about how the economy and societies work (C1), as well as the endorsement of additional normative principle and social ideals (C4) such as human rights and ecological sustainability. Hence the human development paradigm is much more powerful as a policy paradigm than the capability approach, since it is much more comprehensive (taking many more aspects into account then merely people's functionings and capabilities) and it is much more powerful in policy or political terms (being informed about what works and what doesn't).

In sum, I think it is not correct to equate the capability approach and the human development approach. The two are theoretically and historically related, but they are not exactly the same. For those who work within development studies and are endorsing a critical assessment of the development policies that have been pursued as part of the so-called 'Washington consensus', it is understandable that the two may seem to be the same, or at least so close that they can be merged. But that is only if one looks at the two notions from a specific perspective. Merging the two would do injustice to the work of other thinkers using the capability approach, and it would also ultimately hamper the development of the capability approach over its full scope.

4.10 Can the capability approach change welfare economics?

Of all the (sub)disciplines where the capability approach is relevant, welfare economics may well be the one where it is most difficult to describe its impact. The reason is that the capability approach could be seen in two very different lights, depending on one's own position towards the current state of economics: either as an improved modification of mainstream welfare economics, or else as a path that could lead us to a very different type of welfare economics, which would radically break with some mainstream assumptions and practices. One could say that the welfare economists interested in the capability approach have two very different agendas: the first group only wants some changes in the normative focus, and possibly in some of the ontological and behavioural assumptions in the theory development, but no methodological or meta-theoretical changes, whereas the second group wants a paradigm change or a scientific revolution, in which there would be meta-theoretical and methodological pluralism (module B7) and much richer or thicker accounts of human agency (module B3) and structural constraints (module B5). In addition, it makes a difference whether we analyse the possibilities for a capabilitarian *theoretical* welfare economics or for a capabilitarian *empirical* welfare economics.

4.10.1 Welfare economics and the economics discipline

Before analysing the reach and limit of the capability approach in these various endeavours, a few general comments are in order about economics in general, and welfare economics in particular. Let us first ask: what is welfare economics? As Sen (1996, 50) writes, "Welfare economics deals with the basis of normative judgements, the foundations of evaluative measurement, and the conceptual underpinnings of policy-making in economics". While, in practice, much of the economics discipline is concerned with policy advice, welfare economics is nevertheless a small subfield of economics, and is by some prominent welfare economists seen as unduly neglected or marginalised by mainstream economics (Atkinson 2001). One important reason is that welfare economics makes explicit the *inevitable* normative dimensions of economic policy analysis and evaluations, and most economists have been socialised to believe that 'modern economics' is value-free, and that anything to do with normativity can be outsourced to ethics or to a democratic vote. In reality, however, the imaginary science-value split that mainstream economists would wish for is, for many economic questions, impossible (Reiss 2013; Hausman, McPherson and Satz 2016). It would therefore be much better to face this inevitability upfront, and understand economics as a moral science (Boulding 1969; Atkinson 2009; Shiller and Shiller 2011) rather than as applied mathematics or a form of value-free modelling. But in economics, as in any other discipline, there are complicated sociological processes conveying views about authority and status, as well as unexamined beliefs about what 'good science' is and which type of objectivity is most desirable: one is not born an economist, but becomes one through one's training, which is in part also a socialisation process (Colander and Klamer 1987; McCloskey 1998; Nelson 2002). Unfortunately, there is empirical evidence that many economists are unwilling to engage with these fundamental questions and hold on to the belief that economics is superior to other social sciences and has little to learn from other disciplines (Fourcade, Ollion and Algan 2015). Many economists who are interested in economic questions but are not endorsing the myth of value-free social science, or who crave more methodological and meta-theoretical freedom, have left for another discipline that offers them those liberties.[15] After all, economists do not have a monopoly on economic topics, and there are many questions about such topics that are analysed by economic sociologists, economic historians, political economists, economic geographers, and economic philosophers. In my view, one cannot analyse the reach and limits of the capability approach in welfare economics if one does not acknowledge the high levels of discontent and methodological conservatism within economics, which cannot be found in any other discipline that engages with the capability approach.

With this background in mind, we can now proceed to ask whether the capability approach can make a difference to welfare economics. First, in section 4.10.2, we will look at the main theoretical contribution of the capability approach to welfare economics: its contribution to the development of non-welfarist welfare economics. In section 4.10.3 we will analyse what kind of empirical analyses a capabilitarian welfare economics could make, and what its challenges and possibilities are. Finally, in section 4.10.4, we analyse what challenges the development of a heterodox capabilitarian welfare economics would face.

4.10.2 Non-welfarism

The main theoretical contribution of the capability approach is that it contributes to the development of *post-welfarism* or *non-welfarism* in welfare economics. Welfarism is the position that social welfare depends exclusively on individual utilities, which are either understood in a hedonic or in a desire-satisfaction sense, and this has been the dominant position in economics for a long time. Post-welfarism broadens the informational basis of interpersonal comparison with non-utility information, such as deontic rights, or objective information such as people's functionings and capabilities. In a series of publications, Sen has offered strong theoretical arguments to move from welfarism to non-welfarism (sometimes also called 'post-welfarism') and has inspired other welfare economists to work on a post-welfarist welfare economics

---

15   There are plenty of academic economists who have moved to history, development studies or philosophy in order to enjoy the greater methodological and paradigmatic freedoms in those disciplines.

(e.g. Gaertner and Xu 2006, 2008; Gotoh and Yoshihara 2003; Gotoh, Suzumura and Yoshihara 2005; Pattanaik 2006; Pattanaik and Xu 1990; Suzumura 2016; Xu 2002). Some reasons for this move are the same as the arguments against desire-satisfaction theories or the happiness approach that we reviewed earlier in sections 3.7 and 3.8. Another argument is that *relevant information* is left out of the informational basis. If two social states have exactly the same utility levels, but social state A has also a set of legal and social norms that discriminate against one group of people, whereas in social state B, the principles of moral equality and non-discrimination are protected, then surely, we should prefer social state B over social state A. But welfarism, because of its *exclusive* focus on utilities, is unable to take any type of non-utility information into account, whether it is the violation of deontic principles, information on rights, liberties and justice, or information on inefficient or unsustainable use of common resources. Many of the welfare economists who have embarked on the development of a post-welfarist welfare economics have focussed on the importance of freedom as an important part of the widening of the informational basis.

Non-welfarist welfare economics requires some changes to our approach to welfare economics. As Sen (1996, 58) noted in his discussion of the contribution of the capability approach to non-welfarist welfare economics, if we move to an informational basis with multiple dimensions of different types (as in the capability approach) then this requires *explicit* evaluations of the different weights to be given to the contributions of the different functionings and capabilities to overall (aggregate) social welfare. For Sen, the way to proceed is by *public reasoning* about those weights. This should probably not be seen as the only and exclusive way to determine them, since not all work in welfare economics is suited for public discussion — for example, it often entails desk-studies of inequalities or the analysis of the welfare effects of certain policy measures, and it is practically impossible to organise an exercise of public reasoning for every desk study that welfare economists make. Luckily, as the survey by Decancq and Lugo (2013) shows, there are various weighting systems possible that can give us the weights that are needed if one wants to aggregate the changes in different functionings and capabilities. For example, Erik Schokkaert (2007) has suggested that we derive the weights of the functionings from the contribution they make to the life-satisfaction of people, after those weights are cleaned of ethically suspicious information.

However, as we saw in section 4.10.1, many (possibly most) economists are unwilling to engage in explicit evaluations, since they believe in the science/value split and believe that economics can be value-free. This makes it harder for welfare economics to engage in such normative work, since they run the risk that their peers will no longer accept their approach as 'economics research'. But it is inconsistent to reject all explicit evaluative exercises. Economists are happy working with GNP per capita and real income metrics as proxies of welfare, which uses market prices as the weights. But this is equally normative: it is assumed that the welfare-value of a certain good for a person is reflected by the price that the good commands on the market. This is problematic, for reasons that have been explained repeatedly in the literature. For one thing, market prices reflect demand and supply (and thus relative scarcity of a good) — diamonds are expensive and water (in non-drought-affected places) is cheap — but this doesn't say anything about their importance for our wellbeing. Moreover, market prices do not take into account negative or positive welfare effects on third parties, the so-called externalities, despite their omnipresence (Hausman 1992).

Of course, it may be that, upon reflection of the various weights available, some capability theorists will conclude that the set of market prices, possibly combined with shadow prices for non-market goods, is the best way to proceed. That is quite possible, and would not be inconsistent with the general claim in the capability approach that weights need to be chosen. The point is rather that the choice of weights needs to be done in a *reflective* way, rather than simply using the weighing scheme that is dominant or customary. I take it that this is the point Sen is trying to make when he argues that "Welfare economics is a major branch of 'practical reason'" (Sen 1996, 61).[16]

---

16   Note also that for welfare economists, an important concern in examining and developing a capabilitarian welfare economics will be the question of how it can be formalized. On formalizations of the capability approach, see Sen (1985a); Kuklys and Robeyns (2005); Basu and López-Calva (2011); Bleichrodt and Quiggin (2013).

4.10.3 Empirical possibilities and challenges

When Amartya Sen introduced the capability approach in economics, there was some scepticism about its potential for empirical research. For example, Robert Sugden (1993, 1953) famously wrote:

> Given the rich array of functionings that Sen takes to be relevant, given the extent of disagreement among reasonable people about the nature of the good life, and given the unresolved problem of how to value sets, it is natural to ask how far Sen's framework is operational. Is it a realistic alternative to the methods on which economists typically rely — measurement of real income, and the kind of practical cost-benefit analysis which is grounded in Marshallian consumer theory?

What Sugden and other early welfare economic critics of the capability approach, such as John Roemer (1996, 191–93) were looking for, is a theory that is fully formalised and provides a neat algorithm to address questions of evaluation and/or (re-)distribution, resulting in a complete ranking of options. That requires two things: first, to be able to put the capability approach in a fully formalized model which can be econometrically estimated. This requires us to move beyond the welfare economic models as we know them, and may also require the collection of new data (Kuklys 2005). In addition, it requires us to accept that the different dimensions (functionings and/or capabilities) are commensurable, that is, have a common currency that allows us to express the value of one unit of one dimension in relation to the value of one unit of another dimension. One-dimensional or aggregated evaluative spaces are, ultimately, a necessary condition for conducting empirical work in contemporary mainstream welfare economics. Yet there may well be a trade-off between the number of dimensions and the informational richness of the evaluative space on the one hand, and the degree to which the theory can be formalised and can provide complete orderings of interpersonal comparisons on the other hand. Some welfare economists are working on the question of how to aggregate the many dimensions such that one has, in the end, one composite dimension to work with, but it should be obvious that this is not the only way to develop capabilitarian welfare economics. The alternative is to stick to the view that wellbeing is inherently multidimensional, which requires other methods and techniques that allow for fuzziness, vagueness and complexity (Chiappero-Martinetti 2008, 2000, 1994, 2006; Clark and Qizilbash 2005; Qizilbash and Clark 2005). One could also advance work on dominance rankings or incomplete rankings, which Sen has been defending in his social choice work for several decades (e.g. Sen 2017). As a consequence, there are several ways to develop a capabilitarian welfare economics, and to make the capability approach "operational" (Atkinson 1999, 185).

Sugden's objection can be best answered by looking at the applications that have already been developed, and which have been listed in several overviews of the empirical literature (e.g. Kuklys and Robeyns 2005; Robeyns 2006b; Chiappero-Martinetti and Roche 2009; Lessmann 2012).[17] However, whether the applications discussed in those surveys satisfy the critics depends on what one expects from empirical work in capabilitarian welfare economics. As was already shown in chapter 1, empirical applications of the capability approach *do make* a substantive difference to research using other normative frameworks, such as income-based metrics. But from that it doesn't follow that capabilitarian welfare economics will be able to deliver alternatives for each and every existing welfarist study in economics. It may well be that sometimes the informational riches of the capability approach clash with requirements regarding measurability that certain empirical applications put upon the scholar.

4.10.4 Towards a heterodox capabilitarian welfare economics?

In the last two sections, we discussed how the capability approach can make a difference to contemporary welfare economics both theoretically and empirically. Those debates by and large stay within the mainstream of contemporary welfare economics, even though as Amartya Sen (1996, 61) notes, they require us "to go more and more in these pluralist and

---

17   In addition to the first, rather rough empirical application in the Appendix of Sen's (1985a) *Commodities and Capabilities*, the literature on empirical applications in welfare economics that used individual-level data started off with the paper by Schokkaert and Van Ootegem (1990), in which they showed that unemployment benefits may restore an unemployed person's income level, but do not restore all of her functionings to the level they were at before she become unemployed.

heterodox directions, taking note of a variety of information in making the wide-ranging judgements that have to be made". The reference to 'heterodoxy' that Sen makes here is limited to the informational basis of evaluations, yet in other work he has challenged some of the behavioural assumptions underlying mainstream welfare economics (e.g. Sen 1977a, 1985b). However, other economists believe that we need a much more radical heterodox and pluralist turn in economics, which would also affect meta-theoretical views, the range of methods that can be used (e.g. including qualitative methods), giving up on the belief that economics can be value-free, and engaging much more — and much more respectfully — with the other social sciences, and indeed also with the humanities. What can these heterodox economists expect from the capability approach?

The answer to that question flows from the description of the state of economics that was given in section 4.10.1. The unwillingness of mainstream welfare economics to genuinely engage with other disciplines (Fourcade, Ollion and Algan 2015; Nussbaum 2016) clashes with the deeply interdisciplinary nature of the capability approach. The modular view of the capability approach that was presented in chapter 2 makes it possible to see that a heterodox capabilitarian welfare economics is certainly possible. It could not only, as all non-welfarist welfare economics does, include functionings and/or capabilities as ends in the evaluations (A1) and possibly include other aspects of ultimate value too (A6), but it could also include a rich account of human diversity (B3), a richly informed account of agency and structural constraints (B4 and B5) and it could widen its meta-theoretical commitments (B7) to become a discipline that is broader and more open to genuine interdisciplinary learning. Yet the modular account also makes it very clear that mainstream welfare economists can make a range of choices in those modules that are more in line with the status quo in current welfare economics, which would result in a very different type of capabilitarian welfare economics.

In short, while both types of capabilitarian welfare economics will depart in some sense from welfarist welfare economics, we are seeing the emergence of both mainstream capabilitarian welfare economics and heterodox capabilitarian welfare economics. The problem for the first is that it will have few means of communication with other capability theories, since it does not adopt many of the interdisciplinary choices that most other capability theories make. The problem for the latter is that it will not be taken seriously by mainstream economics, since it does not meet the narrow requirements of what counts as economics according to the vast majority of mainstream economists. Taking everything together, a capabilitarian welfare economics is possible, but (a) it will be harder to develop the capability approach in welfare economics than in some other disciplines because of the methodological and meta-theoretical clashes and restrictions, and (b) the difficult position that welfare economics occupies within mainstream economics will become even more challenging, since moving in the direction of the capability approach conflicts with the criteria that the gatekeepers in mainstream economists impose on anyone who wants to do something considered 'economics'. This may also explain why there is much less work done in welfare economics on the capability approach, compared to some other disciplines or fields in which the capability approach has made a much bigger impact.

4.11 Taking stock

In this chapter, we have engaged with a range of critiques that have been voiced about the capability approach, or debates that have developed in the capability literature. While I hope that I have been fair in representing all viewpoints, I have in many cases argued for a particular way of looking at the problem, and in a significant number of cases argued that critiques must be reformulated in order to be sound, or did not sufficiently appreciate the modular structure of the general capability approach or the distinction between the capability *approach* and capability *theories*. Several of the critiques presented in this chapter had bite as a critique of a particular type of capability theory, but not of the capability approach in general.

The next and final (and very short!) chapter will not provide a summary of the previous chapters, but rather offer some thoughts and speculations on what the future of the capability approach could look like, which issues will need to be addressed to unlock its full potential, and which limitations will always need to be reckoned with.

5. Which Future for the Capability Approach?

In the last two decades, much time and intellectual energy has been spent on trying to answer some basic questions about the capability approach. What difference does it make to existing normative frameworks? Can it really make a difference to welfare economics as we know it? How should we select capabilities, and how should these dimensions be aggregated? Is the capability approach not too individualistic? Can it properly account for power? And can it properly account for the importance of groups and the collective nature of many processes that are crucial for people's capabilities?

I believe that many of the debates that kept capability scholars busy in the last two decades have been settled, and we can move to another phase in developing the capability approach and using it to study the problems that need addressing. As many capability scholars have acknowledged (sometimes implicitly) for a very long time, and as this book has illustrated in detail, there are a variety of capability theories possible. As a consequence, one capability theory does not need to be a direct rival of another capability theory: we do not necessarily need to choose between them, and it will often be a mistake to see them as rivals. Many different capability theories can coexist. This theory-pluralism should be embraced, rather than attacked by trying to put the capability approach into a straightjacket. There is, of course, the real risk that *any* theory that is somehow 'broadening' the informational basis of evaluations and comparisons is seen as a capability theory — hence a real risk of inflation. However, the modular understanding of the

https://doi.org/10.11647/OBP.0130.05

capability approach clearly lays out the properties that *every* capability theory, application or analysis should meet, and thereby provides a powerful response to the risk of the inflation of the term 'capability theory'.

Having sorted all of this out, we are free to put the capability approach to good use. It is impossible for one person to know all the interesting paths that the capability approach should take (even if that one person benefited from comments and many helpful discussions with others). But as a start, let me just mention some lines of further thinking, research and interventions that would be interesting to explore.

First, within the disciplines in which the capability has been discussed and developed, there are plenty of opportunities to see what difference it can make if pushed all the way to its limits. In some fields, such as educational studies, the capability approach is well-developed and widely applied. But there are others in which the capability approach has so far merely been introduced, rather than being used to develop mature and complete theories. One question, which remains unanswered after our discussion in section 4.10, is whether the capability approach can provide an equally powerful alternative to utility-based welfare economics. In the literature on theories of justice, which we discussed in section 3.13, the capability approach is widely debated, but there are hardly any fully developed capabilitarian theories of justice, apart from Nussbaum's (2006b) and the theory of disadvantage by Wolff and De-Shalit (2007). We need book-length accounts of capabilitarian theories of justice, capabilitarian theories of institutional evaluation, capabilitarian theories of welfare economics, and so forth.

Second, the capability approach is, so far, almost exclusively used for evaluative and normative purposes — such as studies evaluating whether certain people are better off than others, studies trying to propose a certain policy or institution (for the effect it has on people's functionings and capabilities) rather than others, or studies arguing for justice in terms of people's capabilities. But one could also use the capability approach for *explanatory* studies, e.g. to examine which institutions or policies foster certain capabilities, or using the notions of functionings and capabilities in the analysis of people's behaviour and decision making. For example, labour economists model the decision about a person's labour supply — how many hours she would be willing to work — by looking at the costs and benefits of working more or fewer hours, but wouldn't it make much more sense to also ask how the capabilities of different options compare? For example, many adults are happy to work an equal number of hours for less pay if the work is more intrinsically rewarding or if it contributes to the creation of a public good. Another example is how we explain a parent's decision not to use formal child care, or to use it only for a very limited number of hours. If we explain this exclusively in terms of financial costs and benefits (as some policy analysts do) we don't capture the fact that the capabilities of affiliation and social relations are very different in the two scenarios. A general model of people's behaviour and decision-making should therefore not only look at the pecuniary costs and benefits of different options, but also at the different levels of valuable functionings, and the absence of functionings with a negative value, that the different options offer. The challenge of this approach is, of course, that capabilities are often merely qualitative variables, and this hampers the explanatory models that many social scientists use. But if our decision-making and behaviour is largely influenced by the capabilities that characterize different options, then surely, we should prefer (i) a more muddy and vaguer explanatory model that takes all important aspects into account above (ii) a more elegant and neat model that gives us a distorted picture of how persons act and live.[1] Some of this is already done, of course, since there is a large literature about certain functionings taken individually, e.g. in explanatory research on people's health. The suggestion I'm making here is to look at those functionings in a more systematic way, and to integrate functionings and capabilities as general categories in theories of behaviour and decision making, next to other categories such as resources and preference-satisfaction.

Third, the capability approach may well have a very important role to play in the current quest for a truly interdisciplinary conceptual framework for the social sciences and humanities. Despite the fact that universities are still to a large extent organized along disciplinary lines, there is an increasing recognition that many important questions cannot be studied properly without a unified framework or conceptual language in which all the social sciences and humanities can find their

---

1   This is a methodological point that Amartya Sen has been pressing for a very long time.

place. The capability approach may well form the nexus connecting existing disciplinary frameworks, precisely because its concepts bring together people's wellbeing and the material resources they have, the legal rules and social norms that constrain their capability sets, and so forth. The approach thereby offers important conceptual and theoretical bridges between disciplines. And it could also link evaluative and normative frameworks to descriptive and explanatory frameworks, rather than leaving the normative frameworks implicit, as is now too often done in the social sciences.

Fourth, the capability approach should be more extensively used in designing new policy tools. Citizens who endorse a broad understanding of the quality of life that gives non-material aspects a central place have been annoyed for many years by the constant assessment of economic growth as an end in itself, rather than as a means to human flourishing and the meeting of human needs. They have been saying, rightly in my view, that whether economic growth is a good thing depends, among other things, on how it affects the overall quality of life of people, as well as how other public values fare, such as ecological sustainability, and that we have very good reasons to take seriously the limits to economic growth (Jackson 2016). But those who want to put the ends of policies at the centre of the debate, and focus policy discussions more on these ultimate ends rather than on means, need to move from mere critique to developing tools that can fashion constructive proposals. The alternatives to GDP, which I briefly discussed in chapter 1, are one element that can help, but other tools are also needed.

Fifth, we have to investigate which capability theories are logically possible, but empirically implausible. The argument in this book has been that the capability approach can be developed in a wide range of capability theories and applications, and is not committed to a particular set of political or ideological commitments. But that is as far as its logical structures go, and it doesn't take a stance on empirical soundness. We need to investigate which capability theories may be logically possible, but nevertheless should be ruled out, given what we know about the plausibility of our empirical assumptions regarding conversion factors, human diversity, and structural constraints. It is highly likely that there are capability theories that are logically conceivable, yet inconsistent with some 'basic facts' about human nature and societies.

This is especially important since we want to avoid the hijacking of the capability approach by powerful societal actors or organisations who will start to propagate a very uncritical and reductionist version of the approach, and push that as the only right interpretation of it. The general account of the capability approach that I have defended in this book tries to be as politically and ideologically neutral as possible; but that doesn't mean that I personally, as a scholar who has written a lot on questions of injustice, believe that all possible capability theories are equally plausible. In fact, my own substantive work in which I have used the capability approach confirms that I do not, and that I think that a critical account of social structures and power is needed (e.g. Robeyns 2003, 2010, 2017b, 2017a). But I think we should then argue *directly* about the unjust nature of social structures, economic institutions, or social norms. I hope that the modular view presented in this book makes clear that many of the intellectual and ideological battles actually take place in arguing about the B-modules and the C-modules.

Sixth and finally, the capability approach should be used in guiding existing practices on the ground, in many different segments of society, and in many different societies of the world. This is not easy, since there are quite significant challenges for theorists to bridge the gap between their work and practices on the ground, as several theorists who engaged in such theory-practice collaborations have pointed out (e.g. Koggel 2008; Wolff 2011). Yet if the capability approach aspires to make a difference in practice — which many capability scholars do — then thinking carefully about how to move to practice without diluting the essence of the framework is crucial. Luckily, there are signs that more of these 'on-the-ground applications' are being developed, and that the capability approach is not only of interest to scholars and policy makers, but also for practitioners and citizens. One example is Solava Ibrahim's (2017) recent model for grassroots-led development, which is primarily a conceptual and theoretical framework, yet is also based on ten years of fieldwork. Another example is the practical field of social work in the Netherlands, where social work professionals have recently argued that the field is in need of a new moral compass, in order to counter the technocratic developments that, it is argued, have dominated changes in social work in recent decades. Some social workers argue that the human rights framework could provide a useful theory (Hartman, Knevel and

Reynaert 2016), while others believe that capabilities could be helpful in restoring ethical and political dimensions to the practice of social work (Braber 2013). As the discussion in section 3.14 has shown, there need not be a conflict between those two frameworks. Yet it remains to be seen in the years to come if and how the capability approach is able to guide the effective change of the entire sector of social work in countries where the traditional welfare state is under pressure.

However, with all these future extensions of the capability approach, it remains important to explicitly acknowledge its limitations. This book has shown what the capability approach has to offer, but also what needs to be added before the vague and underspecified capability framework can be developed into a more powerful capability theory or capability application. Especially the choices made in the B-modules, but also the additions made in the C-modules C1 (additional explanatory and ontological theories) and C4 (additional normative claims and principles) will be crucial for many capabilitarian theories and applications to become powerful.

There is no point in pretending that the capability approach can do more than it is able to do, since this would blind us to the *necessary* collaborations with other theories and insights that are needed. It is in those collaborations with complementary powerful theories and frameworks that the success of the future of the capability approach lies.

References

Addabbo, Tindara, Diego Lanzi and Antonella Picchio. 2010. 'Gender Budgets: A Capability Approach'. *Journal of Human Development and Capabilities* 11 (4), 479–501. http://dx.doi.org/10.1080/19452829.2010.520900

Alexandrova, Anna. 2013. 'Doing Well in the Circumstances'. *Journal of Moral Philosophy* 10 (3), 307–28. https://doi.org/10.1163/174552412X628814

Alkire, Sabina. 2002. *Valuing Freedoms. Sen's Capability Approach and Poverty Reduction*. Oxford: Oxford University Press. https://doi.org/10.1093/0199245797.001.0001

Alkire, Sabina. 2005. 'Why the Capability Approach?' *Journal of Human Development* 6 (1), 115–35. https://doi.org/10.1080/146498805200034275

Alkire, Sabina. 2008. 'Using the Capability Approach: Prospective and Evaluative Analyses'. In *The Capability Approach: Concepts, Measures, Applications*, edited by Flavio Comim, Mozaffar Qizilbash and Sabina Alkire, pp. 26–49. Cambridge: Cambridge University Press. https://doi.org/10.1017/cbo9780511492587.002

Alkire, Sabina. 2016. 'The Capability Approach and Wellbeing Measurement for Public Policy'. In *The Oxford Handbook of Wellbeing and Public Policy*, edited by Matthew D. Adler and Marc Fleurbaey, pp. 615–44. Oxford: Oxford University Press. https://doi.org/10.1093/oxfordhb/9780199325818.013.18

Alkire, Sabina and Séverine Deneulin. 2009a. 'A Normative Framework for Development'. In *An Introduction to the Human Development and Capability Approach*, edited by Séverine Deneulin and Lila Shahani, pp. 3–21. London: Earthscan.

Alkire, Sabina and Séverine Deneulin. 2009b. 'The Human Development and Capability Approach'. In *An Introduction to the Human Development and Capability Approach*, edited by Séverine Deneulin and Lila Shahani, pp. 22–48. London: Earthscan.

Alkire, Sabina and James Foster. 2011. 'Counting and Multidimensional Poverty Measurement'. *Journal of Public Economics* 95 (7), 476–87. https://doi.org/10.1016/j.jpubeco.2010.11.006

Alkire, Sabina, James Foster, Suman Seth, Maria Emma Santos, José Manuel Roche and Paola Ballon. 2015. *Multidimensional Poverty Measurement and Analysis*. New York: Oxford University Press. https://doi.org/10.1093/acprof:oso/9780199689491.001.0001

Alkire, Sabina, Mozaffar Qizilbash and Flavio Comim. 2008. 'Introduction'. In *The Capability Approach: Concepts, Measures, Applications*, edited by Flavio Comim, Mozaffar Qizilbash and Sabina Alkire, pp. 1–25. Cambridge: Cambridge University Press. https://doi.org/10.1017/cbo9780511492587.001

Anand, Sudhir and Amartya Sen. 1994. 'Sustainable Human Development'. Unpublished paper written in preparation for the 1994 Human Development Report. New York: United Nations Human Development Report Office.

Anand, Sudhir and Amartya Sen. 2000. 'Human Development and Economic Sustainability'. *World Development* 28 (12), 2029–49. https://doi.org/10.1016/s0305-750x(00)00071-1

Anderson, Elizabeth. 1999. 'What Is the Point of Equality?' *Ethics* 109 (2), 287–337. https://doi.org/10.1086/233897

Anderson, Elizabeth. 2000a. 'Beyond Homo Economicus: New Developments in Theories of Social Norms'. *Philosophy & Public Affairs* 29 (2), 170–200. https://doi.org/10.1111/j.1088-4963.2000.00170.x

Anderson, Elizabeth. 2000b. 'Optional Freedoms'. In *What's Wrong with a Free Lunch?*, edited by Joshua Cohen and Joel Rogers, pp. 70–74. Boston: Beacon Press. http://bostonreview.net/forum/basic-income-all/elizabeth-anderson-optional-freedoms

Anderson, Elizabeth. 2010. 'Justifying the Capability Approach to Justice'. In *Measuring Justice*, edited by Harry Brighouse and Ingrid Robeyns, pp. 81–100. Cambridge: Cambridge University Press. https://doi.org/10.1017/cbo9780511810916.004

Apsan Frediani, Alexandre, Alejandra Boni and Des Gasper. 2014. 'Approaching Development Projects from a Human Development and Capability Perspective'. *Journal of Human Development and Capabilities* 15 (1), 1–12. https://doi.org/10.1080/19452829.2013.879014

Ariely, Dan. 2010. *Perfectly Irrational: The Unexpected Ways We Defy Logic at Work and at Home*. London: Harper.

Arneson, Richard. 2010. 'Two Cheers for the Capabilities Approach'. In *Measuring Justice*, edited by Harry Brighouse and Ingrid Robeyns, pp. 101–27. Cambridge: Cambridge University Press. https://doi.org/10.1017/cbo9780511810916.005

Arneson, Richard. 2013. 'From Primary Goods to Capabilities to Wellbeing'. *Critical Review of International Social and Political Philosophy* 16 (2), 179–95. https://doi.org/10.1080/13698230.2012.757910

Arrow, Kenneth J., Amartya Sen and Kotaro Suzumura. 2002. *Handbook of Social Choice and Welfare*. Vol. 1. Amsterdam: Elsevier.

Arrow, Kenneth J., Amartya Sen and Kotaro Suzumura. 2010. *Handbook of Social Choice and Welfare*. Vol. 2. Amsterdam: Elsevier.

Atkinson, Anthony B. 1999. 'The Contributions of Amartya Sen to Welfare Economics'. *The Scandinavian Journal of Economics* 101 (2), 173–90. https://doi.org/10.1111/1467-9442.00151

Atkinson, Anthony B. 2001. 'The Strange Disappearance of Welfare Economics'. *Kyklos* 54 (2-3), 193–206. https://doi.org/10.1111/1467-6435.00148

Atkinson, Anthony B. 2009. 'Economics as a Moral Science'. *Economica* 76, 791–804. https://doi.org/10.1111/j.1468-0335.2009.00788.x

Barclay, Linda. 2003. 'What Kind of Liberal Is Martha Nussbaum?' *SATS: Northern European Journal of Philosophy* 4 (2), 5–24.

Barclay, Linda. 2016. 'The Importance of Equal Respect: What the Capabilities Approach Can and Should Learn from Human Rights Law'. *Political Studies* 64 (2), 385–400. https://doi.org/10.1111/1467-9248.12175

Barry, Brian. 1995. *Justice as Impartiality*. Oxford: Oxford University Press.

Barry, Brian. 2005. *Why Social Justice Matters*. Cambridge: Polity.

Barry, Brian and Matt Matravers. 2011. 'Justice'. *Routledge Encyclopedia of Philosophy*. https://www.rep.routledge.com/articles/thematic/justice/v-1

Basu, Kaushik. 1987. 'Achievements, Capabilities and the Concept of Wellbeing'. *Social Choice and Welfare* 4 (1), 69–76.

Basu, Kaushik and Luis López-Calva. 2011. 'Functionings and Capabilities'. In *Handbook of Social Choice and Welfare*, edited by Kenneth Arrow, Amartya Sen and Kotaro Suzumura, 2, pp. 153–87. Amsterdam: Elsevier. https://doi.org/10.1016/s0169-7218(10)00016-x

Baujard, Antoinette and Muriel Gilardone. 2017. 'Sen Is Not a Capability Theorist'. *Journal of Economic Methodology* 24 (1), 1–19. https://doi.org/10.1080/1350178x.2016.1257821

Berlin, Isaiah. 1969. *Four Essays on Liberty*. Oxford: Oxford University Press.

Béteille, André. 1993. 'Amartya Sen's Utopia'. *Economic and Political Weekly* 28 (16), 753–56.

Bhanu Mehta, Pratap. 2009. '"Doing" Justice'. *Outlook India*, 17 August 2009. http://www.outlookindia.com/magazine/story/doing-justice/261172

Bhargava, Rajeev. 1992. *Individualism in Social Science. Forms and Limits of a Methodology*. Oxford: Clarendon Press.

Binder, Christina and Constanze Binder. 2016. 'A Capability Perspective on Indigenous Autonomy'. *Oxford Development Studies*, 44 (3), 297–314. https://doi.org/10.1080/13600818.2016.1167178

Bleichrodt, Han and John Quiggin. 2013. 'Capabilities as Menus: A Non-Welfarist Basis for QALY Evaluation'. *Journal of Health Economics* 32 (1), 128–37. https://doi.org/10.1016/j.jhealeco.2012.10.004

Bockstael, Erika and Krushil Watene. 2016. 'Indigenous Peoples and the Capability Approach: Taking Stock'. *Oxford Development Studies* 44 (3), 265–70. https://doi.org/10.1080/13600818.2016.1204435

Boelhouwer, Jeroen. 2002. 'Quality of Life and Living Conditions in the Netherlands'. *Social Indicators Research* 58 (1–3), 113–38.

Boelhouwer, Jeroen and Ineke Stoop. 1999. 'Measuring Wellbeing in the Netherlands: The SCP Index from 1974 to 1997'. *Social Indicators Research* 48 (1), 51–75.

Boni, Alejandra and Melanie Walker. 2013. *Human Development and Capabilities: Re-Imagining the University of the Twenty-First Century*. London: Routledge. https://doi.org/10.4324/9780203075081

Boulding, Kenneth E. 1969. 'Economics as a Moral Science'. *The American Economic Review* 59 (1), 1–12.

Braber, Collin den. 2013. 'The Introduction of the Capability Approach in Social Work across a Neoliberal Europe'. *Journal of Social Intervention: Theory and Practice* 22 (4), 61–77. https://doi.org/10.18352/jsi.380

Brighouse, Harry. 2006. *On Education*. London: Routledge. https://doi.org/10.4324/9780203390740

Brighouse, Harry and Ingrid Robeyns. 2010. *Measuring Justice: Primary Goods and Capabilities*. Cambridge: Cambridge University Press. https://doi.org/10.1017/cbo9780511810916

Brock, Gillian and Soran Reader. 2002. 'Needs-Centered Ethical Theory'. *The Journal of Value Inquiry* 36 (4), 425–34. https://doi.org/10.1023/a:1021910832459

Browne, Jude and Marc Stears. 2005. 'Capabilities, Resources, and Systematic Injustice: A Case of Gender Inequality'. *Politics, Philosophy & Economics* 4 (3), 355–73. https://doi.org/10.1177/1470594x05056608

Burchardt, Tania. 2004. 'Capabilities and Disability: The Capabilities Framework and the Social Model of Disability'. *Disability & Society* 19 (7), 735–51. https://doi.org/10.1080/0968759042000284213

Burchardt, Tania. 2005. 'Are One Man's Rags Another Man's Riches? Identifying Adaptive Expectations Using Panel Data'. *Social Indicators Research* 74 (1), 57–102. https://doi.org/10.1007/s11205-005-6519-y

Burchardt, Tania. 2006. 'Happiness and Social Policy: Barking up the Right Tree in the Wrong Neck of the Woods'. In *Social Policy Review 18: Analysis and Debate in Social Policy, 2006*, edited by Linda Bauld, Karen Clarke and Tony Maltby, pp. 144–59. Bristol: Policy Press. https://doi.org/10.1332/policypress/9781861348449.003.0008

Burchardt, Tania. 2009. 'Agency Goals, Adaptation and Capability Sets'. *Journal of Human Development and Capabilities* 10 (1), 3–19. https://doi.org/10.1080/14649880802675044

Burchardt, Tania. 2010. 'Time, Income and Substantive Freedom: A Capability Approach'. *Time & Society* 19 (3), 318–44. https://doi.org/10.1177/0961463x10369754

Burchardt, Tania and Polly Vizard. 2011. '"Operationalizing" the Capability Approach as a Basis for Equality and Human Rights Monitoring in Twenty-first-century Britain'. *Journal of Human Development and Capabilities* 12 (1), 91–119. https://doi.org/10.1080/19452829.2011.541790

Byskov, Morten Fibieger. Forthcoming. 'Methods for the Selection of Capabilities and Functionings'. In *New Frontiers of the Capability Approach*, edited by Flavio Comim, Shailaja Fennel and P. B. Anand. Cambridge: Cambridge University Press.

Byskov, Morten Fibieger. 2017. 'Democracy, Philosophy, and the Selection of Capabilities'. *Journal of Human Development and Capabilities* 18 (1), 1–16. https://doi.org/10.1080/19452829.2015.1091809

Caney, Simon. 2016. 'The Struggle for Climate Justice in a Non-Ideal World'. *Midwest Studies in Philosophy* 40 (1), 9–26. https://doi.org/10.1111/misp.12044

Canoy, Marcel, Frédéric Lerais and Erik Schokkaert. 2010. 'Applying the Capability Approach to Policy-Making: The Impact Assessment of the EU-Proposal on Organ Donation'. *The Journal of Socio-Economics* 39 (3), 391–99.

Carter, Ian. 2014. 'Is the Capability Approach Paternalist?' *Economics and Philosophy* 30 (1), 75–98. https://doi.org/10.1017/S0266267114000054

Chiappero-Martinetti, Enrica. 1994. 'A New Approach to Evaluation of Wellbeing and Poverty by Fuzzy Set Theory'. *Giornale Degli Economisti E Annali Di Economia* 7 (9), 367–88.

Chiappero-Martinetti, Enrica. 2000. 'A Multidimensional Assessment of Wellbeing Based on Sen's Functioning Approach'. *Rivista Internazionale Di Scienze Sociali* 108 (2), 207–39.

Chiappero-Martinetti, Enrica. 2006. 'Capability Approach and Fuzzy Set Theory: Description, Aggregation and Inference Issues'. In *Fuzzy Set Approach to Multidimensional Poverty Measurement*, edited by Chille Lemmi and Gianni Betti, pp. 93–113. New York: Springer. https://doi.org/10.1007/978-0-387-34251-1_6

Chiappero-Martinetti, Enrica. 2008. 'Complexity and Vagueness in the Capability Approach: Strength or Weakness?' In *The Capability Approach: Concepts, Measures, Applications*, edited by Flavio Comim, Mozaffar Qizilbash and Sabina Alkire, pp. 268–309. Cambridge: Cambridge University Press. https://doi.org/10.1017/cbo9780511492587.010

Chiappero-Martinetti, Enrica and José Manuel Roche. 2009. 'Operationalization of the Capability Approach, from Theory to Practice: A Review of Techniques and Empirical Applications'. In *Debating Global Society. Reach and Limit of the Capability Approach*, edited by Enrica Chiappero-Martinetti, pp. 157–201. Milan: Feltrinelli.

Claassen, Rutger. 2009. 'Institutional Pluralism and the Limits of the Market'. *Politics, Philosophy & Economics* 8 (4), 420–47. https://doi.org/10.1177/1470594x09345479

Claassen, Rutger. 2011. 'Making Capability Lists: Philosophy versus Democracy'. *Political Studies* 59 (3), 491–508. https://doi.org/10.1111/j.1467-9248.2010.00862.x

Claassen, Rutger. 2014. 'Capability Paternalism'. *Economics and Philosophy* 30 (1), 57–73. https://doi.org/10.1017/s0266267114000042

Claassen, Rutger. 2015. 'The Capability to Hold Property'. *Journal of Human Development and Capabilities* 16 (2), 220–36. https://doi.org/10.1080/19452829.2014.939061

Claassen, Rutger. 2016. 'An Agency-Based Capability Theory of Justice'. *European Journal of Philosophy* 24 (3), Early View. http://dx.doi.org/10.1111/ejop.12195

Claassen, Rutger and Marcus Düwell. 2013. 'The Foundations of Capability Theory: Comparing Nussbaum and Gewirth'. *Ethical Theory and Moral Practice* 16 (3), 493–510. https://doi.org/10.1007/s10677-012-9361-8

Clark, David A. 2002. *Visions of Development: A Study of Human Values*. Cheltenham: Edward Elgar Publishing.

Clark, David A. 2005. 'Sen's Capability Approach and the Many Spaces of Human Wellbeing'. *The Journal of Development Studies* 41 (8), 1339–68. https://doi.org/10.1080/00220380500186853

Clark, David A. 2009. 'Adaptation, Poverty and Well-being: Some Issues and Observations with Special Reference to the Capability Approach and Development Studies'. *Journal of Human Development and Capabilities* 10 (1), 21–42. https://doi.org/10.1080/14649880802675051

Clark, David A. and Mozaffar Qizilbash. 2005. 'Core Poverty, Basic Capabilities and Vagueness: An Application to the South African Context', Global Poverty Research Group Working Paper Series, 26. https://ora.ox.ac.uk/objects/uuid:3d2942da-fdce-47a0-880c-80591fe85d8c

Coast, Joanna, Terry N. Flynn, Lucy Natarajan, Kerry Sproston, Jane Lewis, Jordan J. Louviere and Tim J. Peters. 2008. 'Valuing the ICECAP Capability Index for Older People'. *Social Science & Medicine* 67 (5), 874–82. https://doi.org/10.1016/j.socscimed.2008.05.015

Coast, Joanna, Richard D Smith and Paula Lorgelly. 2008. 'Welfarism, Extra-Welfarism and Capability: The Spread of Ideas in Health Economics'. *Social Science & Medicine* 67 (7), 1190–98. https://doi.org/10.1016/j.socscimed.2008.06.027

Cohen, G. A. 1993. 'Equality of What? On Welfare, Goods and Capabilities'. In *The Quality of Life*, edited by Martha Nussbaum and Amartya Sen, pp. 9–29. Oxford: Clarendon Press. https://doi.org/10.1093/0198287976.003.0002

Colander, David and Arjo Klamer. 1987. 'The Making of an Economist'. *The Journal of Economic Perspectives* 1 (2), 95–111. https://doi.org/10.1257/jep.1.2.95

Conradie, Ina. 2013. 'Can Deliberate Efforts to Realise Aspirations Increase Capabilities? A South African Case Study'. *Oxford Development Studies* 41 (2), 189–219. https://doi.org/10.1080/13600818.2013.790949

Conradie, Ina and Ingrid Robeyns. 2013. 'Aspirations and Human Development Interventions'. *Journal of Human Development and Capabilities* 14 (4), 559–80. https://doi.org/10.1080/19452829.2013.827637

Coyle, Diane. 2015. *GDP: A Brief but Affectionate History*. Princeton: Princeton University Press. https://doi.org/10.1515/9781400873630

Crabtree, Andrew. 2012. 'A Legitimate Freedom Approach to Sustainability: Sen, Scanlon and the Inadequacy of the Human Development Index'. *International Journal of Social Quality* 2 (1), 24–40. https://doi.org/10.3167/ijsq.2012.020103

Crabtree, Andrew. 2013. 'Sustainable Development: Does the Capability Approach Have Anything to Offer? Outlining a Legitimate Freedom Approach'. *Journal of Human Development and Capabilities* 14 (1), 40–57. https://doi.org/10.1080/19452829.2012.748721

Cripps, Elizabeth. 2010. 'Saving the Polar Bear, Saving the World: Can the Capabilities Approach Do Justice to Humans, Animals and Ecosystems?' *Res Publica* 16, 1–22. https://doi.org/10.1007/s11158-010-9106-2

Crisp, Roger. 2017. 'Wellbeing'. *Stanford Encyclopedia of Philosophy*. https://plato.stanford.edu/archives/fall2017/entries/wellbeing/

Crocker, David A. 1992. 'Functioning and Capability: The Foundations of Sen's and Nussbaum's Development Ethic'. *Political Theory* 20 (4), 584–612. https://doi.org/10.1177/0090591792020004003

Crocker, David A. 1995. 'Functioning and Capability: The Foundations of Sen's and Nussbaum's Development Ethic. Part 2'. In *Women, Culture and Development: A Study of Human Capabilities*, edited by Martha Nussbaum and Jonathan Glover, pp. 153–98. Oxford: Clarendon Press. https://doi.org/10.1093/0198289642.003.0007

Crocker, David A. 2008. *Ethics of Global Development. Agency, Capability, and Deliberative Democracy*. Cambridge: Cambridge University Press. https://doi.org/10.1017/cbo9780511492594

Crocker, David A. and Ingrid Robeyns. 2009. 'Capability and Agency'. In *Amartya Sen*, edited by Christopher W. Morris, pp. 60–90. Cambridge: Cambridge University Press. https://doi.org/10.1017/cbo9780511800511.005

Cudd, Ann E. 2014. 'Commitment as Motivation: Amartya Sen's Theory of Agency and the Explanation of Behaviour'. *Economics and Philosophy* 30 (1), 35–56. https://doi.org/10.1017/s0266267114000030

Cummins, Robert A., Richard Eckersley, Julie Pallant, Jackie Van Vugt and Roseanne Misajon. 2003. 'Developing a National Index of Subjective Wellbeing: The Australian Unity Wellbeing Index'. *Social Indicators Research* 64 (2), 159–90. https://doi.org/10.1023/a:1024704320683

De Herdt, Tom. 2008. 'Social Policy and the Ability to Appear in Public without Shame: Some Lessons from a Food Relief Programme in Kinshasa'. In *The Capability Approach. Concepts, Measures, and Applications*, edited by Flavio Comim, Mozaffar Qizilbash and Sabina Alkire, pp. 458–88. Cambridge: Cambridge University Press. https://doi.org/10.1017/cbo9780511492587.016

Decancq, Koen and María Ana Lugo. 2013. 'Weights in Multidimensional Indices of Wellbeing: An Overview'. *Econometric Reviews* 32 (1), 7–34. https://doi.org/10.1080/07474938.2012.690641

Deneulin, Séverine. 2006a. 'Individual Wellbeing, Migration Remittances and the Common Good'. *The European Journal of Development Research* 18 (1), 45–58. https://doi.org/10.1080/09578810600572353

Deneulin, Séverine. 2006b. *The Capability Approach and the Praxis of Development*. Houndmills: Palgrave Macmillan. https://doi.org/10.1057/9780230627253

Deneulin, Séverine. 2014. *Wellbeing, Justice and Development Ethics*. London: Earthscan. https://doi.org/10.4324/9781315867090

Deneulin, Séverine and Frances Stewart. 2002. 'Amartya Sen's Contribution to Development Thinking'. *Studies in Comparative International Development* 37 (2), 61–70. https://doi.org/10.1007/bf02686262

Deveaux, Monique. 2015. 'The Global Poor as Agents of Justice'. *Journal of Moral Philosophy* 12 (2), 125–50. https://doi.org/10.1163/17455243-4681029

Di Tommaso, Maria Laura. 2007. 'Children Capabilities: A Structural Equation Model for India'. *The Journal of Socio-Economics* 36 (3), 436–50. https://doi.org/10.1016/j.socec.2006.12.006

Diener, Ed and Martin E. P. Seligman. 2004. 'Beyond Money: Toward an Economy of Wellbeing'. *Psychological Science in the Public Interest* 5 (1), 1–31. https://doi.org/10.1111/j.0963-7214.2004.00501001.x

Doyal, Len and Ian Gough. 1991. *A Theory of Human Need*. New York: Palgrave Macmillan. https://doi.org/10.1007/978-1-349-21500-3

Drèze, Jean and Amartya Sen. 1996. *India: Economic Development and Social Opportunity*. Oxford: Clarendon Press.

Drèze, Jean and Amartya Sen. 2002. *India: Development and Participation*. New Delhi: Oxford University Press. https://doi.org/10.1093/acprof:o so/9780199257492.001.0001

Drèze, Jean and Amartya Sen. 2013. *An Uncertain Glory. India and Its Contradictions*. London: Alan Lane.

Driver, Julia. 2014. 'The History of Utilitarianism'. *Stanford Encyclopedia of Philosophy*. https://plato.stanford.edu/archives/win2014/entries/ utilitarianism-history/

Drydyk, Jay. 2011. 'Responsible Pluralism, Capabilities, and Human Rights'. *Journal of Human Development and Capabilities* 12 (1), 39–61. https://doi.org/10 .1080/19452829.2011.541734

Drydyk, Jay. 2012. 'A Capability Approach to Justice as a Virtue'. *Ethical Theory and Moral Practice* 15 (1), 23–38. https://doi.org/10.1007/s10677-011-9327-2

Drydyk, Jay. 2013. 'Empowerment, Agency, and Power'. *Journal of Global Ethics* 9 (3), 249–62. https://doi.org/10.1080/17449626.2013.818374

Dryzek, John S. 2000. *Deliberative Democracy and Beyond: Liberals, Critics, Contestations*. Oxford: Oxford University Press. https://doi. org/10.1093/019925043x.001.0001

Dworkin, Ronald. 1981. 'What Is Equality? Part 2: Equality of Resources'. *Philosophy & Public Affairs*, 10 (4), 283–345.

Dworkin, Ronald. 2000. *Sovereign Virtue: The Theory and Practice of Equality*. Cambridge, MA: Harvard University Press.

Elster, Jon. 1983. *Sour Grapes*. Cambridge: Cambridge University Press. https:// doi.org/10.1017/cbo9781139171694

Elster, Jon. 1989. *The Cement of Society: A Survey of Social Order*. Cambridge: Cambridge University Press. https://doi.org/10.1017/cbo9780511624995

English, Jane. 1975. 'Abortion and the Concept of a Person'. *Canadian Journal of Philosophy* 5 (2), 233–43. https://doi.org/10.1080/00455091.1975.10716109

Engster, Daniel. 2007. *The Heart of Justice. Care Ethics and Political Theory*. New York: Oxford University Press. https://doi.org/10.1093/acprof:o so/9780199214358.001.0001

Entwistle, Vikki A. and Ian S. Watt. 2013. 'Treating Patients as Persons: A Capabilities Approach to Support Delivery of Person-Centered Care'. *The American Journal of Bioethics* 13 (8), 29–39. https://doi.org/10.1080/15265161. 2013.802060

Eriksson, Lina, James Mahmud Rice and Robert E. Goodin. 2007. 'Temporal Aspects of Life Satisfaction'. *Social Indicators Research* 80 (3), 511–33. https:// doi.org/10.1007/s11205-006-0005-z

Evans, Peter. 2002. 'Collective Capabilities, Culture, and Amartya Sen's Development as Freedom'. *Studies in Comparative International Development* 37 (2), 54–60. https://doi.org/10.1007/bf02686261

Feldman, Shelley and Paul Gellert. 2006. 'The Seductive Quality of Central Human Capabilities: Sociological Insights into Nussbaum and Sen's Disagreement'. *Economy and Society* 35 (3), 423–52. https://doi.org/10.1080/03085140600845008

Fernández-Baldor, Álvaro, Alejandra Boni, Pau Lillo and Andrés Hueso. 2014. 'Are Technological Projects Reducing Social Inequalities and Improving People's Wellbeing? A Capability Approach Analysis of Renewable Energy-Based Electrification Projects in Cajamarca, Peru'. *Journal of Human Development and Capabilities* 15 (1), 13–27. https://doi.org/10.1080/19452829.2013.837035

Ferrer-i-Carbonell, Ada. 2005. 'Income and Wellbeing: An Empirical Analysis of the Comparison Income Effect'. *Journal of Public Economics* 89 (5), 997–1019. https://doi.org/10.1016/j.jpubeco.2004.06.003

Ferrer-i-Carbonell, Ada and John M. Gowdy. 2007. 'Environmental Degradation and Happiness'. *Ecological Economics* 60 (3), 509–16. https://doi.org/10.1016/j.ecolecon.2005.12.005

Fletcher, Guy. 2015. *The Routledge Handbook of Philosophy of Wellbeing*. London and New York: Routledge.

Fleurbaey, Marc. 2002. 'Development, Capabilities and Freedom'. *Studies in Comparative International Development* 37 (2), 71–77. https://doi.org/10.1007/bf02686263

Fleurbaey, Marc. 2009. 'Beyond GDP: The Quest for a Measure of Social Welfare'. *Journal of Economic Literature* 47 (4), 1029–75. https://doi.org/10.1257/jel.47.4.1029

Fleurbaey, Marc and Didier Blanchet. 2013. *Beyond GDP: Measuring Welfare and Assessing Sustainability*. Oxford: Oxford University Press. https://doi.org/10.1093/acprof:oso/9780199767199.001.0001

Folbre, Nancy. 1994. *Who Pays for the Kids?: Gender and the Structures of Constraint*. New York: Routledge. https://doi.org/10.4324/9780203168295

Folbre, Nancy. 2008. *Valuing Children*. Harvard University Press.

Folbre, Nancy and Michael Bittman. 2004. *Family Time: The Social Organization of Care*. London: Routledge. https://doi.org/10.4324/9780203411650

Fourcade, Marion, Etienne Ollion and Yann Algan. 2015. 'The Superiority of Economists'. *The Journal of Economic Perspectives* 29 (1), 89–113. https://doi.org/10.1257/jep.29.1.89

Freeman, Samuel. 2006. 'Bookreview: Frontiers of Justice'. *Texas Law Review* 85, 385–430.

Frey, Bruno S. and Alois Stutzer. 2002. 'What Can Economists Learn from Happiness Research?' *Journal of Economic Literature* 40 (2), 402–35. https://doi.org/10.1257/jel.40.2.402

Fukuda-Parr, Sakiko. 2003. 'The Human Development Paradigm: Operationalizing Sen's Ideas on Capabilities'. *Feminist Economics* 9 (2–3), 301–17. https://doi.org/10.1080/1354570022000077980

Fukuda-Parr, Sakiko. 2009. 'Human Rights and Human Development'. In *Arguments for a Better World. Essays in Honor of Amartya Sen. Volume II: Society, Institutions, and Development*, edited by Kaushik Basu and Ravi Kanbur, pp. 76–99. Oxford: Oxford University Press. https://doi.org/10.1093/acprof:o so/9780199239979.003.0006

Fukuda-Parr, Sakiko. 2011. 'The Metrics of Human Rights: Complementarities of the Human Development and Capabilities Approach'. *Journal of Human Development and Capabilities* 12 (1), 73–89. https://doi.org/10.1080/19452829. 2011.541750

Fukuda-Parr, Sakiko and A. K. Shiva Kumar. 2003. 'Introduction'. In *Readings in Human Development*, edited by Sakiko Fukuda-Parr and A. K. Shiva Kumar, pp. xxi–xxxi. New Delhi: Oxford University Press.

Gaertner, Wulf. 2009. *A Primer in Social Choice Theory: Revised Edition*. Oxford: Oxford University Press.

Gaertner, Wulf and Yongsheng Xu. 2006. 'Capability Sets as the Basis of a New Measure of Human Development'. *Journal of Human Development* 7 (3), 311–21. https://doi.org/10.1080/14649880600815891

Gaertner, Wulf and Yongsheng Xu. 2008. 'A New Class of Measures of the Standard of Living Based on Functionings'. *Economic Theory* 35 (2), 201–15. https://doi.org/10.1007/s00199-007-0229-4

Gandjour, Afschin. 2008. 'Mutual Dependency between Capabilities and Functionings in Amartya Sen's Capability Approach'. *Social Choice and Welfare* 31 (2), 345–50. https://doi.org/10.1007/s00355-007-0283-7

Gasper, Des. 1997. 'Sen's Capability Approach and Nussbaum's Capabilities Ethic'. *Journal of International Development* 9 (2), 281–302. https://doi. org/10.1002/(sici)1099-1328(199703)9:2%3C281::aid-jid438%3E3.0.co;2-k

Gasper, Des. 2004. *The Ethics of Development. From Economism to Human Development*. Edinburgh: Edinburgh University Press.

Gasper, Des. 2007. 'What Is the Capability Approach? Its Core, Rationale, Partners and Dangers'. *The Journal of Socio-Economics* 36, 335–59. https://doi. org/10.1016/j.socec.2006.12.001

Gasper, Des. 2010. 'Understanding the Diversity of Conceptions of Wellbeing and Quality of Life'. *The Journal of Socio-Economics* 39 (3), 351–60. https://doi. org/10.1016/j.socec.2009.11.006

Gasper, Des and Irene Van Staveren. 2003. 'Development as Freedom — and as What Else?' *Feminist Economics* 9 (2–3), 137–61. https://doi. org/10.1080/1354570032000078663

Gheaus, Anca. 2011. 'Arguments for Nonparental Care for Children'. *Social Theory and Practice* 37 (3), 483–509. https://doi.org/10.5840/soctheorpract201137328

Gheaus, Anca and Ingrid Robeyns. 2011. 'Equality-Promoting Parental Leave'. *Journal of Social Philosophy* 42 (2), 173–91. https://doi.org/10.1111/j.1467-9833.2011.01525.x

Gilabert, Pablo. 2009. 'The Feasibility of Basic Socioeconomic Human Rights: A Conceptual Exploration'. *The Philosophical Quarterly* 59 (237), 659–81. https://doi.org/10.1111/j.1467-9213.2008.590.x

Gilabert, Pablo. 2013. 'The Capability Approach and the Debate between Humanist and Political Perspectives on Human Rights. A Critical Survey'. *Human Rights Review* 14 (4), 299–325. https://doi.org/10.1007/s12142-013-0269-z

Gill, Kaveri. 2010. *Of Poverty and Plastic. Scavenging and Scrap Trading Entrepreneurs in India's Urban Informal Economy.* New Delhi: Oxford University Press. https://doi.org/10.1093/acprof:oso/9780198060864.001.0001

Gore, Charles. 1997. 'Irreducibly Social Goods and the Informational Basis of Amartya Sen's Capability Approach'. *Journal of International Development* 9 (2), 235–50. https://doi.org/10.1002/(sici)1099-1328(199703)9:2%3C235::aid-jid436%3E3.0.co;2-j

Gore, Charles. 2000. 'The Rise and Fall of the Washington Consensus as a Paradigm for Developing Countries'. *World Development* 28 (5), 789–804. https://doi.org/10.1016/s0305-750x(99)00160-6

Gotoh, Reiko, Kotaro Suzumura and Naoki Yoshihara. 2005. 'Extended Social Ordering Functions for Rationalizing Fair Allocation Rules as Game Forms in the Sense of Rawls and Sen'. *International Journal of Economic Theory* 1 (1), 21–41. https://doi.org/10.1111/j.1742-7363.2005.00003.x

Gotoh, Reiko and Naoki Yoshihara. 2003. 'A class of fair distribution rules à la Rawls and Sen'. *Economic Theory* 22 (1), 63–88. https://doi.org/10.1007/s00199-002-0280-0

Grewal, Ini, Jane Lewis, Terry Flynn, Jackie Brown, John Bond and Joanna Coast. 2006. 'Developing Attributes for a Generic Quality of Life Measure for Older People: Preferences or Capabilities?' *Social Science & Medicine* 62 (8), 1891–901. https://doi.org/10.1016/j.socscimed.2005.08.023

Gutmann, Amy and Dennis Thompson. 2004. *Why Deliberative Democracy?* Princeton: Princeton University Press. https://doi.org/10.1515/9781400826339

Hagerty, Michael R., Robert A. Cummins, Abbott L. Ferriss, Kenneth Land, Alex C. Michalos, Mark Peterson, Andrew Sharpe, Joseph Sirgy and Joachim Vogel. 2001. 'Quality of Life Indexes for National Policy: Review and Agenda for Research'. *Social Indicators Research* 55 (1), 1–96. https://doi.org/10.1023/a:1010811312332

Harnacke, Caroline. 2013. 'Disability and Capability: Exploring the Usefulness of Martha Nussbaum's Capabilities Approach for the UN Disability Rights Convention'. *The Journal of Law, Medicine & Ethics* 41 (4), 768–80. https://doi.org/10.1111/jlme.12088

Hart, Caroline S. 2009. 'Quo Vadis? The Capability Approach and New Directions for the Philosophy of Educational Research'. *Studies in Philosophy of Education* 28 (5), 391–402. https://doi.org/10.1007/s11217-009-9128-4.

Hart, Caroline S. 2012. 'The Capability Approach and Education'. *Cambridge Journal of Education* 42 (3), 275–82. http://dx.doi.org/10.1080/030576 4X.2012.706393

Hartman, Jeannette, Jeroen Knevel and Didier Reynaert. 2016. 'Manifest: Stel Mensenrechten Centraal in Sociaal Werk'. *Sociale Vraagstukken,* 26 May 2016. http://www.socialevraagstukken.nl/stel-mensenrechten-centraal-in-het-sociaal-werk

Hausman, Daniel. 1992. 'When Jack and Jill Make a Deal'. *Social Philosophy and Policy* 9 (1), 95–113. https://doi.org/10.1017/s0265052500003617

Hausman, Daniel, Michael McPherson and Debra Satz. 2017. *Economic Analysis, Moral Philosophy, and Public Policy.* Cambridge: Cambridge University Press. https://doi.org/10.1017/cbo9780511754289

Heath, Joseph. 2006. 'The Benefits of Cooperation'. *Philosophy & Public Affairs* 34 (4), 313–51. https://doi.org/10.1111/j.1088-4963.2006.00073.x

Hees, M. van. 2013. 'Rights, Goals, and Capabilities'. *Politics, Philosophy and Economics* 12 (3), 247–59. https://doi.org/10.1177/1470594x12447787

Hick, Rod and Tania Burchardt. 2016. 'Capability Deprivation'. In *The Oxford Handbook of the Social Science of Poverty,* edited by David Brady and Linda M. Burton, pp. 75–92. Oxford: Oxford University Press. https://doi.org/10.1093/oxfordhb/9780199914050.013.5

Hill, Marianne. 2003. 'Development as Empowerment'. *Feminist Economics* 9 (2–3), 117–35. https://doi.org/10.1080/1354570022000077962

Hochschild, Adam. 1999. *King Leopold's Ghost: A Story of Greed, Terror, and Heroism in Colonial Africa.* Boston: Mariner Books.

Holland, Breena. 2008. 'Justice and the Environment in Nussbaum's "Capabilities Approach": Why Sustainable Ecological Capacity Is a Meta-Capability'. *Political Research Quarterly* 61 (2), 319–32. https://doi.org/10.1177/1065912907306471

Holland, Breena. 2014. *Allocating the Earth. A Distributive Framework for Protecting Capabilities in Environmental Law and Policy.* Oxford: Oxford University Press. https://doi.org/10.1093/acprof:oso/9780199692071.001.0001

Holland, Breena and Amy Linch. 2016. 'Cultivating Human and Non-Human Capabilities'. In *The Oxford Handbook of Environmental Political Theory,* edited by Teena Gabrielson, Cheryl Hall, John M. Meyer and David Schlosberg, pp. 413–28. Oxford: Oxford University Press. https://doi.org/10.1093/oxfordhb/9780199685271.013.9

Ibrahim, Solava. 2006. 'From Individual to Collective Capabilities: The Capability Approach as a Conceptual Framework for Self-help'. *Journal of Human Development* 7 (3), 397–416. https://doi.org/10.1080/14649880600815982

Ibrahim, Solava. 2009. 'Self-Help: A Catalyst for Human Agency and Collective Capabilities'. In *Debating Global Society. Reach and Limit of the Capability Approach*, edited by Enrica Chiappero-Martinetti, pp. 233–65. Milan: Feltrinelli.

Ibrahim, Solava. 2011. 'A Tale of Two Egypts: Contrasting State-Reported Macro-Trends with Micro-Voices of the Poor'. *Third World Quarterly* 32 (7), 1347–68. https://doi.org/10.1080/01436597.2011.600108

Ibrahim, Solava. 2017. 'How to Build Collective Capabilities: The 3C-Model for Grassroots-Led Development'. *Journal of Human Development and Capabilities* 18 (2), 197–222. https://doi.org/10.1080/19452829.2016.1270918

Jackson, Tim. 2016. *Prosperity without Growth. Economics for a Finite Planet.* Second edition. London: Taylor and Francis. https://doi.org/10.4324/9781849774338

Jaggar, Alison M. 2002. 'Challenging Women's Global Inequalities: Some Priorities for Western Philosophers'. *Philosophical Topics* 30 (2), 229–52. https://doi.org/10.5840/philtopics20023022

Jaggar, Alison M. 2006. 'Reasoning about Well-being: Nussbaum's Methods of Justifying the Capabilities'. *Journal of Political Philosophy* 14 (3), 301–22. https://doi.org/10.1111/j.1467-9760.2006.00253.x

Kagan, Shelly. 1998. 'Rethinking Intrinsic Value'. *The Journal of Ethics* 2 (4), 277–97. https://doi.org/10.1023/a:1009782403793

Kahneman, Daniel. 2011. *Thinking Fast and Slow.* London: Penguin Books.

Kahneman, Daniel and Alan B. Krueger. 2006. 'Developments in the Measurement of Subjective Wellbeing'. *The Journal of Economic Perspectives* 20 (1), 3–24. https://doi.org/10.1257/089533006776526030

Kahneman, Daniel, Alan B. Krueger, David Schkade, Norbert Schwarz and Arthur A. Stone. 2006. 'Would You Be Happier If You Were Richer? A Focusing Illusion'. *Science* 312 (5782), 1908–10. https://doi.org/10.1126/science.1129688

Kamm, F. M. 2011. 'Sen on Justice and Rights: A Review Essay'. *Philosophy & Public Affairs* 39 (1), 82–104. https://doi.org/10.1111/j.1088-4963.2011.01199.x

Karnein, Anja. 2014. 'Putting Fairness in Its Place: Why There Is a Duty to Take up the Slack'. *The Journal of Philosophy* 111 (11), 593–607. https://doi.org/10.5840/jphil20141111138

Kaufman, Alexander. 2005. 'What Goods Do to (and for) People'. In *Capabilities Equality. Basic Issues and Problems*, edited by Alexander Kaufman, pp. 117–29. New York: Routledge. https://doi.org/10.4324/9780203799444

Kaufman, Alexander. 2005 *Capabilities Equality: Basic Issues and Problems.* New York: Routledge. https://doi.org/10.4324/9780203799444

Khader, Serene J. 2009. 'Adaptive Preferences and Procedural Autonomy'. *Journal of Human Development and Capabilities* 10 (2), 169–87. https://doi.org/10.1080/19452820902940851

Khader, Serene J. 2011. *Adaptive Preferences and Women's Empowerment.* New York: Oxford University Press. https://doi.org/10.1093/acprof:o so/9780199777884.001.0001

Khader, Serene J. 2012. 'Must Theorising about Adaptive Preferences Deny Women's Agency?' *Journal of Applied Philosophy* 29 (4), 302–17. https://doi. org/10.1111/j.1468-5930.2012.00575.x

Khader, Serene J. 2013. 'Identifying Adaptive Preferences in Practice: Lessons from Postcolonial Feminisms'. *Journal of Global Ethics* 9 (3), 311–27. https:// doi.org/10.1080/17449626.2013.818379

Kittay, Eva Feder. 1999. *Love's Labor: Essays on Women, Equality and Dependency.* New York: Routledge. https://doi.org/10.4324/9781315021218

Klasen, Stephan. 1994. '"Missing Women" Reconsidered'. *World Development* 22 (7), 1061–71. https://doi.org/10.1016/0305-750x(94)90148-1

Klasen, Stephan. 2000. 'Measuring Poverty and Deprivation in South Africa'. *Review of Income and Wealth* 46 (1), 33–58. https://doi. org/10.1111/j.1475-4991.2000.tb00390.x

Klasen, Stephan and Claudia Wink. 2003. '"Missing Women": Revisiting the Debate'. *Feminist Economics* 9 (2/3), 263–99. https://doi. org/10.1080/1354570022000077999

Kleine, Dorothea. 2010. 'ICT4WHAT? — Using the Choice Framework to Operationalise the Capability Approach to Development'. *Journal of International Development* 22 (5), 674–92. https://doi.org/10.1002/jid.1719

Kleine, Dorothea. 2011. 'The Capability Approach and the "Medium of Choice": Steps Towards Conceptualising Information and Communication Technologies for Development'. *Ethics and Information Technology* 13 (2), 119–30. https://doi.org/10.1007/s10676-010-9251-5

Kleine, Dorothea. 2013. *Technologies of Choice?: ICTs, Development, and the Capabilities Approach.* Cambridge, MA: MIT Press.

Knight, Carl. 2017. 'Reflective Equilibrium'. In *Methods in Analytical Political Theory,* edited by Adrian Blau, pp. 46–64. Cambridge: Cambridge University Press. https://doi.org/10.1017/9781316162576.005

Koggel, Christine. 2003. 'Globalization and Women's Paid Work: Expanding Freedom?' *Feminist Economics* 9 (2–3), 163–84. https://doi. org/10.1080/1354570022000077935

Koggel, Christine. 2008. 'Theory to Practice and Practice to Theory? Lessons from Local NGO Empowerment Projects in Indonesia'. *The Southern Journal of Philosophy* 46 (S1), 111–30. https://doi.org/10.1111/j.2041-6962.2008.tb00158.x

Koggel, Christine. 2013. 'A Critical Analysis of Recent Work on Empowerment: Implications for Gender'. *Journal of Global Ethics* 9 (3), 263–75. https://doi.org /10.1080/17449626.2013.818383

Krishnakumar, Jaya. 2007. 'Going Beyond Functionings to Capabilities: An Econometric Model to Explain and Estimate Capabilities'. *Journal of Human Development* 8 (1), 39–63. https://doi.org/10.1080/14649880601101408

Krishnakumar, Jaya and Paola Ballon. 2008. 'Estimating Basic Capabilities: A Structural Equation Model Applied to Bolivia'. *World Development* 36 (6), 992–1010. https://doi.org/10.1016/j.worlddev.2007.10.006

Krishnakumar, Jaya and Anirudh Lal Nagar. 2008. 'On Exact Statistical Properties of Multidimensional Indices Based on Principal Components, Factor Analysis, MIMIC and Structural Equation Models'. *Social Indicators Research* 86 (3), 481–96. https://doi.org/10.1007/s11205-007-9181-8

Kukathas, Chandran. 2007. 'Liberty'. In *A Companion to Contemporary Political Philosophy*, edited by Robert E. Goodin, Philip Pettit and Thomas Pogge, Second edition, Volume II, pp. 685–98. Oxford: Blackwell. https://doi.org/10.1111/b.9781405136532.2007.00040.x

Kuklys, Wiebke. 2005. *Amartya Sen's Capability Approach: Theoretical Insights and Empirical Applications*. Berlin: Springer. https://doi.org/10.1007/3-540-28083-9

Kuklys, Wiebke and Ingrid Robeyns. 2005. 'Sen's Capability Approach to Welfare Economics'. In *Amartya Sen's Capability Approach: Theoretical Insights and Empirical Applications*, by Wiebke Kuklys, pp. 9–30. Berlin: Springer. https://doi.org/10.1007/3-540-28083-9_2

Kynch, Jocelyn and Amartya Sen. 1983. 'Indian Women: Wellbeing and Survival'. *Cambridge Journal of Economics*, 7 (3/4), 363–80. https://doi.org/10.1093/cje/7.3-4.363

Laderchi, Caterina Ruggeri. 1997. 'Poverty and Its Many Dimensions: The Role of Income as an Indicator'. *Oxford Development Studies* 25 (3), 345–60. https://doi.org/10.1080/13600819708424139

Laderchi, Caterina Ruggeri, Ruhi Saith and Frances Stewart. 2003. 'Does It Matter That We Do Not Agree on the Definition of Poverty? A Comparison of Four Approaches'. *Oxford Development Studies* 31 (3), 243–74. https://doi.org/10.1080/1360081032000111698

Lavaque-Manty, Mika. 2001. 'Food, Functioning and Justice: From Famines to Eating Disorders'. *Journal of Political Philosophy* 9 (2), 150–67. https://doi.org/10.1111/1467-9760.00122

Layard, Richard. 2011. *Happiness: Lessons from a New Science*. London: Penguin UK.

Le Grand, Julian. 1990. 'Equity versus Efficiency: The Elusive Trade-Off'. *Ethics* 100 (3), 554–68. https://doi.org/10.1086/293210

Lessmann, Ortrud. 2012. 'Applying the Capability Approach Empirically: An Overview with Special Attention to Labor'. *Management Revue* 23 (2), 98–118.

Lessmann, Ortrud and Felix Rauschmayer. 2013. 'Re-Conceptualizing Sustainable Development on the Basis of the Capability Approach: A Model and Its Difficulties'. *Journal of Human Development and Capabilities* 14 (1), 95–114. https://doi.org/10.1080/19452829.2012.747487

Lewis, Jane and Susanna Giullari. 2005. 'The Adult Worker Model Family, Gender Equality and Care: The Search for New Policy Principles and the Possibilities and Problems of a Capabilities Approach'. *Economy and Society* 34 (1), 76–104. https://doi.org/10.1080/0308514042000329342

List, Christian and Laura Valentini. 2016. 'The Methodology of Political Theory'. In *The Oxford Handbook of Philosophical Methodology*, edited by Herman Cappelen, Tamar Szabó and John Hawthorne, pp. 525–53. Oxford: Oxford University Press. https://doi.org/10.1093/oxfordhb/9780199668779.013.10

Loots, Sonja and Melanie Walker. 2015. 'Shaping a Gender Equality Policy in Higher Education: Which Human Capabilities Matter?' *Gender and Education* 27 (4), 361–75. https://doi.org/10.1080/09540253.2015.1045458

Loots, Sonja and Melanie Walker. 2016. 'A Capabilities-Based Gender Equality Policy for Higher Education: Conceptual and Methodological Considerations'. *Journal of Human Development and Capabilities* 17 (2), 260–77. https://doi.org/10.1080/19452829.2015.1076777

Lozano, J. Felix, Alejandra Boni, Jordi Peris and Andrés Hueso. 2012. 'Competencies in Higher Education: A Critical Analysis from the Capabilities Approach'. *Journal of Philosophy of Education* 46 (1), 132–47. https://doi.org/10.1111/j.1467-9752.2011.00839.x

Marmot, Michael. 2005. 'Social Determinants of Health Inequalities'. *The Lancet* 365 (9464), 1099–104. https://doi.org/10.1016/s0140-6736(05)71146-6

Marmot, Michael, Sharon Friel, Ruth Bell, Tanja A. J. Houweling, Sebastian Taylor and Commission on Social Determinants of Health. 2008. 'Closing the Gap in a Generation: Health Equity through Action on the Social Determinants of Health'. *The Lancet* 372 (9650), 1661–69. https://doi.org/10.1016/s0140-6736(08)61690-6

Marquis, Don. 1989. 'Why Abortion Is Immoral'. *The Journal of Philosophy* 86 (4), 183–202. https://doi.org/10.2307/2026961

McCleery, Robert K. and Fernando De Paolis. 2008. 'The Washington Consensus: A Post-Mortem'. *Journal of Asian Economics* 19 (5), 438–46. https://doi.org/10.1016/j.asieco.2008.09.004

McCloskey, Deirdre N. 1998. *The Rhetoric of Economics*. Madison: University of Wisconsin Press.

McCowan, Tristan. 2011. 'Human Rights, Capabilities and the Normative Basis of "Education for All"'. *Theory and Research in Education* 9 (3), 283–98. https://doi.org/10.1177/1477878511419566

Menon, Nivedita. 2002. 'Universalism without Foundations?' *Economy and Society* 31 (1), 152–69. https://doi.org/10.1080/03085140120109295

Miller, David. 1999. *Principles of Social Justice*. Cambridge, MA: Harvard University Press.

Mitchell, Paul Mark, Hareth Al-Janabi, Sarah Byford, Willem Kuyken, Jeff Richardson, Angelo Iezzi and Joanna Coast. 2017. 'Assessing the Validity of the ICECAP-A Capability Measure for Adults with Depression'. *BMC Psychiatry* 17 (1), 46. https://doi.org/10.1186/s12888-017-1211-8

Mitchell, Paul Mark, Tracy E. Roberts, Pelham M. Barton and Joanna Coast. 2016. 'Applications of the Capability Approach in the Health Field: A Literature Review'. *Social Indicators Research* 133(1), 1–27.

Mitra, Sophie. 2006. 'The Capability Approach and Disability'. *Journal of Disability Policy Studies* 16 (4), 236–47. https://doi.org/10.1177/104420730601 60040501

Mueller, Dennis C. 2003. *Public Choice III*. Cambridge: Cambridge University Press. https://doi.org/10.1017/cbo9780511813771

Murphy, Michael. 2014. 'Self-Determination as a Collective Capability: The Case of Indigenous Peoples'. *Journal of Human Development and Capabilities* 15 (4), 320–34. https://doi.org/10.1080/19452829.2013.878320

Mutanga, Oliver and Melanie Walker. 2015. 'Towards a Disability-Inclusive Higher Education Policy through the Capabilities Approach'. *Journal of Human Development and Capabilities* 16 (4), 501–17. https://doi.org/10.1080/19 452829.2015.1101410

Naess, Arne. 1973. 'The Shallow and the Deep, Long-range Ecology Movement. A Summary'. *Inquiry* 16 (1–4), 95–100. https://doi. org/10.1080/00201747308601682

Naess, Arne. 1984. 'A Defence of the Deep Ecology Movement'. *Environmental Ethics* 6 (3), 265–70. https://doi.org/10.5840/enviroethics19846330

Nelson, Julie. 1995. *Feminism, Objectivity and Economics*. New York: Routledge. https://doi.org/10.4324/9780203435915

Nickel, James. 2014. 'Human Rights'. *Stanford Encyclopedia of Philosophy*. https:// plato.stanford.edu/archives/spr2017/entries/rights-human/

Nielsen, Lasse and David V. Axelsen. 2017. 'Capabilitarian Sufficiency: Capabilities and Social Justice'. *Journal of Human Development and Capabilities* 18 (1), 46–59. https://doi.org/10.1080/19452829.2016.1145632

Nozick, Robert. 1974. *Anarchy, State, and Utopia*. New York: Basic Books.

Nussbaum, Martha C. 1988. 'Nature, Function, and Capability: Aristotle on Political Distribution'. *Oxford Studies in Ancient Philosophy, Supplementary Volume I*, pp. 145–84.

Nussbaum, Martha C. 1992. 'Human Functioning and Social Justice: In Defence of Aristotelian Essentialism'. *Political Theory* 20 (2), 202–46. https://doi.org/10.1177/0090591792020002002

Nussbaum, Martha C. 1997. 'Capabilities and Human Rights'. *Fordham Law Review* 66, 273.

Nussbaum, Martha C. 2000. *Women and Human Development: The Capabilities Approach.* Cambridge: Cambridge University Press. https://doi.org/10.1017/cbo9780511841286

Nussbaum, Martha C. 2002a. 'Capabilities and Disabilities'. *Philosophical Topics* 30 (2), 133–65. https://doi.org/10.5840/philtopics200230218

Nussbaum, Martha C. 2002b. 'Education for Citizenship in an Era of Global Connection'. *Studies in Philosophy and Education* 21 (4/5), 289–303. https://doi.org/10.1023/a:1019837105053

Nussbaum, Martha C. 2003a. 'Capabilities as Fundamental Entitlements: Sen and Social Justice'. *Feminist Economics* 9 (2–3), 33–59. https://doi.org/10.1080/1354570022000077926

Nussbaum, Martha C. 2003b. 'Political Liberalism and Respect: A Response to Linda Barclay'. *SATS* 4 (2), 25–44. https://doi.org/10.1515/sats.2003.25

Nussbaum, Martha C. 2006a. 'Education and Democratic Citizenship: Capabilities and Quality Education'. *Journal of Human Development* 7 (3), 385–95. https://doi.org/10.1080/14649880600815974

Nussbaum, Martha C. 2006b. *Frontiers of Justice.* Cambridge, Massachusetts: The Belknap Press.

Nussbaum, Martha C. 2011a. 'Capabilities, Entitlements, Rights: Supplementation and Critique'. *Journal of Human Development and Capabilities* 12 (1), 23–37. https://doi.org/10.1080/19452829.2011.541731

Nussbaum, Martha C. 2011b. 'Perfectionist Liberalism and Political Liberalism'. *Philosophy and Public Affairs* 39 (1), 3–45. https://doi.org/10.1111/j.1088-4963.2011.01200.x

Nussbaum, Martha C. 2011c. *Creating Capabilities. The Human Development Approach.* Cambridge, MA: Belknap Press of Harvard University Press. https://doi.org/10.4159/harvard.9780674061200

Nussbaum, Martha C. 2012. *Not for Profit: Why Democracy Needs the Humanities.* Princeton: Princeton University Press. https://doi.org/10.1515/9781400883509

Nussbaum, Martha C. 2014. 'Introduction: Capabilities, Challenges, and the Omnipresence of Political Liberalism'. In *Capabilities, Gender, Equality,* edited by Flavio Comim and Martha Nussbaum, pp. 1–16. Cambridge: Cambridge University Press. https://doi.org/10.1017/cbo9781139059138.002

Nussbaum, Martha C. 2016. 'Economics Still Needs Philosophy'. *Review of Social Economy* 74 (3), 229–47. https://doi.org/10.1080/00346764.2015.1044843

Okin, Susan Moller. 1989. *Justice, Gender, and The Family*. New York: Basic Books.

Okin, Susan Moller. 2003. 'Poverty, Well-being, and Gender: What Counts, Who's Heard?' *Philosophy & Public Affairs* 31 (3), 280–316. https://doi.org/10.1111/j.1088-4963.2003.00280.x

O'Neill, John. 2011. 'The Overshadowing of Needs'. In *Sustainable Development: Capabilities, Needs, Wellbeing*, edited by Felix Rauschmayer, Ines Omann and Johannes Frühmann, pp. 25–42. London: Routledge.

O'Neill, Onora. 1996. *Towards Justice and Virtue. A Constructivist Account of Practical Reasoning*. Cambridge: Cambridge University Press. https://doi.org/10.1017/cbo9780511621239

O'Neill, Onora. 2001. 'Agents of Justice'. *Metaphilosophy* 32 (1-2), 180–95. https://doi.org/10.1111/1467-9973.00181

O'Neill, Onora. 2009. 'Applied Ethics: Naturalism, Normativity and Public Policy'. *Journal of Applied Philosophy* 26 (3), 219–30. https://doi.org/10.1111/j.1468-5930.2009.00446.x

Oosterlaken, Ilse. 2009. 'Design for Development: A Capability Approach'. *Design Issues* 25 (4), 91–102. https://doi.org/10.1162/desi.2009.25.4.91

Oosterlaken, Ilse. 2011. 'Inserting Technology in the Relational Ontology of Sen's Capability Approach'. *Journal of Human Development and Capabilities* 12 (3), 425–32. https://doi.org/10.1080/19452829.2011.576661

Oosterlaken, Ilse. 2015. *Technology and Human Development*. London: Routledge.

Osmani, Siddiqur Rahman. 2000. 'Human Rights to Food, Health, and Education'. *Journal of Human Development* 1 (2), 273–98. https://doi.org/10.1080/713678042

Osmani, Siddiqur Rahman. 2005. 'Poverty and Human Rights: Building on the Capability Approach'. *Journal of Human Development* 6 (2), 205–19. https://doi.org/10.1080/14649880500120541

Parfit, Derek. 1984. *Reasons and Persons*. Oxford: Oxford University Press. https://doi.org/10.1093/019824908x.001.0001

Pattanaik, Prasanta K. 2006. 'On Comparing Functioning Bundles and Capability Sets'. In *Human Development in the Era of Globalization: Essays in Honor of Keith B. Griffin*, edited by James K. Boyce, Stephen Cullenberg, Prasanta K. Pattanaik and Robert Pollin, pp. 181–98. Northampton: Edward Elgar Publishing. https://doi.org/10.4337/9781845429867.00018

Pattanaik, Prasanta K. and Yongsheng Xu. 1990. 'On Ranking Opportunity Sets in Terms of Freedom of Choice'. *Recherches Économiques de Louvain* 56 (3–4), 383–90.

Peppin Vaughan, Rosie. 2016. 'Education, Social Justice and School Diversity: Insights from the Capability Approach'. *Journal of Human Development and Capabilities* 17 (2), 206–24. https://doi.org/10.1080/19452829.2015.1076775

Peppin Vaughan, Rosie and Melanie Walker. 2012. 'Capabilities, Values and Education Policy'. *Journal of Human Development and Capabilities* 13 (3), 495–512. https://doi.org/10.1080/19452829.2012.679648

Pettit, Philip. 2001. 'Capability and Freedom: A Defence of Sen'. *Economics and Philosophy* 17 (1), 1–20. https://doi.org/10.1017/s0266267101000116

Pettit, Philip. 2003. 'Agency-Freedom and Option-Freedom'. *Journal of Theoretical Politics* 15 (4), 387–403. https://doi.org/10.1177/0951692803154003

Pettit, Philip. 2009. 'Freedom in the Spirit of Sen'. In *Amartya Sen*, edited by Christopher W. Morris, pp. 91–114. Cambridge: Cambridge University Press. https://doi.org/10.1017/cbo9780511800511.006

Phillips, Anne. 2004. 'Defending Equality of Outcome'. *Journal of Political Philosophy* 12 (1), 1–19. https://doi.org/10.1111/j.1467-9760.2004.00188.x

Phipps, Shelley. 2002. 'The Well-Being of Young Canadian Children in International Perspective: A Functionings Approach'. *Review of Income and Wealth* 48 (4), 493–515. https://doi.org/10.1111/1475-4991.00065

Phipps, Shelley and Peter Burton. 1995. 'Sharing within Families: Implications for the Measurement of Poverty among Individuals in Canada'. *Canadian Journal of Economics* 28(1), 177–204. https://doi.org/10.2307/136028

Pierik, Roland. 2012. 'State Neutrality and the Limits of Religious Symbolism'. In *The Lautsi Papers: Multidisciplinary Reflections on Religious Symbols in the Public School Classroom*, edited by Jeroen Temperman, pp. 201–18. Leiden: Brill/Martinus Nijhoff. https://doi.org/10.1163/9789004222519_010

Pierik, Roland and Wibren van der Burg. 2011. 'The Neutral State and the Mandatory Crucifix'. *Religion & Human Rights* 6 (3), 267–72. https://doi.org/10.1163/187103211x599427

Pierik, Roland and Ingrid Robeyns. 2007. 'Resources versus Capabilities: Social Endowments in Egalitarian Theory'. *Political Studies* 55 (1), 133–52. https://doi.org/10.1111/j.1467-9248.2007.00646.x

Pogge, Thomas W. 2002. 'Can the Capability Approach Be Justified?' *Philosophical Topics* 30 (2), 167–228. https://doi.org/10.5840/philtopics200230216

Pogge, Thomas W. 2008. *World Poverty and Human Rights*. Cambridge: Polity.

Qizilbash, Mozaffar. 1996. 'Capabilities, Well-being and Human Development: A Survey'. *The Journal of Development Studies* 33 (2), 143–62. https://doi.org/10.1080/00220389608422460

Qizilbash, Mozaffar. 2002. 'A Note on the Measurement of Poverty and Vulnerability in the South African Context'. *Journal of International Development* 14 (6), 757–72. https://doi.org/10.1002/jid.922

Qizilbash, Mozaffar. 2005. 'Sen on Freedom and Gender Justice'. *Feminist Economics* 11 (3), 151–66. https://doi.org/10.1080/13545700500301551

Qizilbash, Mozaffar. 2011. 'Disability and Human Development'. In *Arguing about the World: The Work and Legacy of Meghnad Desai*, edited by Mary Kaldor and Polly Vizard, pp. 99–118. London: Bloomsbury Academic. https://doi.org/10.5040/9781849665469

Qizilbash, Mozaffar. 2012. 'The Capability Approach: Its Interpretations and Limitations'. In *The Capability Approach. Development Practice and Public Policy in the Asian-Pacific Region*, edited by Francesca Panzironi and Katharine Gelber, pp. 9–22. London: Routledge. https://doi.org/10.4324/9780203116159

Qizilbash, Mozaffar. 2013. 'On Capability and the Good Life: Theoretical Debates and Their Practical Implications'. *Philosophy and Public Policy Quarterly* 31 (2), 35–42.

Qizilbash, Mozaffar. 2016. 'Capability, Objectivity and "False Consciousness": On Sen, Marx and JS Mill'. *International Journal of Social Economics* 43 (12), 1207–18. https://doi.org/10.1108/ijse-04-2016-0127

Qizilbash, Mozaffar and David A. Clark. 2005. 'The Capability Approach and Fuzzy Poverty Measures: An Application to the South African Context'. *Social Indicators Research* 74 (1), 103–39. https://doi.org/10.1007/s11205-005-6527-y

Rabinowicz, Wlodek and Toni Rønnow-Rasmussen. 2000. 'A Distinction in Value: Intrinsic and For Its Own Sake'. *Proceedings of the Aristotelian Society* 100, 33–51. https://doi.org/10.1111/1467-9264.00064

Rauschmayer, Felix, Ines Omann and Johannes Frühmann. 2012. *Sustainable Development: Capabilities, Needs, and Wellbeing*. London: Routledge.

Rawls, John. 1988. 'The Priority of Right and Ideas of the Good'. *Philosophy & Public Affairs* 17(4), 251–76.

Rawls, John. 1999. *Law of Peoples*. Cambridge, MA: Harvard University Press.

Rawls, John. 2009. *A Theory of Justice*. Cambridge, MA: Harvard University Press.

Reader, Soran. 2006. 'Does a Basic Needs Approach Need Capabilities?' *Journal of Political Philosophy* 14 (3), 337–50. https://doi.org/10.1111/j.1467-9760.2006.00259.x

Reader, Soran and Gillian Brock. 2004. 'Needs, Moral Demands and Moral Theory'. *Utilitas* 16 (3), 251–66. https://doi.org/10.1017/s0953820804001165

Reddy, Sanjay G., Sujata Visaria and Muhammad Asali. 2009. 'Inter-Country Comparisons of Income Poverty Based on a Capability Approach'. In *Arguments for a Better World. Essays in Honor of Amartya Sen*, edited by Kaushik Basu and Ravi Kanbur, Volume I, pp. 7–29. New Delhi: Oxford University Press. https://doi.org/10.1093/acprof:oso/9780199239979.003.0002

Reiss, Julian. 2013. *Philosophy of Economics: A Contemporary Introduction*. London: Routledge. https://doi.org/10.4324/9780203559062

Richardson, Henry S. 2000. 'Some Limitations of Nussbaum's Capabilities'. *Quinnipiac Law Review* 19, 309–32.

Richardson, Henry S. 2007. 'The Social Background of Capabilities for Freedoms'. *Journal of Human Development* 8 (3), 389–414. https://doi.org/10.1080/14649880701462213

Richardson, Henry S. 2015. 'Using Final Ends for the Sake of Better Policy-Making'. *Journal of Human Development and Capabilities* 16 (2), 161–72. https://doi.org/10.1080/19452829.2015.1036846

Richardson, Henry S. 2016. 'Capabilities and the Definition of Health: Comments on Venkatapuram'. *Bioethics* 30 (1), 1–7. https://doi.org/10.1111/bioe.12219

Robeyns, Ingrid. 2003. 'Sen's Capability Approach and Gender Inequality: Selecting Relevant Capabilities'. *Feminist Economics* 9 (2–3), 61–92. https://doi.org/10.1080/1354570022000078024

Robeyns, Ingrid. 2005a. 'Selecting Capabilities for Quality of Life Measurement'. *Social Indicators Research* 74, 191–215. https://doi.org/10.1007/s11205-005-6524-1

Robeyns, Ingrid. 2005b. 'The Capability Approach: A Theoretical Survey'. *Journal of Human Development* 6 (1), 93–117. https://doi.org/10.1080/146498805200034266

Robeyns, Ingrid. 2006a. 'Measuring Gender Inequality in Functionings and Capabilities: Findings from the British Household Panel Survey'. In *Gender Disparity: Manifestations, Causes and Implication*, edited by Premananda Bharati and Manoranjan Pal, pp. 236–77. New Delhi: Anmol.

Robeyns, Ingrid. 2006b. 'The Capability Approach in Practice'. *Journal of Political Philosophy* 14 (3), 351–76. https://doi.org/10.1111/j.1467-9760.2006.00263.x

Robeyns, Ingrid. 2006c. 'Three Models of Education Rights, Capabilities and Human Capital'. *Theory and Research in Education* 4 (1), 69–84. https://doi.org/10.1177/1477878506060683

Robeyns, Ingrid. 2008a. 'Ideal Theory in Theory and Practice'. *Social Theory and Practice* 34 (3), 341–62. https://doi.org/10.5840/soctheorpract200834321

Robeyns, Ingrid. 2008b. 'Justice as Fairness and the Capability Approach'. In *Arguments for a Better World: Essays in Honor of Amartya Sen*, edited by Kaushik Basu and Ravi Kanbur, Volume II, pp. 397–413. New Delhi: Oxford University Press. https://doi.org/10.1093/acprof:oso/9780199239115.003.0022

Robeyns, Ingrid. 2008c. 'Sen's Capability Approach and Feminist Concerns'. In *The Capability Approach: Concepts, Measures, Applications*, edited by Sabina Alkire, Flavio Comin and Mozaffar Qizilbash, pp. 82–104. Cambridge: Cambridge University Press. https://doi.org/10.1017/cbo9780511492587.004

Robeyns, Ingrid. 2009. 'Capabilities and Theories of Social Justice'. In *Debating Global Society. Reach and Limit of the Capability Approach*, edited by Enrica Chiappero-Martinetti, pp. 61–89. Milan: Feltrinelli.

Robeyns, Ingrid. 2010. 'Social Justice and the Gendered Division of Labour: Possibilities and Limits of the Capability Approach'. In *Gender Inequalities, Households and the Production of Wellbeing in Modern Europe*, edited by Tindara Addabbo, Marie-Pierre Arrizabalaga, Cristina Borderías and Alastair Owens, pp. 25–40. Farnham: Ashgate. https://doi.org/10.4324/9781315584058

Robeyns, Ingrid. 2011. 'Review of Martha Nussbaum, Creating Capabilities'. *Notre Dame Philosophy Reviews* 2011.09.23 http://ndpr.nd.edu/news/creating-capabilities-the-human-development-approach-2/

Robeyns, Ingrid. 2016a. 'Book Review of B. Holland (2014), Allocating the Earth'. *Ethics* 126 (4), 1100–04. https://doi.org/10.1086/686060

Robeyns, Ingrid. 2016b. 'Capabilitarianism'. *Journal of Human Development and Capabilities* 17 (3), 397–414. https://doi.org/10.1080/19452829.2016.1145631

Robeyns, Ingrid. 2016c. 'Conceptualising Wellbeing for Autistic Persons'. *Journal of Medical Ethics* 42 (6), 383–90. https://doi.org/10.1136/medethics-2016-103508

Robeyns, Ingrid. 2016d. 'The Capability Approach'. *The Stanford Encyclopedia of Philosophy*. https://plato.stanford.edu/archives/win2016/entries/capability-approach/

Robeyns, Ingrid. 2017a. 'Freedom and Responsibility — Sustainable Prosperity through a Capabilities Lens'. Center for the Understanding of Sustainable Prosperity. https://www.cusp.ac.uk/essay/m1-4

Robeyns, Ingrid. 2017b. 'Having Too Much'. In *NOMOS LVIII: Wealth*, edited by Jack Knight and Melissa Schwartzberg, pp. 1–45. Yearbook of the American Society for Political and Legal Philosophy. New York: New York University Press.

Robeyns, Ingrid and Robert-Jan Van der Veen. 2007. *Sustainable Quality of Life. Conceptual Analysis for a Policy-Relevant Empirical Specification*. Bilthoven: Netherlands Environmental Assessment Agency. http://www.pbl.nl/sites/default/files/cms/publicaties/550031006.pdf

Rodogno, Raffaele. 2015a. 'Prudential Value or Wellbeing'. In *Handbook of Value: Perspectives from Economics, Neuroscience, Philosophy, Psychology and Sociology*, edited by Tobias Brosch and David Sander, pp. 287–312. Oxford: Oxford University press. https://doi.org/10.1093/acprof:oso/9780198716600.003.0014

Rodogno, Raffaele. 2015b. 'Wellbeing, Science, and Philosophy'. In *Wellbeing in Contemporary Society*, edited by Johnny H. Søraker, Jan-Willem van der Reijt, Jelle de Boer, Pak-Hang Wong, and Philip Brey, pp. 39–57. Berlin: Springer. https://doi.org/10.1007/978-3-319-06459-8_3

Roemer, John E. 1996. *Theories of Distributive Justice*. Cambridge, MA: Harvard University Press.

Roy, Arundhati. 2014. *Capitalism: A Ghost Story*. Chicago: Haymarket Books.

Ruger, Jennifer Prah. 2006. 'Toward a Theory of a Right to Health: Capability and Incompletely Theorized Agreements'. *Yale Journal of Law & the Humanities* 18 (2), article 3. http://digitalcommons.law.yale.edu/cgi/viewcontent. cgi?article=1313&context=yjlh

Ruger, Jennifer Prah. 2010. 'Health Capability: Conceptualization and Operationalization'. *American Journal of Public Health* 100 (1), 41–49. https:// doi.org/10.2105/ajph.2008.143651

Saito, Madoka. 2003. 'Amartya Sen's Capability Approach to Education: A Critical Exploration'. *Journal of the Philosophy of Education* 37, 17–33. https:// doi.org/10.1111/1467-9752.3701002

Schinkel, Anders. 2008. 'Martha Nussbaum on Animal Rights'. *Ethics & the Environment* 13 (1), 41–69. https://doi.org/10.2979/ete.2008.13.1.41

Schkade, David A. and Daniel Kahneman. 1998. 'Does Living in California Make People Happy? A Focusing Illusion in Judgments of Life Satisfaction'. *Psychological Science* 9 (5), 340–46. https://doi.org/10.1111/1467-9280.00066

Schlosberg, David. 2012. 'Climate Justice and Capabilities: A Framework for Adaptation Policy'. *Ethics & International Affairs* 26 (4), 445–61. https://doi. org/10.1017/s0892679412000615

Schlosberg, David and David Carruthers. 2010. 'Indigenous Struggles, Environmental Justice, and Community Capabilities'. *Global Environmental Politics* 10 (4), 12–35. https://doi.org/10.1162/glep_a_00029

Schokkaert, Erik. 2007. 'Capabilities and Satisfaction with Life'. *Journal of Human Development* 8 (3), 415–30. https://doi.org/10.1080/14649880701462239

Schokkaert, Erik and Luc Van Ootegem. 1990. 'Sen's Concept of the Living Standard Applied to the Belgian Unemployed'. *Recherches Économiques de Louvain/Louvain Economic Review* 45 (3–4), 429–50.

Scholtes, Fabian. 2010. 'Whose Sustainability? Environmental Domination and Sen's Capability Approach'. *Oxford Development Studies* 38 (3), 289–307. https://doi.org/10.1080/13600818.2010.505683

Schultz, Emily, Marius Christen, Lieske Voget-Kleschin and Paul Burger. 2013. 'A Sustainability-Fitting Interpretation of the Capability Approach: Integrating the Natural Dimension by Employing Feedback Loops'. *Journal of Human Development and Capabilities* 14 (1), 115–33. https://doi.org/10.1080/ 19452829.2012.747489

Sen, Amartya. 1970a. *Collective Choice and Social Welfare*. San Fransisco: Holden-Day.

Sen, Amartya. 1970b. 'The Impossibility of a Paretian Liberal'. *Journal of Political Economy* 78 (1), 152–57. https://doi.org/10.1086/259614

Sen, Amartya. 1976. 'Liberty, Unanimity and Rights'. *Economica* 43 (171), 217–45. https://doi.org/10.2307/2553122

Sen, Amartya. 1977a. 'Rational Fools: A Critique of the Behavioral Foundations of Economic Theory'. *Philosophy & Public Affairs* 6 (4), 317–44.

Sen, Amartya. 1977b. 'Social Choice Theory: A Re-Examination'. *Econometrica: Journal of the Econometric Society* 45(1), 53–89. https://doi.org/10.2307/1913287

Sen, Amartya. 1979. 'Utilitarianism and Welfarism'. *Journal of Philosophy* 76 (9), 463–89. https://doi.org/10.2307/2025934

Sen, Amartya. 1980. 'Equality of What?' In *The Tanner Lectures on Human Values*, edited by S. McMurrin, pp. 196–220. Salt Lake City: University of Utah Press.

Sen, Amartya. 1982. 'Rights and Agency'. *Philosophy and Public Affairs* 11 (1), 3–39.

Sen, Amartya. 1983. 'Liberty and Social Choice'. *The Journal of Philosophy* 80 (1), 5–28. https://doi.org/10.2307/2026284

Sen, Amartya. 1984a. *Resources, Values, and Development*. Oxford: Basil Blackwell.

Sen, Amartya. 1984b. 'Rights and Capabilities'. In *Resources, Values and Development*, pp. 307–24. Cambridge, MA: Harvard University Press.

Sen, Amartya. 1984c. 'The Living Standard'. *Oxford Economic Papers* 36, 74–90. https://doi.org/10.1093/oxfordjournals.oep.a041662

Sen, Amartya. 1985a. *Commodities and Capabilities*. Oxford: Oxford University Press.

Sen, Amartya. 1985b. 'Goals, Commitment, and Identity'. *Journal of Law, Economics and Organisation* 1 (2), 341–56. https://doi.org/10.1093/oxfordjournals.jleo.a036895

Sen, Amartya. 1985c. 'Wellbeing, Agency and Freedom: The Dewey Lectures 1984'. *The Journal of Philosophy* 82 (4), 169–221. https://doi.org/10.2307/2026184

Sen, Amartya. 1986. 'Social Choice Theory'. *Handbook of Mathematical Economics* 3, 1073–181. https://doi.org/10.1016/s1573-4382(86)03004-7

Sen, Amartya. 1987. *The Standard of Living*. Edited by Geoffrey Hawthorn. Cambridge University Press. https://doi.org/10.1017/cbo9780511570742

Sen, Amartya. 1990a. 'Justice: Means versus Freedoms'. *Philosophy and Public Affairs* 19 (2), 111–21.

Sen, Amartya. 1990b. 'More Than 100 Million Women Are Missing'. *The New York Review of Books*, 20 December 1990.

Sen, Amartya. 1990c. 'Welfare, Freedom and Social Choice: A Reply'. *Recherches Économiques de Louvain/Louvain Economic Review* 56 (3–4), 451–85.

Sen, Amartya. 1992a. *Inequality Reexamined*. Oxford: Clarendon Press. https://doi.org/10.1093/0198289286.001.0001

Sen, Amartya. 1992b. 'Missing Women'. *British Medical Journal* 304, 587–88. https://doi.org/10.1136/bmj.304.6827.587

Sen, Amartya. 1992c. 'Minimal Liberty'. *Economica* 59 (234), 139–59. https://doi.org/10.2307/2554743

Sen, Amartya. 1993a. 'Capability and Wellbeing'. In *The Quality of Life*, edited by Martha Nussbaum and Amartya Sen, pp. 30–53. Oxford: Clarendon Press. https://doi.org/10.1093/0198287976.003.0003

Sen, Amartya. 1993b. 'Markets and Freedoms: Achievements and Limitations of the Market Mechanism in Promoting Individual Freedoms'. *Oxford Economic Papers*, 45 (4), 519–41. https://doi.org/10.1093/oxfordjournals.oep.a042106

Sen, Amartya. 1996. 'On the Foundations of Welfare Economics: Utility, Capability, and Practical Reason'. In *Ethics, Rationality, and Economic Behaviour*, edited by Francesco Farina, Frank Hahn and Stefano Vannucci, pp. 50–65. Oxford: Clarendon Press.

Sen, Amartya. 1999a. *Development as Freedom*. New York: Knopf.

Sen, Amartya. 1999b. *Reason Before Identity: The Romanes Lecture*. Oxford: Oxford University Press.

Sen, Amartya. 1999c. 'The Possibility of Social Choice'. *The American Economic Review* 89 (3), 349–78. https://doi.org/10.1257/aer.89.3.349

Sen, Amartya. 2000. 'Social Justice and the Distribution of Income'. In *Handbook of Income Distribution*, edited by Anthony B. Atkinson and Francois Bourguinon, pp. 59–85. Amsterdam: Elsevier. https://doi.org/10.1016/s1574-0056(00)80004-4

Sen, Amartya. 2002a. *Rationality and Freedom*. Cambridge, MA: The Belknap Press.

Sen, Amartya. 2002b. 'Response to Commentaries'. *Studies in Comparative International Development* 37 (2), 78–86. https://doi.org/10.1007/bf02686264

Sen, Amartya. 2003a. 'Foreword'. In *Readings in Human Development*, edited by Sakiko Fukuda-Parr and A. K. Shiva Kumar, pp. vii–xiii. New Delhi: Oxford University Press.

Sen, Amartya. 2003b. 'Missing Women — revisited'. *BMJ: British Medical Journal* 327 (7427), 1297–98. https://doi.org/10.1136/bmj.327.7427.1297

Sen, Amartya. 2004a. 'Capabilities, Lists, and Public Reason: Continuing the Conversation'. *Feminist Economics* 10 (3), 77–80. https://doi.org/10.1080/1354570042000315163

Sen, Amartya. 2004b. 'Elements of a Theory of Human Rights'. *Philosophy and Public Affairs* 32 (4), 315–56. https://doi.org/10.1111/j.1088-4963.2004.00017.x

Sen, Amartya. 2005. 'Human Rights and Capabilities'. *Journal of Human Development* 6 (2), 151–66. https://doi.org/10.1080/14649880500120491

Sen, Amartya. 2006. 'What Do We Want from a Theory of Justice?' *Journal of Philosophy* 103 (5), 215–38. https://doi.org/10.5840/jphil2006103517

Sen, Amartya. 2008. 'The Economics of Happiness and Capability'. In *Capabilities and Happiness*, edited by Luigino Bruni, Flavio Comim and Maurizio Pugno, pp. 16–27. Oxford: Oxford University Press.

Sen, Amartya. 2009a. 'Capability: Reach and Limit'. In *Debating Global Society: Reach and Limits of the Capability Approach*, pp. 15–28. Milan: Fondazione Giangiacomo Feltrinelli.

Sen, Amartya. 2009b. 'The Fog of Identity'. *Politics, Philosophy and Economics* 8 (3), 285–88. https://doi.org/10.1177/1470594x09105388

Sen, Amartya. 2009c. *The Idea of Justice*. London: Allen Lane.

Sen, Amartya. 2013. 'The Ends and Means of Sustainability' *Journal of Human Development and Capabilities* 14 (1), 6–20. http://dx.doi.org/10.1080/19452829 .2012.747492

Sen, Amartya. 2017. *Collective Choice and Social Welfare: Expanded Edition*. London: Penguin.

Sen, Amartya and Sunil Sengupta. 1983. 'Malnutrition of Rural Children and the Sex Bias'. *Economic and Political Weekly* 18, 855–64.

Shiller, Robert J. and Virginia M. Shiller. 2011. 'Economists as Worldly Philosophers'. *The American Economic Review* 101 (3), 171–75. https://doi. org/10.1257/aer.101.3.171

Singer, Peter. 2004. *One World. The Ethics of Globalization*. Second edition. New Haven: Yale University Press.

Singer, Peter. 2010. *The Life You Can Save: How to Do Your Part to End World Poverty*. New York: Random House.

Sinnott-Armstrong, Walter. 2015. 'Consequentialism'. *Stanford Encyclopedia of Philosophy*. https://plato.stanford.edu/entries/consequentialism

Stemplowska, Zofia. 2008. 'What's Ideal about Ideal Theory?' *Social Theory and Practice* 34 (3), 319–40. https://doi.org/10.5840/soctheorpract200834320

Stewart, Frances. 2005. 'Groups and Capabilities'. *Journal of Human Development* 6 (2), 185–204. https://doi.org/10.1080/14649880500120517

Stewart, Frances. 2006. 'Basic Needs Approach'. In *The Elgar Companion to Development Studies*, edited by David A. Clark, pp. 14–18. Cheltenham: Edward Elgar. http://dx.doi.org/10.4337/9781847202864.00014

Stiglitz, Joseph E., Amartya Sen and Jean-Paul Fitoussi. 2010. *Mismeasuring Our Lives: Why GDP Doesn't Add up*. New York: The New Press.

Streeten, Paul. 1995. 'Foreword'. In *Reflections on Human Development*, edited by Mahbub ul Haq, pp. vii–xvi. New York: Oxford.

Sugden, Robert. 1993. 'Welfare, Resources, and Capabilities: A Review [Inequality Reexamined]'. *Journal of Economic Literature* 31 (4), 1947–62.

Sumner, Leonard Wayne. 1996. *Welfare, Happiness, and Ethics*. Oxford: Clarendon Press. https://doi.org/10.1093/acprof:oso/9780198238782.001.0001

Suzumura, Kotaro. 2016. *Choice, Preferences, and Procedures*. Cambridge, MA: Harvard University Press. https://doi.org/10.4159/9780674726307

Swift, Adam. 2008. 'The Value of Philosophy in Nonideal Circumstances'. *Social Theory and Practice* 34 (3), 363–87. https://doi.org/10.5840/soctheorpract200834322

Taylor, Alan. 1979. 'What's Wrong with Negatlive Liberty?' In *The Idea of Freedom*, edited by Alan Ryan, pp. 175–93. Oxford: Oxford University Press.

Terzi, Lorella. 2005. 'Beyond the Dilemma of Difference: The Capability Approach to Disability and Special Educational Needs'. *Journal of Philosophy of Education* 39 (3), 443–59. https://doi.org/10.1111/j.1467-9752.2005.00447.x

Terzi, Lorella. 2007. 'Capability and Educational Equality: The Just Distribution of Resources to Students with Disabilities and Special Educational Needs'. *Journal of Philosophy of Education* 41 (4), 757–73. https://doi.org/10.1111/j.1467-9752.2007.00589.x

Terzi, Lorella. 2010. *Justice and Equality in Education: A Capability Perspective on Disability and Special Educational Needs*. London: Bloomsbury Publishing. https://doi.org/10.5040/9781472541178

Teschl, Miriam and Flavio Comim. 2005. 'Adaptive Preferences and Capabilities: Some Preliminary Conceptual Explorations'. *Review of Social Economy* 63 (2), 229–47. https://doi.org/10.1080/00346760500130374

Teschl, Miriam and Laurent Derobert. 2008. 'Does Identity Matter? On the Relevance of Identity and Interaction for Capabilities'. In *The Capability Approach: Concepts, Measures, Applications*, edited by Flavio Comim, Mozaffar Qizilbash and Sabina Alkire, pp. 125–56. Cambridge: Cambridge University Press. https://doi.org/10.1017/cbo9780511492587.006

Thomson, Judith Jarvis. 1971. 'A Defense of Abortion'. *Philosophy & Public Affairs* 1 (1), 47–66.

Tooley, Michael. 1972. 'Abortion and Infanticide'. *Philosophy & Public Affairs* 2 (1), 37–65.

Trommlerová, Sofia Karina, Stephan Klasen and Ortrud Leßmann. 2015. 'Determinants of Empowerment in a Capability-Based Poverty Approach: Evidence from the Gambia'. *World Development* 66, 1–15. https://doi.org/10.1016/j.worlddev.2014.07.008

Tronto, Joan C. 1987. 'Beyond Gender Difference to a Theory of Care'. *Signs: Journal of Women in Culture and Society* 12 (4), 644–63. https://doi.org/10.1086/494360

United Nations Development Program. 1990–2017. *Human Development Reports*. New York: UNDP.

Unterhalter, Elaine. 2003a. 'Crossing Disciplinary Boundaries: The Potential of Sen's Capability Approach for Sociologists of Education'. *British Journal of Sociology of Education* 24 (5), 665–69. https://doi.org/10.1080/0142569032000148708

Unterhalter, Elaine. 2003b. 'The Capabilities Approach and Gendered Education An Examination of South African Complexities'. *Theory and Research in Education* 1 (1), 7–22. https://doi.org/10.1177/1477878503001001660

Unterhalter, Elaine. 2009. 'What Is Equity in Education? Reflections from the Capability Approach'. *Studies in Philosophy and Education* 28 (5), 415–24. https://doi.org/10.1007/s11217-009-9125-7

Unterhalter, Elaine. 2013. 'Educating Capabilities'. *Journal of Human Development and Capabilities* 14 (1), 185–88. https://doi.org/10.1080/19452829.2013.762183

Valentini, Laura. 2012. 'Ideal vs. Non-ideal Theory: A Conceptual Map'. *Philosophy Compass* 7 (9), 654–64. https://doi.org/10.1111/j.1747-9991.2012.00500.x

Vallentyne, Peter. 2005. 'Debate: Capabilities versus Opportunities for Well-being'. *Journal of Political Philosophy* 13 (3), 359–71. https://doi.org/10.1111/j.1467-9760.2005.00227.x

Vallentyne, Peter and Bas Van der Vossen. 2014. 'Libertarianism'. In *Stanford Encyclopedia of Philosophy*. https://plato.stanford.edu/entries/libertarianism

Van Parijs, Philippe. 1995. *Real Freedom for All. What (If Anything) Can Justify Capitalism?* Oxford: Oxford University Press. https://doi.org/10.1093/0198293577.001.0001

Van Praag, Bernard M. S. and Ada Ferrer-i-Carbonell. 2004. *Happiness Quantified: A Satisfaction Calculus Approach.* Oxford: Oxford University Press. https://doi.org/10.1093/0198286546.001.0001

Van Zanden, Jan Luiten, Joerg Baten, Marco Mira d'Ercole, Auke Rijpma, Conal Smith and Marcel Timmer. 2014. *How Was Life? Global Wellbeing since 1820.* Paris: Organisation for Economic Co-operation and Development. http://dx.doi.org/10.1787/9789264214262-en

Vaughan, Donna. 2011. 'The Importance of Capabilities in the Sustainability of Information and Communications Technology Programs: The Case of Remote Indigenous Australian Communities'. *Ethics and Information Technology* 13 (2), 131–50. https://doi.org/10.1007/s10676-011-9269-3

Veenhoven, Ruut. 1996. 'Happy Life-Expectancy'. *Social Indicators Research* 39 (1), 1–58. https://doi.org/10.1007/bf00300831

Venkatapuram, Sridhar. 2009. 'A Bird's Eye View. Two Topics at the Intersection of Social Determinants of Health and Social Justice Philosophy'. *Public Health Ethics* 2 (3), 224–34. https://doi.org/10.1093/phe/php031

Venkatapuram, Sridhar. 2011. *Health Justice. An Argument from the Capability Approach.* Cambridge: Polity Press.

Venkatapuram, Sridhar. 2013. 'Health, Vital Goals, and Central Human Capabilities'. *Bioethics* 27 (5), 271–79. https://doi.org/10.1111/j.1467-8519.2011.01953.x

Vizard, Polly. 2006. *Poverty and Human Rights. Sen's 'Capability Perspective' Explored.* Oxford: Oxford University Press. https://doi.org/10.1093/acprof:o so/9780199273874.001.0001

Vizard, Polly. 2007. 'Specifying and Justifying a Basic Capability Set: Should the International Human Rights Framework Be given a More Direct Role?' *Oxford Development Studies* 35 (3), 225–50. https://doi.org/10.1080/13600810701514787

Vizard, Polly, Sakiko Fukuda-Parr and Diane Elson. 2011. 'Introduction: The Capability Approach and Human Rights'. *Journal of Human Development and Capabilities* 12 (1), 1–22. https://doi.org/10.1080/19452829.2010.541728

Voget-Kleschin, Lieske. 2013. 'Employing the Capability Approach in Conceptualizing Sustainable Development'. *Journal of Human Development and Capabilities* 14 (4), 483–502. https://doi.org/10.1080/19452829.2013.827635

Voget-Kleschin, Lieske. 2015. 'Reasoning Claims for More Sustainable Food Consumption: A Capabilities Perspective'. *Journal of Agricultural and Environmental Ethics* 28 (3), 455–77. https://doi.org/10.1007/s10806-014-9503-1

Walker, Melanie. 2003. 'Framing Social Justice in Education: What Does the Capabilities Approach Offer?' *British Journal of Educational Studies* 51 (2), 168–87. https://doi.org/10.1111/1467-8527.t01-2-00232

Walker, Melanie. 2005. 'Amartya Sen's Capability Approach and Education'. *Educational Action Research* 13 (1), 103–10. https://doi.org/10.1080/09650790500200279

Walker, Melanie. 2008. 'A Human Capabilities Framework for Evaluating Student Learning'. *Teaching in Higher Education* 13 (4), 477–87. https://doi.org/10.1080/13562510802169764

Walker, Melanie. 2010. 'Critical Capability Pedagogies and University Education'. *Educational Philosophy and Theory* 42 (8), 898–917. https://doi.org/10.1111/j.1469-5812.2007.00379.x

Walker, Melanie. 2012a. 'A Capital or Capabilities Education Narrative in a World of Staggering Inequalities?' *International Journal of Educational Development* 32 (3), 384–93. https://doi.org/10.1016/j.ijedudev.2011.09.003

Walker, Melanie. 2012b. 'Universities and a Human Development Ethics: A Capabilities Approach to Curriculum'. *European Journal of Education* 47 (3), 448–61. https://doi.org/10.1111/j.1465-3435.2012.01537.x

Walker, Melanie and Elaine Unterhalter. 2007. *Amartya Sen's Capability Approach and Social Justice in Education.* Basingstoke: Palgrave Macmillan. https://doi.org/10.1057/9780230604810

Walsh, Vivian. 2000. 'Smith after Sen'. *Review of Political Economy* 12 (1), 5–25. https://doi.org/10.1080/095382500106795

Walzer, Michael. 1983. *Spheres of Justice*. New York: Basic Books.

Wasserman, David. 2005. 'Disability, Capability, and Thresholds for Distributive Justice'. In *Capabilities Equality: Basic Issues and Problems*, edited by Alexander Kaufman, pp. 214–34. London: Routledge. https://doi.org/10.4324/9780203799444

Watene, Krushil. 2016. 'Valuing Nature: Māori Philosophy and the Capability Approach'. *Oxford Development Studies* 44 (3), 287–96. https://doi.org/10.1080/13600818.2015.1124077

Watene, Krushil and Jay Drydyk, eds. 2016. *Theorizing Justice. Critical Insights and Future Directions*. London: Rowman & Littlefield.

Weiler, Joseph H. H. 2010. 'Lautsi: Crucifix in the Classroom Redux'. *The European Journal of International Law* 21, 1–6. https://doi.org/10.1093/ejil/chq032

Weinberg, Justin. 2009. 'Norms and the Agency of Justice'. *Analyse & Kritik* 31 (2), 319–38. https://doi.org/10.1515/auk-2009-0207

Wiggins, David. 1998. *Needs, Values, Truth: Essays in the Philosophy of Value*. Oxford: Oxford University Press.

Wigley, Simon and Arzu Akkoyunlu-Wigley. 2006. 'Human Capabilities versus Human Capital: Gauging the Value of Education in Developing Countries'. *Social Indicators Research* 78 (2), 287–304. https://doi.org/10.1007/s11205-005-0209-7

Wilkinson, Richard G. and Michael Marmot. 2003. *Social Determinants of Health: The Solid Facts*. Geneva: World Health Organization.

Williams, Andrew. 2002. 'Dworkin on Capability'. *Ethics* 113 (1), 23–39. https://doi.org/10.1086/341323

Wilson-Strydom, Merridy and Melanie Walker. 2015. 'A Capabilities-Friendly Conceptualisation of Flourishing in and through Education'. *Journal of Moral Education* 44 (3), 310–24. https://doi.org/10.1080/03057240.2015.1043878

Wissenburg, Marcel. 2011. 'The Lion and the Lamb: Ecological Implications of Martha Nussbaum's Animal Ethics'. *Environmental Politics* 20 (3), 391–409. https://doi.org/10.1080/09644016.2011.573361

Wolff, Jonathan. 2011. *Ethics and Public Policy. A Philosophical Inquiry*. London: Routledge. https://doi.org/10.4324/9780203816387

Wolff, Jonathan and Avner De-Shalit. 2007. *Disadvantage*. Oxford: Oxford University Press. https://doi.org/10.1093/acprof:oso/9780199278268.001.0001

Wolff, Jonathan and Avner De-Shalit. 2013. 'On Fertile Functionings: A Response to Martha Nussbaum'. *Journal of Human Development and Capabilities* 14 (1), 161–65. https://doi.org/10.1080/19452829.2013.762177

Woolley, Frances R. and Judith Marshall. 1994. 'Measuring Inequality within the Household'. *Review of Income and Wealth* 40 (4), 415–31. https://doi.org/10.1111/j.1475-4991.1994.tb00084.x

Xu, Yongsheng. 2002. 'Functioning, Capability and the Standard of Living: An Axiomatic Approach'. *Economic Theory* 20 (2), 387–99. https://doi.org/10.1007/s001990100221

Zaidi, Asghar and Tania Burchardt. 2005. 'Comparing Incomes When Needs Differ: Equivalization for the Extra Costs of Disability in the UK'. *Review of Income and Wealth* 51 (1), 89–114. https://doi.org/10.1111/j.1475-4991.2005.00146.x

Zheng, Yingqin. 2009. 'Different Spaces for E-development: What Can We Learn from the Capability Approach?' *Information Technology for Development* 15 (2), 66–82. https://doi.org/10.1002/itdj.20115

Zheng, Yingqin and Bernd Carsten Stahl. 2011. 'Technology, Capabilities and Critical Perspectives: What Can Critical Theory Contribute to Sen's Capability Approach?' *Ethics and Information Technology* 13 (2), 69–80. https://doi.org/10.1007/s10676-011-9264-8

Index

Printed in June 2021
by Rotomail Italia S.p.A., Vignate (MI) - Italy